MEDIEVAL FRENCH PLAYS

MEDIEVAL FRENCH PLAYS

Translated by

RICHARD AXTON

and

JOHN STEVENS

OXFORD
BASIL BLACKWELL
1971

Cloth edition ISBN 0 631 12970 7

Paperback edition ISBN 0 631 13920 6

Library of Congress Number 70-129587

Printed in Great Britain
by Western Printing Services Ltd., Bristol
and bound at the Kemp Hall Bindery

CONTENTS

TRANSLATORS' PREFACE

The medieval French plays of the twelfth and thirteenth centuries should belong to actors as well as to students of *langue d'oïl*. Our aim has been to provide actable English translations which we hope will also be useful to students of the Middle Ages who cannot read the originals. These eight plays are probably the earliest surviving in Old French; their interest and general excellence has long been recognized; their variety of dramatic effect is striking. But, to our knowledge, only two of the plays (*Adam* and *Robin et Marion*) have ever been published in English translation before, and these are not easily accessible. The original texts present considerable difficulty: the accidents of survival and the quirks of medieval manuscript production account for the lack of original stage directions in most of the plays; in some of them the dialogue is not even properly divided among the speakers. Many of these obscurities have been removed by editors of the original texts and other scholars to whom we are indebted.

We have tried to visualize the plays in performance and our Introductions and added stage directions are intended to make the dramatic possibilities of the texts readily apparent. A close study of the original stage directions for *Adam* is by far the best introduction to these plays and one only wishes that all the texts had been as well rubricated by their medieval scribes. But, since they have not, we have provided each play with a separate Introduction, outlining the evidence for the original staging and suggesting how this might be adapted for modern production. To the texts themselves we have added minimal stage directions. All

stage directions are printed in italics; those which are
editorial are also enclosed in brackets. Our stage directions
are intended to elucidate the essential action implied by the
dialogue; we have avoided the producer's territory of
interpretative 'business', except where the dialogue was
obscure. The Notes to the plays, printed at the end of the
book, are meant to gloss any difficulties in the dialogue,
to explain important topical allusions and, occasionally, to
justify our readings or interpretations of the text. Brief
suggestions for further reading and reference are given at
the end of the General Introduction. A list of texts and
principal authorities used in the preparation of each translation is given at the end of each play.

The Old French drama was poetic. All the authors are
competent versifiers, while the *Adam* playwright, Jehan
Bodel, Rutebeuf, and Adam de la Halle, are among the
finest poets of their time. They use a great variety of metrical
forms, but the most common is the octosyllabic couplet,
the basic metre of contemporary romance and fabliau. The
Old French octosyllabic gives form and control to the
raciest tavern dialogue of *Le Jeu de Saint Nicolas* or to the
impromptu of Adam de la Halle's plays; it is intrinsic to
their effect. To translate the plays into modern prose would
be misleading, but the choice of an appropriate English
metre presented a problem. Rhymed octosyllabic couplets
seemed to us too inflexible for modern English dialogue, and
the rhyme words of modern English too epigrammatically
bright to convey the easy flow of the original. The staple of
English drama, blank verse, seemed altogether too stately
and threatened to bring with it echoes of Elizabethan drama
irrelevant to these plays. As an equivalent for the octosyllabic we have chosen an unrhymed four-stress line, with
rhyme or assonance only where greater formality was
required. We have reserved pentameters for the Old French
decasyllabics and alexandrines; the various other metres and
verse forms of the originals we have imitated as closely as
possible.

We have tried to achieve a modern spoken idiom, as

natural as possible within the discipline of metre. Departures from the literal sense were sometimes necessary in translating the swiftly varying tenses and impersonal constructions of Old French, idiomatic expressions and oaths. We started, like all translators, in the excitement of the illusion that we could capture the spirit of the originals—easy, elegant, unpretentious, racy, and dignified by turns. We finished by realizing that we could satisfy no one completely, least of all ourselves.

All the translations and commentaries are the result of a constant collaboration. John Stevens provided the music for the book and was largely responsible for the texts of *Le Jeu d'Adam*, *Le Garçon et l'Aveugle* and *Robin et Marion*. Richard Axton provided the Introductions and Notes to all the plays, and was largely responsible for the texts of *La Seinte Resureccion*, *Courtois d'Arras*, *Le Miracle de Théophile* and *Le Jeu de la Feuillée*. The labours of *Le Jeu de Saint Nicolas* were evenly divided from the start.

We would like to express our warm thanks to Dr. R. C. D. Perman for his expert advice on points of linguistic difficulty and for saving us from many mistakes. In a few instances, and at our own peril, we have presumed to differ from him in choosing a particular reading or interpretation, or a phrase that we thought important for the style of the translation. For help with the plain-song adaptations for *Le Jeu d'Adam* we are grateful to Mother Thomas More.

In preparing the translations we have also been greatly helped by hearing the lines of *Adam* spoken in two separate Cambridge productions. Our thanks are due to Caroline Lee and to Alan Horrox for the many suggestions and emendations which were the result of working with the text in rehearsal. A play changes shape as the skeleton is fleshed out, clothed and animated in performance; the work of translating a play is never really complete. 'Bless the amending hand.'

GENERAL INTRODUCTION

During the period spanned by the plays in this book (the mid-twelfth to the late thirteenth century) vernacular poetry flowered in Western Europe. This century-and-a-quarter includes much of the greatest lyric poetry of the troubadours, trouvères and Minnesingers, most of the finest Arthurian romances in French and German, an abundance of religious poetry, saints' lives and homilies, innumerable tales and fabliaux. The French drama, which brought together traditions of poetry and acting from churches, schools, courts and tavern greens, engaged the talents of three major named poets: Bodel, Rutebeuf and Adam de la Halle. These three would be known to us for their lyric and occasional poetry even if their plays had not survived. They were poets who felt the form and pressure of their times.

Jean Bodel, author of *Le Jeu de Saint Nicolas*, wrote an epic *Chanson des Saxons*, lyrics and *pastourelles*. He was a clerk to the city magistrates of Arras. Prevented from fulfilling his vow to go on Crusade, Bodel bade a poetic farewell to Arras in his *Congé* (1202), begging the mayor and his employers to support him in a leper house. The enigmatic 'Rutebeuf' was a Parisian. Though he seems to have been ambitious for royal patronage, he occupied a humble post and complained of wretched poverty. His poems are often biographical, sometimes topical, satirical or scurrilous, sometimes devotional. The outpourings of personal bitterness combined with self-mockery and technical brilliance suggest the temperament of an earlier Villon. The third playwright whose name is known, Adam de la Halle, was a celebrated musical composer of chansons and motets and the author of witty debate poems on questions of love; a restless, subtle, complex personality, who brought the topical, mock-autobiographical art of the Arras poets to the height of its achievement. As a married *clerc* (a tonsured man with a clerical education, though not in orders), caught between the law of ecclesiastical and secular courts, Adam was spokesman for a group of literate Arrageois malcontents who criticized the corrupt patrician government of the city during a period of social upheaval. He travelled to Southern Italy as court musician to Robert II, Count of Artois, in about 1283. Adam, Rutebeuf and Bodel between them are responsible for four of the eight earliest plays—for half the extant Old French drama.

The number of French plays to have survived is small because their chance of survival was small, compared with that of the 'official' Latin drama of the medieval Church. At this date vernacular plays were mostly by definition ephemeral, occasional pieces intended for non-clerical audiences. Only if they were particularly successful did they become 'reading pieces' in manuscript collections. Thus Rutebeuf's 'repentance' and 'prayer' in the *Miracle de Théophile* and Adam de la Halle's set piece on the delusions of love in the *Jeu de la Feuillée* were taken out of the plays in which they belonged and anthologized. By contrast, the Church's Latin drama formed part of the liturgical services on major feast days, the most usual place for these liturgical plays being before the final *Te Deum* of Matins.[1] The texts of these Latin plays and sometimes their music (the portions, at least, which would have been unfamiliar to the singers) were carefully written into service books, together with rubrics specifying costumes, properties and ceremonial movements, for yearly use at a monastery or church. It was a traditional and conventional drama; it derived its form and its meaning from an intimate relationship with Christian (especially monastic) worship; it belonged to certain moments of

[1] The habit of singing the *Te Deum* at the conclusion of any play with a religious subject, whatever the auspices of its performance, was continued into the sixteenth century.

celebration in the Church's liturgical year. The *Adam* owes a debt to this liturgical tradition, although it is composed in Anglo-Norman or Norman French and was acted outdoors: the play requires a choir skilled in singing liturgical plain chant, and the author's detailed 'stage directions' call for the use of liturgical vestments.

The true liturgical drama was international and a small number of dramatically simple plays for use at Christmas, Epiphany and Easter were known throughout Europe. Indeed, in the late twelfth century it was quite possible that the same liturgical play was being performed almost simultaneously in churches ranging from the north of England to Sicily. However, since the essential qualities of this drama were elaborate liturgical ceremony, poetic composition in Latin, and creative musical adaptation, it is not surprising that most of the greatest liturgical plays were the products of the famous cathedral schools in Northern France and Germany.

If only because of their language, vernacular plays had geographically more limited audiences. For instance, two thirteenth-century English manuscripts contain fragments of play speeches written in both French and English verse; it seems from this that the same group of actors played in different languages according to the area or social class of their audiences. Nevertheless, French was an international language, and the fluid unity of Angevin culture meant that priests and clercs as well as English kings and queens constantly travelled between England and the Continent. It is possible that the quasi-liturgical *Adam* and the popular *La Seinte Resureccion* were known on both sides of the Channel in the twelfth century. Recent scholars have not yet decided whether the author of *Adam* was Norman or Anglo-Norman; the distinction is perhaps not a valid one to make.

It is clear from the existence of these two plays that there was a fully-developed vernacular religious drama in England in the second half of the twelfth century; that is, more than two centuries earlier than the surviving English mystery-play cycles. Like the Middle English cycle-plays of York,

Wakefield and Chester, the Anglo-Norman plays are concerned to show the divine plan of history enacted in human terms. The play of *Adam*, which links together 'scenes' of the Fall, and of Cain and Abel, with brief appearances of the Prophets of Christ, has been considered a prototype of the Old Testament play-cycles in fourteenth-century England and France. Whether or not one accepts this teleological view, it is certain that the same 'figural' principle of structure is at work in *Adam* and in the later play-cycles. The events dramatized are chosen for their traditional significance in worship and iconography as prefigurations of the events of the New Testament, particularly of Christ's Passion and Resurrection. In the drama, as in medieval theology and art, the Fall is seen as a necessary prelude to the Redemption and as an implicit reminder of it. The Adam of our play puts Satan to flight with words that echo those of Christ: 'Fui tei de ci! Tu es Sathan.' (*Adam* 196) Later in the play he hints at his own deliverance from hell by the Son of Mary (381–2). Satan's temptation of Eve with the title 'queen of heaven', which the audience would immediately recognize as appropriate to the Virgin Mary, shows the same habit of mind and dramatic method. In the *Resureccion* (443ff.) a guard boasts that though Jesus be as strong as old Samson he will not escape from the Sepulchre; the audience is thus reminded of one of the best known Old Testament *figurae*, or foreshadowings, of Christ's Resurrection.

The Anglo-Norman drama anticipates the subsequent drama in other ways. The treatment of the Resurrection story and the staging techniques in *La Seinte Resureccion* are similar in many respects to those of the fourteenth- and fifteenth-century French Passion plays and those of the English and Cornish play-cycles. The revised text of the *Resureccion* that we have translated here was made in the mid-thirteenth century, probably at Canterbury. This revision, together with the existence of the two bilingual fragments mentioned above and other scraps of evidence, suggests that a vernacular tradition in England was continuous.

Turning to the other side of the Channel, the dramatic landscape is dominated by Arras: four of the plays (*Le Jeu de Saint Nicolas*, c. 1200, *Courtois d'Arras*, c. 1200, *Le Jeu de la Feuillée*, c. 1276, *Robin et Marion*, c. 1283) belong to that prosperous city in Northern France, where all forms of poetic entertainment met with eager patronage from a large and literate bourgeoisie. Since the early twelfth century there had existed a *Confrérie* or *Carité des Ardents*, which was a guild 'of jongleurs and bourgeois of Arras'. It provided collective aid for sick and needy members and intercessions for the souls of the departed, but it also organized feasts, civic entertainments and poetic competitions. The interests of the worldly, commercial-minded burgher audiences are firmly stamped in the 'realism' of the Arras plays. This 'realism'—the mirroring of the audience's life and manner of speech in the plays—is most striking in the Arras plays, but it is a quality common to all the French plays, something intimately connected with their use of the vernacular.

If one compares any of the early French plays with the contemporary liturgical Latin drama, the independence of the vernacular traditions is immediately arresting. The liturgical Latin drama is ceremonial, highly formalized; it is acted and sung in church as a lyrical and symbolic celebration of historical events which are held to be timelessly significant. The vernacular drama is, to overstate the contrast, popular and representational: it is directly imitative of real human life. Even the most strictly 'religious' of the French plays owe little to liturgical drama. Although *Adam* is often referred to as 'semi-liturgical', no Latin liturgical play of the Genesis story has ever come to light; moreover, the construction and dramatic method of the play are unique. The poet's free use of apocryphal matter, the rich stylistic variety of his dialogue, the penetrating psychological realism of his evocation of a triangular relationship involving Adam and Eve and Satan, and of the relationship between Cain and Abel—these features come from the traditions of vernacular poetry and, perhaps, from the traditions of a lost vernacular drama. In bringing two modes of drama together the playwright sets real human life within an arch which frames the whole of Christian history.

Of the other plays, only *La Seinte Resureccion* and *Le Jeu de Saint Nicolas* deal with themes that are also found in Latin plays. But again the differences in the scope, aims, and methods of the Latin and vernacular dramas are all important. The *Resureccion* is only a fragment, but its detail suggests a far more extensive treatment of the Resurrection story than is found in any surviving Latin play. A cast of at least fifty would have been needed and the play would have lasted well over three hours. The staging gives some idea of its popular appeal: whereas Latin plays of the Resurrection used only an Easter Sepulchre and Crucifix, the Anglo-Norman play lays out its open-air acting place like a diagram of Jerusalem and includes the famous medieval Tower of David. Bodel's *Jeu de Saint Nicolas* similarly owes little to earlier Latin plays of the miraculous icon. It was Bodel's own invention to dramatize a heroic conflict between Christians and pagans as the setting for the miracle, and to place the thieves of the story firmly in an Arras tavern. By linking the conventions of crusading epic with those of tavern buffoonery through the agency of the Saint, Bodel triumphantly fashioned perhaps the first double-plot in modern drama.

The originality of the remaining plays in the volume may serve to counter any easy generalizations about the hypothetical 'evolution' of medieval drama from religious to secular, and from Latin to vernacular forms. *Le Miracle de Théophile* is the first known miracle play of the Virgin; it dramatizes in intricately wrought lyric verse-forms the legend of a priest who sold his soul to the devil. The brutally realistic *Courtois d'Arras* is the only known medieval play of the parable of the prodigal son. *Le Jeu de la Feuillée* is the first known satirical 'revue'; at the same time it anticipates *A Midsummer Night's Dream* and other court comedies with its medley of fairies and rude mechanics, its play-within-a-play. *Robin et Marion* is, as it were, a miniature 'musical'; it combines the traditional plot of *pastourelle* poetry (the attempted seduction of a shepherdess by a knight) with the antics of a *bergerie* (the courtly make-believe of rustic life, which entailed dressing up to perform rustic songs, games and dances) and intersperses the whole with songs in the popular mode. The range of vernacular achievement is indeed impressive.

No single 'theatre' is suitable for the performance of all these plays, nor would one have been found in the medieval world. It is probable that there was no such thing as a theatre building, intended primarily for the performance of plays, in the thirteenth century. One must imagine instead a great number of potential acting 'places' (to use the playwrights' own term), where an audience might congregate on various occasions to see a dramatic performance. The rubrics of *Adam* indicate that its performance was envisaged on the open ground adjoining a church porch or West door. The prologue of staging directions for the *Resureccion* calls for a large space (possibly a churchyard), carefully allotted to the actors by means of 'houses' and 'places' (perhaps stalls or stages) like so many islands. It was a large spectacle, to be played when the weather was suitable, presumably by priests and clerks, to arouse the devotion of a crowd. On the other hand, *Saint Nicolas*, *Courtois d'Arras* and *Théophile* may all have been intended for meetings of guilds of *clercs*, to be performed indoors in guildhalls as part of the celebrations for a festival.

The farce, *Le Garçon et l'Aveugle*, in which the actors appear to beg from the bystanders, was probably performed wherever two entertainers could drum up an audience: in a market place, at a summer fair, or at a rich man's dinner table. *Le Jeu de la Feuillée*, with its medley of real and fictional characters and its current of topical scandal, seems to belong to a summer festival of the *Confrérie des Ardents*. The recurrent anti-feminism and the battle of the sexes suggest it may have been for a 'men only' night. The play was probably performed in a public square in Arras, barricaded round with the tables and benches of traders to keep out

B

those who did not pay. The actors and revellers may have drunk wine together and the fairies have danced through the city streets after the show, to find a new audience for their make-believe. For Adam's *Robin et Marion* the company is more refined: the court of Count Robert in Naples. It may have been in a banquet hall or in the sunshine of a tilt yard that the songs and dances of Picard *bergerie* reminded the expatriate soldiers of their native country.

These very different 'theatres' (to use the anachronistic word) have in common the use of a 'simultaneous' set: the acting area usually represents more than one scene at the same time, so that action is continuous. Like medieval art or pageantry, medieval staging is symbolic; separate places, times and actions are held together on a single spot and within a single moment. The poet uses his stage as a microcosm of time and space.

It follows that this stage is not naturalistic in the sense in which most European drama has been naturalistic in the last two centuries. The authors animate their symbolic sets with a variety of lively but still stylized imitations, play forms, of real life. The tavern is, after all, as much an 'ideal', a simplification, as the epic battlefield. The audience see their lives patterned and transformed by literary and dramatic convention into a wide diversity of dramatic experience: the grave formality of the marriage of Adam and Eve, a moment of religious solemnity and human tenderness at the beginning of man's history; the diabolical 'courtoisie' of Satan's wooing of Eve; the simple adventure story of Joseph of Arimathia's devotion to the body of Christ, played out like a chess game upon a ground plan of Jerusalem; the vision of crusading Christianity set against a world where the compass of life is reduced to dicing and tavern reckonings; the pastoral artifice of a simple, wholesome, erotic life, filled with music and dance; the brutal knockabout world of the Blind Man perpetually deceived; the bewildering shifts of illusion in the *Feuillée*, with its folkloric fairies and its obscene fantasy.

This rich variety of forms and experiences is the sign of a

drama which seven centuries ago was very much alive and which today needs only to be acted to live again.

Further reading and reference

Grace Frank, *The Medieval French Drama*, Oxford University Press, 1954. [Standard history of the vernacular French drama.]

E. K. Chambers, *The Medieval Stage*, 2 vols., Oxford University Press, 1903. [Survey of dramatic activity from late Roman to Elizabethan times.]

Karl Young, *The Drama of the Medieval Church*, 2 vols., Oxford University Press, 1933. [Standard history and commentary, giving texts of almost all known Latin Church plays.]

O. B. Hardison Jr., *Christian Rite and Christian Drama in the Middle Ages*, Baltimore: Johns Hopkins Press, 1965. [Study of the origins and development of the Resurrection play, comparing liturgical and more popular methods.]

Marie Ungureaunu, *La bourgeoisie naissante; société et littérature bourgeoises d'Arras aux XIIe et XIIIe siècles*, (Mémoires de la Commission des Monuments Historiques du Pas-de-Calais, VIII: i) Arras, 1955. [Detailed study of Arras society, guilds and entertainments.]

C. J. Stratman, *Bibliography of Medieval Drama*, University of California Press, 1954. [A revised edition is in preparation.]

ACKNOWLEDGMENTS

We thank the Cambridge University Press for permission to quote from M. D. Anderson, *Drama and Imagery in English Medieval Churches* (1963), George G. Harrap & Company for permission to use their edition of *Le Jeu de Robin et de Marion*, Manchester University Press for permission to use *Le Mystère d'Adam*, and Librairie Honoré Champion for permission to use their editions of *Courtois d'Arras*, *Le Garçon et l'Aveugle*, *Le Miracle de Théophile* and *Le Jeu de la Feuillée* on which we have based our translations.

LE JEU D'ADAM

PERSONS OF THE PLAY

GOD
ADAM
EVE
SATAN, The Devil
CAIN
ABEL
THE CHOIR
Devils

LE JEU D'ADAM

Text

Adam was composed early in the second half of the twelfth century. The author is not known. He wrote in Norman French; but modern French and English scholars dispute whether his language was continental or Anglo-Norman. The play consists of three parts: the Fall of Adam and Eve, Cain's murder of Abel, and a Prophet play. The first two 'scenes' are not known in any other dramatization before the fourteenth century; here the poet's dramatic skill and subtle characterization are most remarkable. The third 'scene' is a reworking of a kind of play known in Latin liturgical drama from at least the eleventh century. This is a formal procession of 'prophets', each of whom foretells the coming of Christ. We have omitted it from our translation for three reasons: the dramatic interest of this pageant for a modern audience is relatively small; it is questionable whether the Prophets make an aesthetically satisfying conclusion; and, the full extent of the original play is in any case in doubt.

The Latin responds sung in the play by the choir belong to Sexagesima (the Sunday next but one before Ash Wednesday) and the play may have been performed then—although weather conditions in England or Normandy are not auspicious for outdoor performances in February. Easter is another possibility, since by the end of the play Adam and all his descendants and all the patriarchs and prophets are chained in Hell awaiting deliverance; so perhaps the play ended with a Harrowing of Hell. There is a third possibility. The text has survived in a paper manuscript, written in the

South of France in the early thirteenth century. In this manuscript the Prophet play is followed by a popular eschatological sermon on the 'Fifteen Signs of Judgment'. It is conceivable that this sermon may have served on some occasion to conclude a performance of the play during Advent.

The play is edited by Paul Aebischer (TLF, 1963). We have translated this text and followed Aebischer's line numbering.

The dialogue (of which single lines are often skilfully divided between speakers) is chiefly composed in octosyllabic couplets; these are translated into four-stress lines, rhymed in the more formal passages. The passages in decasyllabics grouped in quatrains with a single rhyme, e.g. 49–112, 519–622, are translated into pentameters with alternate rhymes.

Music

While the dialogue is in French, the stage directions are written in Latin; so too are the responds sung by the choir. The music for the play is an integral part of it. Indeed, in an extreme view, the play of *Adam*, at least, can be thought of as an extensive dramatic 'trope' on the responds for the service of Matins at Sexagesima. That is to say, the responds celebrate each particular moment in the story of Creation whilst the dramatic scenes enact and develop their message. The original manuscript contains no actual music; there was no need for it to do so. The music can be supplied from any one of a number of contemporary service-books. In Jacques Chailley's edition, with G. Cohen, *Le Jeu d'Adam et Eve* (Paris, 1936), an antiphonary of the Abbey of Saint-Maur-des-Fosses was used as a source. Slightly different versions of the same chants are supplied by an antiphonary in Worcester Cathedral Library (see J. W. Doyle, S.J., trs., *Adam; A Play* [Sydney, 1948]). These twelfth-century responds are Gregorian chant at its most elaborate and difficult; they cannot be satisfactorily performed except by highly skilled singers with some experience of plainsong.

So, reluctantly, we have set the words of the responds to simpler but still authentic forms of chant (psalm-tones), in the hope that they will take their essential place in any performance of the play. They should be sung in a straightforward, restrained, rather formal manner, in notes of equal length.

The music should not be treated as an extra, nor as a series of interludes, nor as providing atmosphere. It is intimately associated with the utterances of God; the choir are not characters in the ordinary sense but represent, as they stand in the background, the heavenly host, to whom the heavenly praises are entrusted. Whilst they are singing, the dramatic action should be 'frozen', producing a tableau effect. Experience shows that this can be strikingly effective in performance.

Staging

The Latin stage-directions are so explicit and detailed that little comment on the staging is necessary, except upon the initial siting of the acting place and on the theory behind the poet's instructions. The play seems to have been intended for performance outdoors, against either the West door or the side porch of a church. This is the ideal setting. When God is not playing he retires into the church (between lines 112 and 387). The choir may stand inside the church or porch. If the door or porch stands above the churchyard and has a conveniently broad surround this will serve well for the 'fairly high place' of Paradise. Otherwise Paradise should be set up on a raised stage. The open ground between Paradise and the audience is called *platea* (the 'place'); it represents Earth; to one side of it and close to the audience is the 'house' for Hell.

If the play is performed in a church or any other building, a similar spatial relationship between the parts should be maintained because of its symbolic significance. In the original and ideal set the church is God's 'house', whence he comes to animate his creation and from which his Word issues in the sung liturgical responds. Paradise is high because it is 'a very pleasant place' and it is closest to God.

Earth is on a level with the audience. Hell is close to them and the devils are able to make sallies amongst them (after line 204) as well as through the 'place' (after 112 and 172).

The rubrics specify costumes for all except the devils. The omission may show traditional caution in talking about such matters. More importantly, it suggests that the costuming of devils was conventional and could safely be left to the 'producer's' discretion. Twelfth-century poems and representations indicate that the devils should be quasi-human, having grotesque masks, claws and tails. The details of costume and stage action which are laid down in the original show a careful concern for making the spoken word visible. Thus Adam's loss of his fine clothes (after 314) shows his change of state as well as symbolizing his loss of everlasting life. The thorns and thistles which the Devil plants in Adam's patch of dug earth (after 518) are directly evocative in their literalness. The author intended the costumes to carry symbolic meanings too. Adam's robe is red, possibly to signify that he was made of red earth; Eve's is white because she is a bride. God wears a priest's dalmatic (ceremonial robe with wide sleeves), and for the expulsion of Adam and Eve from Paradise, he dons a stole as a twelfth-century priest would have done to expel sinners from the church on Ash Wednesday. Cain's red associates him with fire, anger, bloodshed; Abel's white with the Lamb, innocence and sacrifice.

The method of acting should underline the poet's double concern for realistic and symbolic effect. There is room for two styles, one formalized (for the utterances of God, Adam's lament, and for other speeches in the 'high style'); the other freer and more naturalistic (for the dialogues between Adam, Eve, and Satan, and between Cain and Abel). A third style might be used for the devils, who do not speak, but whose dumb-show is so important a part of the total effect of the play. The ancient histrionic tradition from which these creatures derive their lineage is by no means clear, but the style might effectively be grotesque, vigorous and pantomimic.

ADAM AND EVE

Paradise shall be set up in a fairly high place; curtains and silk cloths shall be hung around it, at such a height that the persons who shall be in Paradise can be seen from the shoulders upwards. Fragrant flowers and leaves shall be planted there; there shall also be various trees with fruit hanging on them, so that it looks a very pleasant place. Then shall come God the Saviour wearing a dalmatic, and Adam and Eve shall be stationed in front of him. Adam shall wear a red tunic, but Eve a woman's garment in white with a white silk scarf; and they shall both stand in front of God—Adam, however, nearer to God with a calm countenance, Eve with face lowered. Adam shall be well trained not to answer too quickly nor too slowly, when he has to answer. Not only Adam but all the actors shall be instructed to control their speech and to make their actions appropriate to the matter they speak of; and, in speaking the verse, not to add a syllable, nor to take one away, but to enunciate everything distinctly, and to say everything in the order laid down. Whenever anyone shall speak of Paradise, he shall look towards it and point it out with his hand.

Then shall the lesson begin:

In principio creavit Deus celum et terram

After which the choir shall sing:

Formavit igitur dominus

And after that God shall say: Adam!
And Adam shall answer: My Lord.

For-ma-vit i-gi-tur Do-mi-nus ho-mi-nem de li-mo ter-rae et in-spi-

ra-vit in fa-ci-em e-jus spi-ra-cu-lum vi-tae * Et fac-tus est

ho-mo in a-ni-mam vi-ven-tem * In prin-ci-pi-o fe-cit De-us ce-lu

et ter-ram et cre-a-vit in e-a ho-mi-nem * Et factus est ho-mo

in a-ni-mam vi-ven-tem.

GOD   Adam!

ADAM   My lord!

GOD   I moulded you
From earthly clay.

ADAM   Yes, this I know.

GOD   I've given you a living soul,
And formed you like myself in all.
Made you from earth in my own form;
You never should be my enemy.

ADAM   I never will, but follow your word,
Obeying my creator, Lord.

GOD   I've given you a good companion:
She is your wife, her name is Eve,
She is your wife and partner; you

10

Must stay faithful to her and true.
May you love her and in turn she
Love you; both will be loved by me.
She must answer to your command,
The two of you be in my hand.
Out of your rib your wife I shaped;
She's born from you and is no stranger.
Straight from your body I made her:
She came from you—not from elsewhere. 20
Govern her by the light of reason;
Between you be there no dissension,
But mutual comfort, mutual love—
Such shall the law of marriage be.
And now to you, Eve, will I speak—
Attend, and listen carefully:
If you desire to take my part,
You'll harbour goodness in your heart.
Honour me, Creator, God!
Acknowledge me to be your Lord! 30
My service must be all your thought,
All your wisdom, all your strength.
Love Adam, hold him dear as life—
He is your husband, you his wife.
To him remain obedient;
Don't go beyond his government.
Serve him and love him well, then sure
You'll be to keep the marriage law.
If you make him a good help-meet,
With him in glory you'll be set. 40

EVE I will do, Lord, as you command;
 I shall not wish to stray beyond.
 I'll recognize your sovereign sway;
 As mate and master him obey.
 I'll always serve him faithfully:
 He'll have the best support from me.
 Your pleasure and Your service, Lord,
 I shall in everything perform.

Then God shall call Adam nearer and shall speak more particularly to him:

GOD   Now listen, Adam, and hear what I shall say!
    I made you, and endow you with this wealth: 50
    You'll live for ever, if you keep my word,
    Feel no disease but always have good health;
      No hunger know; nor drink from any need;
    Never be cold; nor of the heat complain.
    You shall be happy, never tired at all,
    Full of delight, you never shall know pain.
      In joy the days of all your life you'll lead,
    Exist for ever, your life not short but long;
    I tell you this, and wish that Eve may hear;
    If she does not, she does herself a wrong.   60
      You two have lordship over all the earth—
    The birds, the beasts, and all created things.
    Of small account is he who envies you,
    For over all the world you shall be kings.
      Within yourselves I put both good and evil;
    To give you this is still to leave you free.
    Weigh everything in balance fairly now;
    Accept this counsel—keep your faith with me!
      Put aside evil, and give your mind to good.
    Love your good lord, and firmly hold to him.   70
    For no one else's counsel turn from mine;
    If you observe it, then you'll never sin.

ADAM   Great thanks I give to your benignity,
    The God who made me with such kind intent,
    That right and wrong you put within my power.
    To serve you, may my will be always bent.
      You are my Lord; I, your created thing;
    You formed me, I'm the product of your art.
    My will shall never be so hard, so set,
    That serving you shall not take all my heart.   80

Then shall God point out Paradise to Adam with his hand saying:

GOD   Adam!

ADAM   My Lord.

GOD   I'll tell you my design:
    This garden.

ADAM   What's it called?

GOD   Paradise.

ADAM   How fine it is!

GOD   I grew and planted it.
    He who lives here shall always be my friend.
    I entrust it you, to dwell here and to guard it.

Then shall he lead them into Paradise, saying;

    It is for you.

ADAM   Then, can we settle here?

GOD   For all your lives; you need not be afraid.
    Within it neither sickness is, nor death.

The choir shall sing: Tulit ergo dominus hominem

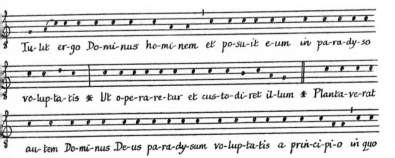

Tu-lit er-go Do-mi-nus ho-mi-nem et po-su-it e-um in pa-ra-dy-so

vo-lup-ta-tis * Ut o-pe-ra-re-tur et cus-to-di-ret il-lum * Planta-ve-rat

au-tem Do-mi-nus Deus pa-ra-dy-sum vo-lup-ta-tis a prin-ci-pi-o in quo

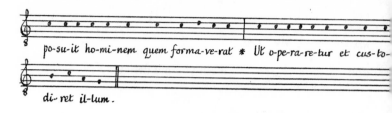

po-su-it ho-mi-nem quem forma-ve-rat * Ut o-pe-ra-re-tur et cus-to-di-ret il-lum.

Then shall God stretch out his hand towards Paradise, saying:

GOD   The nature of this garden I'll recount:
No joy is lacking here as you will find;   90
Whatever good things men in the world desire
Here can be found in measure and in kind.
    No woman shall a husband's anger know,
No husband for his wife feel fear or shame;
The act of love is not for man a sin;
Nor shall a woman here give birth in pain.
    You'll live for ever, in this marvellous place
And not grow any older. Have no fear
Of death here, for it cannot do you harm.
I wish you not to leave; your home is here!   100

The choir shall sing: Dixit Dominus ad Adam.

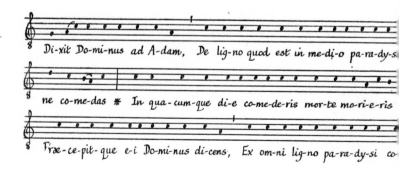

Di-xit Do-mi-nus ad A-dam, De lig-no quod est in me-di-o pa-ra-dy-si ne co-me-das * In qua-cum-que di-e co-me-de-ris mor-te mo-ri-e-ris Præ-ce-pit-que e-i Do-mi-nus di-cens, Ex om-ni lig-no pa-ra-dy-si co-

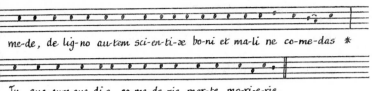

me-de, de lig-no au-tem sci-en-ti-æ bo-ni et ma-li ne co-me-das *

In qua-cum-que di-e co-me-de-ris mor-te mo-ri-e-ris.

Then shall God show Adam the trees of Paradise, saying:

GOD   Of all *that* fruit, eat as it pleases you.

And he shall show him the forbidden tree and its fruit, saying:

GOD   *This* is forbidden! Take no comfort here!
   If you eat this, you shall be dead at once;
   My love you'll lose, and change your happy state.

ADAM   I will observe all that you do command;
   Neither my wife nor I will swerve an inch.
   For a single fruit to lose this place of bliss!
   I should deserve to be thrown headlong out.
   If for one apple I reject your love,
   Then all my life I'll pay for being mad: 110
   He will be rightly judged as traitors are
   Who breaks his faith and thus betrays his Lord.

*Then shall God go into the church, while Adam and Eve walk
up and down, innocently delighting in Paradise. Meanwhile
devils shall run about the 'place', making appropriate gestures:
and they shall come in turn near to Paradise, pointing out the
forbidden fruit to Eve as if persuading her to eat it. Then
shall Satan come to Adam and say to him:*

SATAN   What are you doing, Adam?

ADAM   Enjoying life.

   C

SATAN   All well with you?

ADAM   I feel nothing amiss.

SATAN   It could be better.

ADAM   I can't imagine how.

SATAN   Do you want to know?

ADAM   I've no desire at all.

SATAN   I know, I know *how*.

ADAM   What's that to me?

SATAN   Why not?

ADAM   It means nothing to me.

SATAN   It'll be worth while.

ADAM   I can't see when.

SATAN   I'm in no hurry to let you know.   120

ADAM   Tell me, come on!

SATAN   Certainly not,
   Until you're tired of asking me.

ADAM   I'm really not on fire to know.

SATAN   You don't deserve to have good things;
   The good you have you don't enjoy.

ADAM   I don't—how?

SATAN   Would you like to hear?
  I'll whisper it quietly in your ear.

ADAM   I certainly would like to know.

SATAN   Listen, then, Adam! Listen to me,
  For your own good.   130

ADAM   All right, go on!

SATAN   You *will* believe me?

ADAM   Yes, of course.

SATAN   Absolutely?

ADAM   Except one thing.

SATAN   What thing is that?

ADAM   I'll tell it you.
  I will not act against my God.

SATAN   Are you so afraid?

ADAM   Indeed I am;
  I love and fear him.

SATAN   You're a fool.
  What can he do?

ADAM   Both good and bad.

SATAN   You are a madman, if you think
  Anything bad can come of this.
  In Paradise!—You cannot die.   140

ADAM   God said to me that I should die
  If I transgressed his ordinance.

SATAN   What is this great trangression? Come
   I'd like to hear, and no delay.

ADAM   I'll tell you all about it, all.
   He gave me this command to keep:
   All the fruits in Paradise
   I am allowed to eat, he said,
   Bar one; that is forbidden me—
   I shall not lay a hand upon it.   150

SATAN   And which is that?

Then shall Adam stretch out his hand and show Satan the forbidden fruit, saying:

ADAM   You see that there?
   That one he's quite forbidden me.

SATAN   Do you know why?

ADAM   Indeed I don't.

SATAN   I'll tell you what the real cause is.
   He doesn't care about the rest—

And with his hand let him point to the forbidden fruit, saying to Adam:

SATAN   Only this fruit that hangs up high:
   This is the fruit of Knowledge, this
   Gives insight into everything.
   If you eat this, you will do well.

ADAM   Do well? In what?   160

SATAN   You will soon see.
   At once you will be wide-awake.
   The future—? Like an open book!

You'll gratify your every whim,
It will be wise to pick it now;
Eat it Adam! and you'll do well.
You'll no more be afraid of God,
But, rather, his equal, equal in all.
This is the reason He said no.
Will you believe me? Taste the fruit.

ADAM   I will not.   170

SATAN   A fine thing to hear!
Why won't you?

ADAM   No!

SATAN   You are a fool.
One day you'll say, 'He told me so!'

*Then let the Devil retreat; and he shall go to the other devils
and shall run about the 'place', and after a little while he shall
come back, happy and glad, to tempt Adam, and he shall say
to him:*

SATAN   Well, Adam?—will you change your mind?
Are you still set in your stupid ways?
I meant to say the other day,
God has made you a mere dependant,
And put you here to eat his fruit.
Do you have any other fun?

ADAM   Certainly. Everything I want.

SATAN   Have you got no ambition, man?   180
You set a value on yourself
'Cause God has made you his—gardener!
God's made you keeper of his garden:
Don't you want anything else from life?
Did he make you just for belly-joys?

Hasn't he anything higher in store?
Now listen, Adam, to what I say.
I'll give you some genuine advice—
You can be your very own master
On a level with God himself.   190
To summarize the whole affair—
If you eat this apple here,

Then he shall raise his hand towards Paradise

You shall be king, in majesty,
Sharing power with God himself.

ADAM   Get out of here!

SATAN   What are you saying?

ADAM   Get out of here! You are the devil,
   The foul-mouthed devil.

SATAN   What do you mean?

ADAM   You want to shove me down in hell,
   And put me in the wrong with God,
   End happiness, start misery.   200
   I cannot trust you. Out you go!
   And, Satan—don't you have the nerve
   Ever to come near me again.
   You are a traitor, a faithless thing.

*Then sadly and with downcast look Satan shall leave Adam
and go to the gates of hell, where he shall talk with the other
devils. After that he shall run around among the spectators;
and then he shall approach Paradise, on Eve's side, and with a
pleasant expression on his face suavely address her:*

SATAN   Eve, I've come to talk to you.

EVE   Tell me, Satan, what on earth for?

SATAN   I've come in your best interests.

EVE   God's blessing on it!

SATAN   Don't be afraid.
 I have known for quite a while
 All the secrets of Paradise.   210
 I'll pass on some of them to you.

EVE   Go on, begin, I'm listening.

SATAN   Will you hear me out?

EVE   Why, certainly.
 I shan't put you in a temper.

SATAN   You'll keep it quiet?

EVE   Of course I will.

SATAN   It'll get out.

EVE   It won't through me.

SATAN   I put myself into your hands;
 For me your word is good enough.

EVE   You will be safe—I've promised you.

SATAN   You have been very well brought up.   220
 I've seen Adam—but he's a fool.

EVE   A bit severe.

SATAN   He'll soften up.
 Harder than hell he is just now.

EVE   He's a gentleman.

SATAN   A menial, rather.
  Even if he neglects himself,
  At least he might look after you.
  You're delicate and sensitive,
  Sweeter to look at than a rose;
  A crystal-clear complexion (like
  Snow in an icebound valley falling).   230
  You two! God made a bad match there:
  You have feelings—*Adam* has none.
  All the same, you are the one with sense,
  Mature and wise to the finger-tips.
  Obviously you're the one to deal with;
  I'd like a word.

EVE   You can trust me.

SATAN   No one must know.

EVE   Why, who should know?

SATAN   Not even Adam.

EVE   Not even him.

SATAN   All right, I'll tell you. Listen now.
  There's no one here except us two.   240
  And Adam over there—but he can't hear.

EVE   Speak up, he'll never catch a word.

SATAN   You are the victims of a trick,
  A trick—worked in this very spot.
  The fruit which God has given you—
  There's hardly any goodness in it;
  The fruit you *aren't* allowed to eat
  Has in it most amazing power—
  The very gift of life itself,

Of strength, and of authority,   250
Of all knowledge, both good and evil.

EVE   How does it taste?

SATAN   It's heavenly.
  With your figure and your face
  You deserve a chance like this—
  To be first lady in the world
  Queen of heaven and of hell—
  Knowing all that is to be,
  And being mistress of it all.

EVE   Is that the fruit?

SATAN   Yes, that's the one.

*Then shall Eve look carefully at the forbidden fruit, and
having looked for a long time she shall say:*

EVE   It does me good simply to *see* it.   260

SATAN   Well, just imagine *eating* it!

EVE   I? How can I?

SATAN   You won't believe me!
  Pick it first, give Adam some.
  At once you'll have the crown of heaven,
  Be on a par with Him who made you.
  He'll have no secrets from you then.
  As soon as you have eaten the fruit,
  You'll feel completely different;
  You'll be with God, I guarantee,
  In equal goodness, equal power.   270
  Taste it and see!

EVE   I'm thinking of it.

SATAN　Don't believe Adam.

EVE　　　　　　　　　　　　I will do it.

SATAN　When will you do it?

EVE　　　　　　　　　　　Let me be,
　I'll wait till Adam's having a rest.

SATAN　Come on, eat it, don't be afraid.
　Only children put things off.

Then shall Satan leave Eve and go to hell. Adam, however, shall come to Eve, taking it badly that the Devil has been talking with her, and he shall say to her:

ADAM　Tell me, Eve, what was he after,
　That devil Satan? What did he want?

EVE　He spoke to me of our well-being.

ADAM　Now—don't believe a word he says,　　　280
　He's a traitor, I know he is.

EVE　How do you know?

ADAM　　　　　　　　　I've tried him out.

EVE　What does it matter if I see him?

ADAM　He'll influence the way you think.

EVE　He won't, you know. I shan't believe
　A thing he says until *I've* tried it.

ADAM　Don't let him come near you again!
　He's not a person one can trust;
　He wanted to betray his master,

And put himself in the high command.   290
I shouldn't like that kind of blackguard
To come crawling to you for help.

*Then shall a serpent cunningly contrived climb up the trunk of
the forbidden tree; Eve shall put her ear up to it as if listening
to its advice. Then Eve shall take the apple and offer it to
Adam. Adam, however, shall not yet take it, and Eve shall say
to him:*

EVE   Eat it! You don't know what it's like.
We mustn't lose our opportunity.

ADAM   Is it so good?

EVE   You'll see it is.
You'll never know unless you taste.

ADAM   I'm not so sure.

EVE   Well, leave it!

ADAM   I won't.

EVE   You're a coward to put it off.

ADAM   But I *will* take it.

EVE   Come on, then! Bite!
Full understanding's in your grasp,—   300
Of good and evil. I'll eat it first.

ADAM   And I will afterwards.

EVE   That's right.

Then shall Eve eat part of the apple, and say to Adam:

EVE   I've tasted it. Oh, God! The flavour!

I've never tasted such a sweetness.
This apple has a taste like . . . like. . . .

ADAM   Like what?

EVE   Like no one's ever tasted.
At last my eyes are opened—wide;
I feel like God—God, the almighty.
All past and future circumstance
I have it all, all in my grasp.
Eat, Adam, eat—don't hesitate.   310
It's the best thing you'll ever do.

Then shall Adam take the apple from Eve's hand, saying:

ADAM   I'll trust in you—you are my wife.

EVE   Eat! there's nothing for you to fear.

Then shall Adam eat part of the apple; as soon as it is eaten he shall realize his sin; and, bending down so that the on-lookers cannot see him, he shall take off his fine clothes and put on poor clothes sewn with figleaves. Then simulating the greatest possible grief he shall begin his lament:

ADAM   Oh! What wickedness I've done!
No escape left, but death alone.
No hope of rescue—dead am I.
So evil is my destiny:
Evilly changed, good fortune gone;
I had bright hopes, now I've none.   320
I have betrayed the Lord of life
Through counsel of a wicked wife.
I know my guilt; what shall I do?
My Lord, I cannot look on you.
How can I gaze on holiness
Forsaken through my foolishness?
I never made a worse exchange;

Now I know truly what sin is.
O, death, why don't you seize on me?
Why cannot earth from guilt be free?   330
Why do I cumber up the world?
Into hell I must be hurled.
In hell shall be my dwelling-place
Until He come who shall me save.
In hell thus shall I lead my life;
Whence to me shall come relief?
Whence shall I assistance gain?
Who can release me from this pain?
Why did I as a traitor end?
I am the man without a friend;   340
There is no one to help me out;
I am lost beyond a doubt.
Against my Lord I've done such ill
I cannot plead with him at all,
Since I am wrong and he is right.
Lord! this shall be my cursed plight.
Who'll ever now remember me,
Who wronged the King of Majesty?
The King of Glory I've defied,
No trace of reason on my side.   350
I have no neighbour, have no friend,
Who could reprieve me at the end.
Whom shall I call upon for aid,
Now my wife has me betrayed,
The wife God gave to partner me?
She counselled me to misery.
Oh, Eve.

Then he shall see Eve his wife, and shall say:

ADAM   You wicked woman!
    Why were you ever born, you witch?
    I wish that rib had been burnt up,
    The rib that's plunged me in despair.   360
    It should have been thrown into the fire;

Look at the terrible things it's brought.
When God withdrew it from my side,
Why didn't he burn it and slaughter me?
This rib's betrayed the whole body—
Damaged and ruined from head to foot.
What shall I say? What shall I do?
Unless grace comes to me from heaven
I shall never find release
From this excruciating pain.   370
Ah, Eve, it was an evil hour,
A great unhappiness in store,
When you were given me for wife.
Now through your advice I'm damned,
Utterly ruined because of you—
Down from the mountains to the shadows.
No one will come to rescue me,
Unless it be mighty God himself.
What am I saying? Why name Him?
Will He help, when I've angered Him?   380
No one will ever send me aid,
Except the son of Blessed Mary.
I don't know whom to ask for help
When we've not kept our faith with God.
Now in God's keeping all must be:
There's nothing left for me but death.

Then shall the chorus begin: Dum deambularet

Dum de am-bu-la-ret Domi-nus in pa-ra-dy-so ad au-ram post

me-ri-di-em, cla-ma-vit et di-xit : 'Adam u-bi es?' 'Au-di-vi Do-mi-

ne vo-cem tu-am ♯ Et abscon-di me. Vo-cem tu-am Do-mi-ne au-di-vi in

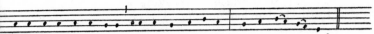

pa-ra-dy-so et ti-mu-i, eo quo nu-dus essem * Et ab-scon-di me.'

*After which God shall come, wearing a stole, and he shall enter
Paradise and look around him, as if searching for Adam. But
Adam and Eve shall hide in a corner of Paradise, as if acknow-
ledging their wretched state, and God shall say:*

GOD   Adam, where are you?

*Then they shall both get up and stand before God, not, how-
ever, completely upright, but stooping a little because of
the shame of their sin, and very sorrowful; and Adam shall
reply:*

ADAM   I'm here, my Lord.
 I've hidden to avoid your anger.
 My nakedness makes me ashamed—
 And so I've shut myself away.   390

GOD   What have you done? How have you sinned?
 Who's snatched you from your happiness?
 What have you done? Why so ashamed?
 Shall we reckon our accounts?
 There was nothing the other day
 Of which you needed feel ashamed,
 And now I see you sad and grey;
 There's no joy in such a life.

ADAM   I'm so ashamed before you, Lord;
 That's why I hide.   400

GOD   You, hide? Now why?

ADAM   I'm so entwined with my disgrace
    I scarcely dare look in your face.

GOD   Why did you go against my ban?
    Have you gained anything at all?
    You are my servant, I your Lord.

ADAM   I cannot contradict the facts.

GOD   I made you in my likeness; why
    Have you transgressed the law I gave?
    I moulded you in my own image;
    Why have you outraged me thus?   410
    My interdiction you've not kept;
    You've broken it quite wantonly.
    You ate the fruit, of which I said
    I plainly had forbidden it.
    Did you think *you* could be my equal?
    I don't think you will boast of it.

Then shall Adam extend his hand towards **God,** *and then
towards Eve, saying:*

ADAM   The woman whom you gave to me,
    She was the first to do this thing;
    She gave it me and then I ate:
    Now, I think, it's turned to gall.   420
    I meddled wrongly with this fruit;
    I've sinned, and it was due to her.

GOD   You trusted in her more than in me;
    You ate the fruit without my leave,
    Now you shall have your recompense:
    The earth shall henceforth bear a curse
    Where you wish to sow your grain:
    It'll fail you when it comes to harvest;
    It shall be cursed beneath your hand.
    You shall work the soil in vain: 430

Your crop will ripen, certainly—
Thorns and thistles it will yield!
Your farming will not be the same;
It will be cursed (I pass this sentence):
With great labour, with great pain,
You will toil to get your bread;
With great hardship, and with great sweat
Both night and day you'll live your life.

*Then shall God turn to Eve and with threatening face say to
her:*

GOD And you, Eve, you wicked wife,
    You quickly took up arms against me,   440
    Lightly regarded my commands.

EVE The wicked serpent set me a trap.

GOD Through him you thought to equal me?
    You know now how to prophecy?
    And once you had the mastery
    Over all things that are alive.
    How quickly you have lost it all!
    I see you sad and miserable:
    Have you won or lost? Now say!
    I wish to render you your due,   450
    Give it to you as servant's hire:
    You shall be plagued in every way.
    In pain your children you shall bear;
    In pain they shall to death endure.
    Your children even in birth shall languish,
    And die amidst the greatest anguish.
    You've pledged to deep disquietude
    Yourself, and all your flesh and blood.
    All, who shall issue from your seed,
    All will lament your sinful deed.   460

And Eve shall reply saying:

    D

EVE   I have done wrong; it was my foolishness:
      A single apple brings me great distress.
      It casts me and my children in deep sorrow;
      A moment's pleasure brings me pain tomorrow.
      If I did wrong, it is no great surprise—
      It was the treacherous serpent closed my eyes.
      He has an evil mind; he is no lamb;
      The man who takes *his* word is bound for doom.
      I took the apple (I know I was a fool)
      Against your word; this act of mine was cruel.   470
      A wicked taste! I now live in your hate:
      I lose my life for one small fruit I ate.

Then shall God threaten the serpent, saying:

GOD   And you, serpent! My curse on you
      Shall rest, till I obtain my due.
      On your belly you shall glide
      Till the last days of your life.
      The dust shall be your only food,
      On heath, in field, in wood.
      Women will hate you to the core—
      An evil thing to have next door.   480
      Even though you bruise her heel,
      She can overcome that ill:
      She'll strike your head a mighty blow
      That will bring you pain and woe.
      She'll undertake all she can do
      To have her just revenge on you.
      You chose unwisely for a friend:
      She will make your neck to bend.
      A mighty Root from her shall rise
      To shatter all your energies.   490

Then God shall expel them from Paradise, saying:

      Now, get you gone from Paradise!
      Your change of country is for worse.

In earth set up your home, for here
You have no right to reappear.
You have no rightful claim to make;
Now, get outside, never come back!
Gone is your privilege—now roam
And find elsewhere a place for home.
Exiled from beatitude,
You shall be tired, you shall crave food. 500
Pain and misery will seek
And find you, seven days in the week.
On earth you'll miserably toil
Only for death at end of all;
And then, when you have tasted death,
Go straight away, to hell beneath.
The body's exiled in this world,
But there the soul's in peril hurled.
Satan will hold you in his power;
No man can help at that dark hour. 510
From whom do you expect rescue,
Unless *I* choose to pity you?

The choir shall sing the Respond:
In sudore vultus tui.

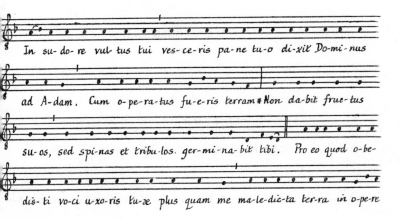

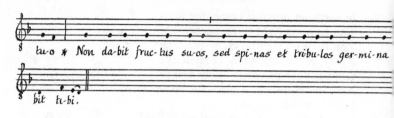

tu-o ＊ Non da-bit fruc-tus su-os, sed spi-nas et tri-bu-los ger-mi-na

bit ti-bi.

Meanwhile an angel shall come, clothed in white, bearing a shining sword in his hand, whom God shall station at the gate of Paradise, saying to him:

GOD   Mount guard on Paradise, and bar
     This outlaw ever entering there.
     See that he has no power nor might
     To lay hands on the fruit of Life.
     Prevent him with your flashing sword
     From setting foot upon this road.

When they are outside Paradise, looking sad and cast down, they shall bend down to the earth over their ankles, and God shall point to them with his hand, his face turned towards Paradise:

And the choir shall begin: Ecce Adam quasi unus

Ec-ce A-dam quasi u-nus ex no-bis fac-tus est   sci-ens bo-num et

ma-lum ＊ Vi-de-te ne for-te su-mat de lig-no vi-tæ et vi-vat in

æ-ter-num ＊ Che-ru-bim et flam-me-um gla-di-um at-que ver-sa-ti-lem

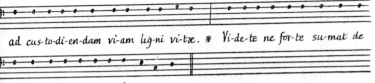

ad cus-to-di-en-dam vi-am lig-ni vi-tæ. * Vi-de-tæ ne for-te su-mat de

lig-no vi-tæ et vi-vat in æ-ter-num.

At the end of which God shall go away to the church. Then Adam shall have a spade and Eve a mattock and they shall begin to cultivate the ground and they shall sow wheat in it. After they have sowed, they shall go and sit somewhere for a little while, as if wearied of work, and, weeping, they shall look back often towards Paradise, striking their breasts. Meanwhile the devil shall come and shall plant thorns and thistles in their plot and go away. When Adam and Eve come to their plot and see the thorns and thistles growing, they shall be seized with violent grief and prostrate themselves on the ground and sitting there they shall beat their breasts and thighs, showing their grief in their actions; and Adam shall begin his lament:

ADAM   Alas! Wretched, that ever I saw this hour
    When sins of mine have overwhelmed me so   520
    That I've forsaken God whom all adore;
    Who'll intercede with Him to help me now?

Here shall Adam look back to Paradise, and shall lift up both his hands towards it and inclining his head devoutly he shall say:

ADAM   Ah!—Paradise, our glorious residence,
    Garden of bliss, beautiful to our sense!
    Exiled I am indeed because of sin;
    I've lost all hope of getting back again.
      I was inside, yet scarcely did enjoy;
    Followed advice which brought me banishment.

Now it's too late—what use is it to sigh?
Though I repent, I have my punishment.   530
　　Where was my wisdom, where my memory,
That I for Satan left the King of Glory?
Now, though I labour, it's no use to me:
My sins will be recounted in man's story.

*Then he shall raise his hand towards Eve, who shall be a little
distant from him, and shaking his head with great indignation
he shall say to her:*

　　O evil woman, with a traitor's heart
Thus did you send me quickly to perdition,
When reasoning and sense you did pervert.
Now I repent, but cannot have remission.
　　Unhappy Eve, how prompt you were to sin,
How swiftly followed counsel from the devil!   540
You brought me death; I lost the life within;
Your sin shall be inscribed in every chronicle.
　　Do you see the signs of chaos come again?
The earth itself feels our disgraceful curse.
We sowed our wheat; and thistles grow, not grain;
Wearily sweated, but the harvest's worse.
　　You saw the start of this our evil end—
A heavy sorrow, yet greater is in store;
To hell we shall be taken. Understand,
Torment and pain we'll suffer evermore.   550
　　O wretched Eve, what do you say now?
These are your winnings, this your heritage.
You'll never have a blessing to bestow—
Unreasonable, perverse, into old age.
　　All those who issue from our mutual seed
Will share the punishment for your misdeed.
It falls on all, although you did the wrong;
Before the doom's reversed, it will be long.

Then shall Eve reply to Adam:

EVE   Adam, my lord, on me reproach you've bent:
　　You blame me for my crime and castigate.   560
　　If I did wrong, I feel the punishment;
　　I am to blame, God is the magistrate.

　　　Both against God and you it was a crime;
　　My wickedness men will for long recall.
　　My sins are hateful to me; great is my blame.
　　A sinner—there's no good in me at all.

　　　I've no excuse; to God how could I defend
　　Myself? No grounds can clear me of this sin.
　　Forgive me, since I cannot make amend:
　　If I were able, I would—with offering   570

　　　Sinful, unhappy, wretched that I am
　　Before God's face I'm overcome with shame.
　　Death, take me now, and let me live no more!
　　I am in peril, and cannot reach the shore.

　　　The wicked serpent, evil-hearted snake,
　　Compelled me of the cursed fruit to take.
　　I gave you some—to do you good, I thought;
　　Sank you in sin and cannot lift you out.

　　　Why could I not Creation's Lord obey?
　　Why did I not accept a husband's care?   580
　　You did wrong too; but first I showed the way.
　　The evil done will take an age to cure.

　　　My wicked deed, my fateful accident,
　　Will make our offspring pay the highest price.
　　The fruit was sweet; but stern the punishment;
　　To eat was wicked, and we were unwise.

　　　Nevertheless, my hope in God I place—
　　For sin there will be reconciliation.
　　God will bestow His favour and His grace;
　　His strength from Hell will bring us to salvation.   590

*Then shall come the devil, and three or four other devils with
him, carrying in their hands iron chains and manacles, which
they shall put round the necks of Adam and Eve. And some of
the devils shall drive them, and others shall drag them, to hell;
yet other devils shall be near hell to meet them as they come,*

and they shall make a great dance amongst themselves at the damnation of Adam and Eve; and some of the devils shall point to them as they come, and shall receive them and despatch them to hell. From hell they shall make a great smoke to arise, and shall shout to each other in their joy; and they shall bang their cauldrons and kettles together so that they can be heard outside. And after a little while the devils shall emerge and run around the 'place'; some, however, shall remain in hell.

Then shall come Cain and Abel. Cain shall be clothed in red garments, but Abel in white, and they shall cultivate the ground which has been prepared. And when he has rested a little from his work, Abel shall address Cain, his brother, in a pleasant friendly way, saying to him:

ABEL   My brother Cain, the two of us are brothers,
   We are the sons of that first man on earth;
   'Adam' was his name; and 'Eve' was our mother's.
   In serving God let us now show our worth!
      In everything our God we must obey:
   So let us serve Him and win back His love,
   Which our own parents lost so foolishly;
   Our mutual friendship firm as His above!
      Let us serve God in ways that best Him please,
   And holding nothing back, give Him His dues.   600
   If, loyal-hearted, we obey Him well,
   We need not fear to lose our souls in hell.
      We'll render tithe and all His just demands:
   First fruits and offerings, gifts and sacrifice.
   But if the greed of holding ties our hands,
   We shall be lost in hell, past help of grace.
      Between us two let loving-kindness reign,
   No covetousness nor slander intervene.
   How should there any quarrel rise between
   Us two, who have the earth as our domain?   610

Then shall Cain look at his brother Abel as if deriding him and shall say to him:

CAIN   Good brother Abel, you're very good at preaching,
      Know how to make a decent speech, no doubt;
      But, anyone who listens to your teaching,—
      It won't be long before he's cleaned right out!
         Giving of tithes was never to my taste.
      Do as you like with what *you* have to waste;
      So far as mine's concerned, I am quite free—
      You won't be sent to hell because of me!
         Nature instructs us we should love each other:
      Between us two let there be no pretence!   620
      Who ever starts a fight against a brother
      Will pay for it—he can have no defence!

Then shall Abel speak to his brother Cain; and insomuch as he Cain has answered more mildly than usual, Abel shall say:

ABEL   Good brother Cain, listen to me!

CAIN   I'm listening. Go ahead. What is it?

ABEL   It's for your good.

CAIN   That's all the better.

ABEL   Don't set yourself up as a rebel!
      Don't exercise your pride on God!
      I'm warning you.

CAIN   I'm very grateful.

ABEL   *Believe* my words! Now let us go
      And make our offering; He likes it so.   630
      If God is truly pleased with us
      Why, then He will not hold us sinners.
      No harm will strike us from above:
      It's a wise step to get His love.

Let's go and offer in good measure
Altar gifts to give Him pleasure.
That He may love us, let us pray,
And keep us safe both night and day.

*Then Cain shall answer as if Abel's counsel pleased him,
saying:*

CAIN It's true, good Abel, all you've said;
  That speech was beautifully made.   640
  I'll certainly take your words to heart:
  It's right to sacrifice—let us depart!
  What will you offer?

ABEL   I? A lamb.
  The best, most perfect specimen,
  That I can find within our pen
  I'll offer. Nothing else will do
  For Him; I'll offer incense too.
  Now my whole plan I've shared with you.
  What will you offer?

CAIN   Me? some corn
  Just like the stuff He's given me, man.   650

ABEL Some of the best?

CAIN   What's that you said?
  I'll need that tonight to make my bread.

ABEL That kind of offering will not seem
  Worthy of God.

CAIN   You live in a dream.

ABEL You are well off. You've got rich stock.

CAIN I have.

ABEL   Why don't you count the lot,
And give to God his one-in-ten?
Offer with all your fervour, when
You're offering to God. This way
You stand to gain, for He'll repay.   660
Well, will you do this?

CAIN   I think you're mad.
[*line missing*]. . . .
One from ten leaves only nine!
Your reasoning's not worth a bean.
Come on, let's offer! each on his own,
Whatever he fancies.

ABEL   All right then.

Then shall they go to two big stones which shall be put ready for the purpose. The stones shall be well apart, so that when God appears, Abel's stone shall be on his right hand, but Cain's stone on his left. Abel shall offer a lamb and incense, from which he shall make smoke ascend. Cain shall offer a handful of corn. God then appearing shall bless Abel's gifts and despise Cain's. Then after the offering Cain shall put on a threatening face against Abel; and, the offerings once made, they shall go to their own places. Then Cain shall come to Abel, wanting to get him outside, craftily, so that he may kill him; and he shall say to Abel:

CAIN   Well, brother! Let us go outside.

ABEL   What for?

CAIN   To take some relaxation,
And have a look round at our crops,
See how they're growing—if they're in flower.   670
Let us be off back to the fields;
We'll feel the better for it, later.

ABEL   I'll go with you, wherever you want.

CAIN   Well, come on then! You won't regret it.

ABEL   You are my elder brother, so—
I'm happy to observe your wishes.

CAIN   You go in front, I'll come behind,
Strolling along, quite at my ease.

*Then shall they both go to a distant place and, as it were, a
hidden one, where Cain like a madman shall attack Abel
wishing to kill him, and shall say to him:*

CAIN   Abel! You're dead.

ABEL   I, dead? How's that?

CAIN   I want to be revenged on you.   680

ABEL   Have I done wrong?

CAIN   Yes, deep wrong.
You're a traitor through and through.

ABEL   I'm certainly not.

CAIN   Do you say 'Not'?

ABEL   I've never had a traitorous thought.

CAIN   You've done one, though.

ABEL   I have? How?

CAIN   You'll soon know!

ABEL   I don't understand.

CAIN   I'll do my best to shed some light.

ABEL   You'll never be able to prove it true.

CAIN   The proof's all ready.

ABEL   God will help me.

CAIN   I'm going to kill you.   690

ABEL   He will know.

*Then shall Cain raise his right hand threateningly against
Abel saying:*

CAIN   See here! This arm will prove my case.

ABEL   My trust is in the God of grace.

CAIN   He'll be no use to you against *me*!

ABEL   He's able to upset your scheme.

CAIN   He cannot rescue you from death.

ABEL   In his will is my only peace.

CAIN   Do you want to hear why I shall kill you?

ABEL   Yes, tell me.

CAIN   Here's the reason then:
        You've worked yourself into God's affections,
        Because of you, I'm in the cold;   700
        Because of you, he spurned my gift.
        D'you think then I shan't pay you back?
        I'll give you proper compensation—
        Your death today upon this sand.

ABEL   If you murder me, that *will* be wrong;
        God will revenge my death on you.

I never wronged you, God is my witness,
I never slandered you to Him;
But rather I told you what to do
To deserve the peace He gives: 710
Give Him all the dues He claims,
Tithes and firstfruits and oblations—
This is the way you'll win His favour.
You did not do it—now you're angry.
But God is faithful: the man who serves Him
Is richly rewarded and loses nothing.

CAIN   You've talked too much. Now you must die.

ABEL   What are you saying? You brought me here.
I came because I trusted you.

CAIN   Your confidence will be wasted now.   720
I'm going to kill you. I challenge you!

ABEL   Pray God have mercy on my soul!

*Then shall Abel genuflect towards the east. And he shall have a
pot hidden in his clothes, which Cain shall strike as if he were
really killing Abel. Abel, moreover, shall lie prostrate, as if
dead.*

The choir shall sing: Ubi est Abel, frater tuus?

*Meanwhile God shall come from the church to Cain and, after
the choir have finished their respond, He shall say to Cain, as
if He were angry:*

GOD   Cain, where is your brother, Abel?
Have you now set up as a rebel?
You have begun to raise up strife
Against me! Show me him alive!

CAIN   How do I know, sir, where he's gone—
Perhaps in the fields, perhaps at home?

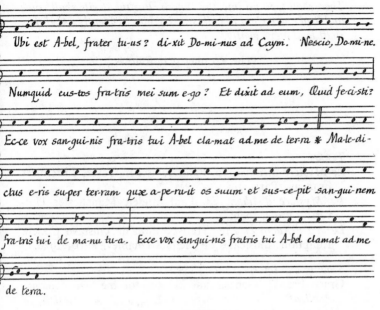

Ubi est A-bel, frater tu-us? di-xit Do-mi-nus ad Caym. Nescio, Do-mi-ne. Numquid cus-tos fra-tris mei sum e-go? Et dixit ad eum, Quid fe-ci-sti? Ec-ce vox san-gui-nis fra-tris tu-i A-bel cla-mat ad me de ter-ra * Ma-le-di-ctus e-ris su-per ter-ram quæ a-pe-ru-it os suum et sus-ce-pit san-gui-nem fra-tris tu-i de ma-nu tu-a. Ecce vox san-gui-nis fratris tui A-bel clamat ad me de terra.

Why should I have him under my eye?
I was never my brother's keeper. 730

GOD   What have you done? Where have you laid
Your brother, for I know you've shed
His blood? it raises up a cry—
The sound has reached me in the sky.
This is an evil thing you've done,
You'll bear my curse till your life is gone.
This curse shall rest continuously.
For such sin, such a penalty:
I wish you to be spared from death;
In sorrow you shall draw your breath. 740
Cain's murderer (who could be so bold?)
Will suffer for it sevenfold.
You've killed your brother who trusted me:
Heavy your penitence shall be.

Then shall God go into the church. But the devils shall come and lead away Cain to hell, striking him frequently; Abel they shall lead more gently.

[The Prophet play follows.]

Texts

Le Mystère d'Adam, ed. Paul Aebischer, Textes Littéraires Français, Paris, 1963.

Le Mystère d'Adam, ed. Paul Studer, Manchester University Press, 1949.

Le Jeu d'Adam et Eve, Transposition de Gustave Cohen, Adaptions musicales de Jacques Chailley, Paris, 1936.

Staging and interpretation

Grace Frank, 'Genesis and Staging of the *Jeu d'Adam*', *Publications of the Modern Language Association of America* LIX (1944), pp. 7–17.

Erich Auerbach, *Mimesis*, translated by Willard Trask, Doubleday Anchor Books, New York, 1957, chapter 7.

LA SEINTE
RESURECCION

PERSONS OF THE PLAY

EXPOSITOR
JOSEPH OF ARIMATHIA
NICODEMUS
LONGINUS
PILATE
FIRST SOLDIER[1]
SECOND SOLDIER[2]
CAIAPHAS
FIRST GUARD[1]
SECOND GUARD[2]
THIRD GUARD
FOURTH GUARD
LEVI, priest of Jewish Law
A MAN

[1] [2] These are just called *miles* in the original. We have distinguished between the Soldiers who arrest Longinus and the Guards who watch the Tomb. These parts may be doubled.

E

LA SEINTE RESURECCION

Text

It is thought that *La Seinte Resureccion* was composed in England *c.* 1180, by a *clerc* writing the Anglo-Norman idiom current at the time. The original must have been a lengthy and ambitious affair, but the two versions of the play that have survived are both incomplete: one, an early fourteenth-century manuscript of an early thirteenth-century revision of the play (the Paris MS., *P*); the other, a mid-thirteenth-century revision, copied down in a Canterbury manuscript (*C*) in about 1275. Both versions are edited in the Anglo-Norman Text Society edition (1943). We have translated the longer, Canterbury version from this edition.

The play is intended for open-air performance before a popular rather than clerical audience. It has little in common with the contemporary Latin liturgical drama of the Resurrection; rather, it makes much of the role of Joseph of Arimathia from the *Apocrypha* and from contemporary romance. The Canterbury fragment ends, excitingly, with Joseph's arrest. We can only surmise how the play ended from the list of 'houses', 'places' and persons in the 'pro-logue'. It would have shown Christ's Harrowing of Hell and liberation of the enchained Patriarchs, the liberation of Joseph from the Tower, Christ's Resurrection, the fright of the Guards and their report to Pilate, the visit of the three Maries and of the Disciples to the empty Tomb, Christ's journey with the Travellers to Emmaus, His meeting with the Disciples in Galilee, and His Ascension to Heaven. It would have been a three-hour spectacle at least.

Both the manuscript texts were apparently intended for

readers rather than prospective producers; as a result, their 'prologues' and rubrics present many problems of interpretation. The *C* 'prologue' describes the outdoor stage-set and the acting parts required in a rather cryptic way. The remaining rubrics consist chiefly of links between the dialogue, narrating the movements of the characters *in the past tense*. It is possible that these lines were actually spoken by a Narrator or Expositor during performance. Such a role seems to have been used in the fragmentary *Passion d'Autun* (*c*. 1300), while the fourteenth-century Cornish plays probably had an 'on stage' prompter directing the action. We have left the puzzling narrative lines in their original tenses and have ascribed them all to an Expositor. In the 'prologue' he speaks in the future, as if advising a prospective producer of the play. During most of the action he speaks in the past tense, as if he were seeing with his inner eye the historical action which the play re-enacts. But sometimes (e.g. 345–8, 411–2) he reverts to a more practical role and describes, or directs, the dramatic action as it unfolds.

Staging

The original staging of the play has been the subject of controversy, partly because of the existence of the two versions of the 'prologue'; in fact, the differences between these two are very slight if the right lay-out is conceived.[1] The *C* 'prologue' distinguishes between 'houses' (*maisuns*), which are structural, and 'places' (*lius*), which are merely areas of ground where characters or groups of characters belong, and which may have been marked out with rope or stones.

The seven 'houses' and eight 'places' are arranged as shown in the diagram, which reconstructs the set as the Expositor describes it.

In a modern production, as the Expositor announces the

---

[1] Our interpretation of the staging for the Canterbury text is indebted to that made by O. B. Hardison, Jr. (*Christian Rite and Christian Drama*, p. 266), with the Paris text as a basis, although it differs from his.

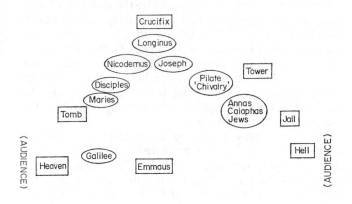

AUDIENCE

inhabitants of each 'place' the actors concerned might walk into their 'houses' and circles, ready for the play to begin.

We know nothing about the size or nature of the 'houses' proposed by the twelfth-century dramatist. It seems likely that the Crucifix was large enough to support the body of an actor, equipped with a bladder of 'blood' (123ff.), playing Christ; he would later rise out of a box-like Tomb by pushing up its lid. Nicodemus climbs 'up' to unfasten Christ's hands (277) and probably employed a small ladder such as is shown in contemporary iconography of the scene. Hell may have been similar to that detailed for *Adam* (they both house devils as well as patriarchs waiting liberation). For the rest a modern producer probably should adopt emblematic properties. The Tower of David and Bartholomew (representing the medieval Tower of David at the Western gate of Jerusalem, made famous by the visits of pilgrims) need be no more than barrel-sized. It was probably used only for the imprisonment of Joseph.

Details of costume are suggested by the medieval illustrations of the Deposition and Resurrection reproduced in Otto Pächt's *Rise of Pictorial Narrative in Twelfth-Century England*, and in those of the *St. Albans Psalter*. This iconography suggests that realistic contemporary costumes were used: the Soldiers and Guards should have chain-mail suits and carry shields, the Jews, long robes, beards and hats, and the Travellers (who do not appear in the fragment) should be dressed as medieval pilgrims.

Clearly the play would be unsatisfactory to perform exactly as it stands. If it is presented as a religious experience, an appropriate place to break off would be after the first part of Joseph's invocation to Christ (i.e. at 484). The play could then be rounded off by the singing of a Resurrection hymn or in some similar manner. Alternatively, the play could be produced simply for the interest of its unusual dramatic technique. In this case the problem of a suitable dramatic conclusion must be faced. It would be possible to show the further episodes in dumb-show, observing the same principles of action (movement between 'places' or 'houses') used in the extant text. Or, a conclusion could be made by using the text of one of the surviving English play cycles. The *Chester Plays* (nos. 17–20) and the plays (nos. 35–39) in the Lincoln cycle (still known misleadingly as *Ludus Coventriae*) are briefest and could be adapted to the *Resureccion* staging. The most attractive solution might be to use a cut version of the fourteenth-century Cornish cycle (ed. E. Norris, *The Ancient Cornish Drama*, vol. 2). The Cornish play alone includes the apocryphal imprisonment and miraculous liberation of Joseph of Arimathia as well as the other episodes listed above; furthermore, like the *Resureccion*, it was played in an outdoor theatre, which was equipped with tents, stages and 'scaffolds'.

LA SEINTE RESURECCION

EXPOSITOR

If, devoutly, you intend,
For God's glory, to represent
The Resurrection before a crowd
And to speak each part of it aloud,
You should arrange an open space
Large enough for the acting place.
Then carefully you should provide
The playing 'places' on each side.
The 'houses' too must be built there,
Set out in order with great care.   10
First, for the Crucifix find room;
The next 'house' is the Holy Tomb,
With its guard, four soldiers brave,
And the Maries who shall visit the grave.
The disciples standing in their stall
Must keep their bearing honourable.
Now there's a 'place' for Nicodemus,
And one for the beggar, blind Longinus;
A 'place' for Joseph of Arimathia,
Pilate and his knights are here;   20
Then Annas, Caiaphas, and the Jews.
The Tower of David and Bartholomew
And a Jail there must also be,
To lock prisoners in captivity.
On one side should be set up Hell,
Which shall be occupied by devils
And by the Patriarchs, who are restrained
By fettering them there in chains.
Do not forget the 'house' for Heaven,

In which the angels have their dwelling.   30
And someone ought to make a 'place'
For Galilee, central in the space,
With Emmaus, a little castle
In which the pilgrims find a hostel.
So, when the crowd has settled down
And on all sides there is no sound,
Then Joseph of Arimathia shall come
To Pilate and shall say to him:

JOSEPH   May God, who from the hands of Pharaoh
    Rescued Moses and Aaron too,   40
    Bless my lord and master Pilate,
    Granting him both rank and fame.

PILATE   May Hercules, who slew the dragon
    And overcame the ancient Gerion,
    Grant him, who greets me with true love,
    Wealth and honour among men.

JOSEPH   My lord Pilate, please believe
    I greet you in all friendliness!
    If ever you want a favour done,
    I'm glad to do it—you know that well.   50
    I'm sure you'd do the same for me
    If I should ask you anything.

PILATE   Courage, man! Put your request—
    I'll listen with a friendly ear.
    It's only right and reasonable,
    Since you have paid me such respect,
    That I should pay you back in kind.
    Believe me, you'll find that it is so.

JOSEPH   Thank you, I'm most grateful, sir.
    I'm glad if I have been of use.   60
    Please don't take offence, my lord,
    If I mention Mary's son to you—

The man on the gallows, over there.
Be sure of this: he was honest
And was a favourite of God's;
And now you've killed him, you and the Jews.
You should be dreadfully afraid
Of some misfortune plaguing you.

PILATE Joseph of Arimathia, my friend,
    I shan't conceal my motives from you: 70
    The Jews were moved by vicious hate
    And undertook this wicked crime.
    I consented out of policy
    So as not to lose my post.
    If I had been accused at Rome,
    I could easily have lost my life.
    As for him, I couldn't deny
    He called himself the King of Jews,
    Opposing Caesar, who's governor
    And emperor of all the world.   80

JOSEPH Since we've begun to talk of that,
    Let me explain, sir, what he meant.
    Jesus called himself a king,
    Not to challenge Caesar's rule,
    Nor to steal his worldly power,
    But to win *him* a heavenly crown.
    If he meant harm, they haven't suffered—
    Those crafty Jews who are such cowards!
    But what does it matter? I beg you please
    To let me have his corpse to bury.   90
    If you see that you've done wrong,
    Ask his mercy, he'll hear you kindly;
    No one begs his mercy in vain.
    But he'll be revenged, however it be.

PILATE Has he passed out of this life?

JOSEPH Yes, my lord, there is no doubt.

PILATE   Get up, you soldiers! Quickly now,
    Run over where that man is hanging—
    The one who has been crucified—
    And ascertain if he is dead.   100

EXPOSITOR
Two of his soldiers then went off,
Carrying lances in their hands,
And said to Longinus, who was blind
And whom they discovered sitting near:

FIRST SOLDIER   Do you want to make some money, friend?

LONGINUS   Yes, thank you sir, indeed I do.

FIRST SOLDIER   Come on, then, you shall have a shilling
    For sticking Jesus in the side.

LONGINUS   I'll go with you most gladly, sir.
    I badly need to earn some money;   110
    I'm very poor—I've got no means;
    I often beg, but don't get much.
    I can't get out and about these days.
    Without my sight, I'm badly off.

FIRST SOLDIER   Give me your hand, I'll lead you there.

LONGINUS   I shall not manage otherwise.

EXPOSITOR
When they had reached the Crucifix,
He put a lance in Longinus' hand.

FIRST SOLDIER   Hold this lance and shove it hard.

LONGINUS   I'll push it right into the heart.   120

FIRST SOLDIER   Make it go through into his lungs,
    Then we shall know if he's dead or not.

EXPOSITOR
He took the lance and pierced the heart;
Blood and water burst out at once,
Flowed down the spear on to his hands.
With the moisture he wetted his face;
When the blood and water touched his eyes,
Longinus recovered his sight and said:

LONGINUS   Jesus! O my noble lord!   130
  I don't know what in the world to say.
  You are a miraculous doctor, when
  You turn your anger into mercy!
  I ought to have died for what I did,
  But you have shown me such great love,
  That my eyes, blind all my life, now see!
  Have mercy on me, I am yours.

EXPOSITOR
Then he prostrated himself in prayer,
And one of the soldiers said to his mate:

FIRST SOLDIER   What's that, my friend? He says he sees?

OTHER SOLDIER   That's what he says—maybe not true.   140
  Longinus, take your dozen pence—
  They're yours.

LONGINUS   I don't need pay—except
  Seeing my lord and master here.
  He is not dead, though he's passed away.

SECOND SOLDIER   Let's go to Pilate and tell him this:
  If he won't believe we'll swear on oath.

(*The two soldiers return to Pilate's 'place'.*)

FIRST SOLDIER   Most mighty prince, you may be sure
  Jesus Christ has left this life.

But we have seen a miracle—
Didn't you see it too, my friend?   150

SECOND SOLDIER   We saw it happen, both of us.

PILATE   Silence, fellows! Not one word more!
    Joseph, my friend, you've served me well;
    Take the body, I grant you leave.

JOSEPH   I thank you, sir, with all my heart.
    I'm glad if I've ever been of service.

EXPOSITOR
When Joseph had taken leave of Pilate,
He went towards Nicodemus' 'place'
And Pilate said to the man he summoned:

PILATE   You, fellow, come here at once!   160
    What's this miracle you've seen?
    Speak up, say what was in your mind
    When I silenced you just now.

FIRST SOLDIER   It was blind Longinus made the wound;
    He shoved the spear in the hanged man's side,
    Put his hands all bloody up to his eyes—
    The luckiest thing he did in his life.
    Was blind before and now he can see—
    No wonder he thinks the man is God.

PILATE   Quiet, you slave! Don't tell a soul.   170
    Pure fantasy—don't trust it at all!
    I tell you, arrest Longinus now
    And shut him up in jail at once
    To stop him preaching this around.

EXPOSITOR
They went at once to find Longinus
And said to him maliciously:

FIRST SOLDIER   Well, friend, you shall go to jail—
  Rough old lodgings for you tonight,
  For believing the fellow on the gallows   180
  And saying he gave you back your sight.

LONGINUS   He really did restore my sight.
  I believe him perfectly,
  Because he's Lord and King of Heaven.

FIRST SOLDIER   It's not true you can see a thing;
  It's a lie, we know that perfectly well.

LONGINUS   What's that? Then I can't see at all?
  One of you doubts that it is true?

FIRST SOLDIER   Pilate thinks it's just a yarn.

LONGINUS   Then Pilate is the devil's son!   190
  May he be damned—the Jews as well,
  For putting God's own son to death!

FIRST SOLDIER   You slandered before, but this is worse;
  You'll have to go to jail for this.
  Get on in front—go quickly now!

LONGINUS   Thanks be to God for what he's done!

EXPOSITOR
When they had reached the prison 'house',
The soldiers spoke these words to him:

FIRST SOLDIER   Get in there, you! You won't get out
  Without losing all you have—   200
  Your life and every single limb—
  Unless you repudiate Mary's son.

LONGINUS   Son of the father, not of flesh,
  Of God the father motherless:

He is the Lord and King of Heaven—
I will affirm what I believe.
I put my life into his hands—
It doesn't matter what they say.

EXPOSITOR
Meanwhile Joseph, that honest man,
Has come to speak with Nicodemus.   210

JOSEPH   Nicodemus, come with me
    To take our king down from the cross.
    Let's not forsake him because he's dead;
    He'll be a comfort to us still.
    He is not dead, but passed away;
    He'll rise again, I know through faith.
    Those who loved and honoured him
    Will be rewarded, you may be sure.
    Let's go together, my dear friend;
    At least let's pay him the respect   220
    Of burying his body honourably
    And placing it inside a tomb.

NICODEMUS   I realize, Joseph, that the Lord
    Whose body hangs upon the cross
    Was truly a prophet, a holy man,
    Filled with the grace and power of God;
    He made me fully understand
    When I came to him to learn.
    But still, I daren't commit myself
    To come with you and take him down.   230
    Even though I dearly wish
    I could do him this great service,
    I am afraid to break the law—
    I daren't have any part in it.

JOSEPH   I have the leave of Pilate himself.

NICODEMUS   But I have not—I'm scared of trouble.

JOSEPH I'll go with you to see him now.
    Come on, then—I'll take you there.

NICODEMUS I'll do it with a calmer mind
    When I hear it from his very mouth.   240

EXPOSITOR
The two of them went to Pilate together,
And Joseph spoke up, saying to him:

JOSEPH My lord, I need a friend to help,
    But I can't unless I have your leave.
    Give this man your guarantee
    He may come with me without fear.

PILATE My good friend, you may proceed;
    Nothing unpleasant will happen to you.
    You may be firmly confident
    You have my warrant for what you do.   250

EXPOSITOR
The two of them went towards the Cross,
Taking with them a pair of servants,
One who carried the implements,
The other a box with the ointment in.
And when they came to the foot of the Cross,
Joseph cried out in a mighty voice:

JOSEPH Jesus, Jesus, son of Mary,
    Blessed Virgin, sweet and holy!
    Judas did a dreadful crime
    To you, and did himself great wrong,   260
    When out of spite he traded you
    To those who bore you little love.
    Judas' soul perished in hell
    When he committed suicide.
    He did not know what powerful help
    Those who ask for mercy have.

Poor wretched Jews, they are my people,
How they shall suffer for this deed!
More cursed than any other race,
Because they put this man to death.   270
Their punishment shall be severe
When they shall come to judgment day.

EXPOSITOR
Nicodemus picked up his tools,
And Joseph told him what to do.

JOSEPH   First, start working on the feet.

NICODEMUS   Certainly, I'll do it gently.

JOSEPH   Climb up to the hands and pull out the nails.

NICODEMUS   Yes, sir, I'll manage both of them.

EXPOSITOR
When Nicodemus had done his part,
He spoke to Joseph, who held the body.   280

NICODEMUS   Take him gently in your arms.

JOSEPH   You may be sure I have him safe.

EXPOSITOR
They lifted the body gently down
And Joseph said to one of his men:

JOSEPH   Hand me the ointment, in that box,
   And I'll embalm this body here.

EXPOSITOR
When the man had handed him the spice,
Nicodemus cried out aloud:

NICODEMUS   O God, O Lord omnipotent,
    Earth and sky and sea and wind   290
    Together in perfect harmony
    Your absolute command obey!
    So do all things which you gave life,
    Except for evil men on earth,
    Who forced this man to suffer torment—
    Condemned to die without fair judgment.
    Harsh vengeance shall be their reward,
    Except you are so gentle, lord.
    Grant that we may worthily
    Give burial to this sacred body.   300

EXPOSITOR
When they had anointed the corpse
They placed it on a funeral bier.

NICODEMUS   Joseph, you are the elder man,
    You take the head, and I the feet,
    And we shall bury him at once.
    Have you seen where he's to lie

JOSEPH   I've made a handsome sepulchre,
    Cut fresh and new out of a rock.
    Now let's carry him to that place,
    Where his body must be buried.   310

EXPOSITOR
When they've arrived, they set down the bier
And Joseph speaks to his friend as follows:

JOSEPH   Nicodemus, I'll tell you now
    About the tomb I have prepared.
    Before I had this sepulchre made
    I saw the miraculous power of the stone
    In a vision, while I slept.
    What a wonderful apparition!
    I thought I saw the angels of heaven—

F

Six or seven, I don't know how many—   320
Descending, radiant with light; they sat
Singing sweetly, upon this rock,
Unfolded a great winding sheet
And spread it out across the stone.
The cloth inside was purest white
And outside coloured red as blood.
When I saw this, I was amazed
And told my father about the dream.
He told me what its meaning was:
A holy corpse should be buried there.   330
And this is why I've made the tomb.

NICODEMUS   Joseph, now it has truly happened—
There never was a holier man
Than this one whom you'll bury here.

JOSEPH   This slab of rock must go on top.
I made it beforehand, ready to fit.
Let's lift it on. Though it's so big,
He'll still rise up when that's his will.
God of Heaven, almighty King,
Christ's body I commend to you.   340
For love of him be our protector
Every day, now and for ever.
May he grant us to serve him loyally,
And in his service to live and die.

EXPOSITOR
These two knights turn back again
And each comes to his proper 'place'.
Meanwhile, Caiaphas gets up
And, coming hot-foot to Pilate, says:

CAIAPHAS   Lord Pilate, listen to my advice—
I should do wrong to keep it from you: 350
That crafty Jesus, deceitful wretch,
Hanged over there like a common thief,

Maintained when he was still alive
(And ignorant fools believe it's true)
He'd rise again after three days.
One must be a fool to believe in that!
But let us have the sepulchre watched
So his followers cannot steal him away
And then say that he's still alive.
They'll mislead poor simpletons.   360
If he gets out, there'll be trouble.

PILATE   Have it guarded, my worthy friend.

EXPOSITOR
One of the sergeants jumped to his feet
And spoke to Pilate in these words:

FIRST GUARD   If anyone offers the job to me,
    I'll keep a guard over the tomb.
    And, if it happens by any chance,
    While I'm on duty, a friend of his
    Should come there hoping to snatch him away,
    He won't depart without some aches!   370
    He won't have an arm or leg left whole.
    And I shan't ask for absolution.

EXPOSITOR
Three of the others leaped up at once
And spoke to the one who took the lead.

SECOND GUARD   We'll go along with you, good friend,
    And help you watch the sepulchre.
    If anyone comes, we shall arrest him.
    If Jesus rises, we'll find out.

THIRD GUARD   Let's go there now, as fast as we can,
    And watch the monument carefully.   380
    If anyone comes—I've got the idea—
    We'll give him a roughish handling.

FOURTH GUARD   By the duty I owe to Pilate—
   And he deserves to have respect—
   If anyone comes to carry him off,
   We'll give him a proper shaking up.

CAIAPHAS   I'll go along with you as well,
   To get this business organized.
   My lord, you agree this should be so?

PILATE   Caiaphas, I agree to this.   390

EXPOSITOR
When Caiaphas had led them there
He gave his orders to the men.

CAIAPHAS   Now, stay here by the sepulchre,
   And keep a sharp look-out all round.
   If you fall asleep and he gets taken,
   We shall never be friends again!
   But first, you must swear upon our Law
   Truly to keep this oath you make:
   If any man is foolish enough
   To come to this place after dusk   400
   Sneaking and spying out the land
   So he can steal the body away—
   Although he tells you it isn't so—
   Swear this solemnly here and now,
   That whoever he is, big or small,
   If he hasn't got the princes' warrant,
   You'll grab him fiercely by the throat.
   And when you've got him, bring him to me.
   Swear you'll loyally keep this oath.
   Where's the Book of Scriptures? Have it brought.   410

EXPOSITOR
Look, there's a priest, Levi by name,
Who has written the Law of Moses down.

LEVI See, here's the Law that Moses made,
   As God himself dictated it;
   Here are all the ten commandments.
   A perjurer will be revealed.

CAIAPHAS All of you, swear upon this book
   To keep the oath that I just spoke.

FIRST GUARD By the Law that's written here,
   If any man comes creeping by,   420
   I undertake to capture him
   As best I can and hand him to you.

SECOND GUARD I swear by the power of the Holy Law
   I'll faithfully keep to your command.

THIRD GUARD If it be the will of God,
   By the Sacred Law I'll keep it too.

FOURTH GUARD So help me both my God and Scripture,
   Then for my part I will keep the oath.

EXPOSITOR
Caiaphas then went away
And the first of the sergeants spoke to the rest.   430

FIRST GUARD You two fellows, keep watch there.
   This man and I will stand over here.
   However stealthily he may rise
   One of us will notice it.

SECOND GUARD Now we have close guard on him,
   He'll never rise with our consent,
   Nor be stolen away by one of his gang.
   Too bad for them if they're found here!

THIRD GUARD By God—and may he save us all!—
   His men will come here far too late.   440

He'll be strung up with a crafty noose
If he's caught escaping on *our* side.
I don't care if he's as strong
As mighty Samson, long ago,
Who ripped the skin clean off a lion;
Then, while he sat inside a castle,
Pulled its gateways crashing down
And walked off among his enemies.
Unless this fellow does the same
He'll never leave this place, because   450
We shall keep him here by force.
Now stay awake, we'll keep the watch!

EXPOSITOR
A man who overheard their talk
Went to Joseph and said to him:

MAN   My lord Joseph of Arimathia—
   God be your guide as long as you live!
   What do you think has happened now?
   They've posted sentries round the grave—
   There are four soldiers, fully armed,
   To keep the corpse from being stolen.   460

JOSEPH   Is this news true?

MAN   Yes, honestly.

JOSEPH   Then I shall go there secretly
   To make certain that the blessed body
   Is never thrown to dogs or swine,
   And to see there's nothing underhand.

MAN   Your lordship shall not go alone—
   I'll go with you if you like.

JOSEPH   Don't do that; you'd better stay.
   I'll go quietly on my own.
   Look, there's a cape. I'll put it on.   470

EXPOSITOR
When he had muffled himself in the cape
He raised his hands and cried aloud:

JOSEPH Jesus! Jesus! My dearest lord!
  You were a doctor whilst you lived
  And once raised Lazarus from the dead.
  What will you do? Will you revive?
  Will you yourself not rise from death?
  You said you would—that comforts me.
  I still have perfect faith in this,
  For you're the Son of God Almighty.   480
  I know with perfect sureness too
  No man's so clever nor so strong
  That he can stop or hinder you
  When you desire to rise again.
  But, all the same, I long to be sure
  That your body will lie peacefully
  And will not be removed from here
  Till from the grave it is raised on high.

EXPOSITOR
When Joseph had come close to the tomb
One of them shouts that he's been seen.   490

FIRST GUARD Jump to it, men! Look—there's a thief!
  If we don't take him we shall be perjured.
  We'll soon have him without a struggle—
  He's all alone if I see right.

EXPOSITOR
They all leaped out to capture him
Together, and angrily said to him:

FIRST GUARD Who are you, peasant? Are you a spy?

JOSEPH No. I am Joseph of Arimathia.

SECOND GUARD You, sir? What are you doing here?

JOSEPH   Guarding the body I buried today   500
   So it cannot be shamefully mauled
   Or carried away to another place.

SECOND GUARD   I'm sorry, sir, that you have come,
   Because we all have sworn on oath
   That whoever we find here we'll arrest
   And take post haste before the council.
   What shall we do?

FIRST GUARD   Take him along—
   Haven't we sworn?

SECOND GUARD   Yes, but still
   He's an important man, you know.

FIRST GUARD   Leave off, you know that makes no odds. 510
   Two of us will escort this man,
   You two stay here and keep the watch.

EXPOSITOR
These two led him before the princes
And, when they had arrived, they said:

FIRST GUARD   Lord Caiaphas, we've kept our oath
   To the best of our ability.
   Joseph of Arimathia is caught—
   His status didn't get him off.

CAIAPHAS   Ah, Joseph! Now it appears for sure
   That you were one of Jesus' men.
   What you're doing's against the law;
   And now at last we have our proof!

(*The text ends here.*)

(*The guards take Joseph and lock him in the Tower of David and Bartholomew.*)

Text
La Seinte Resureccion, ed. T. A. Jenkins, J. M. Manley, M. K. Pope, J. G. Wright, Anglo-Norman Text Society, Oxford, 1943.

Staging and Interpretation
O. B. Hardison Jr., *Christian Rite and Christian Drama in the Middle Ages*, Johns Hopkins Press, Baltimore, 1965, pp. 253–83.

W. Noomen, 'Passages narratifs dans les drames médiévaux français: Essai d'interpretation', *Revue Belge de Philologie et d'Histoire*, XXXI (1958), pp. 761–85.

Omer Jodogne, 'Recherches sur les débuts du théâtre religieux en France', *Cahiers de Civilisation Médiévale Xe–XIIe siècles* (Université de Poitiers), VIII (1965), pp. 1–24.

LE JEU DE
SAINT NICOLAS

by Jean Bodel

PERSONS OF THE PLAY

PREACHER (Prologue)
KING of Africa, Arabia and Saracen lands
SENESCHAL to the King
EMIR OF COINE
EMIR OF ORKENIE
EMIR OF OLIFERNE
EMIR FROM BEYOND THE WITHERED TREE
AUBERON, the courier
CONNART ('cuckold'), crier to the City governors
DURANT, jailer
ANGEL
SAINT NICHOLAS
THE GOOD MAN
CHRISTIANS
FIRST CHRISTIAN
YOUNG CHRISTIAN KNIGHT
TAVERNER
CAIGNET, barman
RAOUL, crier of wine to the townsmen
PINCEDÉ ('Pinchdice')
CLIQUET ('Chatterbox') } thieves
RASOIR ('Rasor')
TERVAGAN, the Saracen idol
Saracen Knights

LE JEU DE SAINT NICOLAS

Text
Le Jeu de Saint Nicolas was probably written between 1199 and 1202, at the time of preparations for the Fourth Crusade. The author, Jean Bodel, was a native of Arras and was employed as a clerk to the city governors. He was a member of the *Confrérie des jongleurs et des bourgeois d'Arras* and composed lyrical poems, a *Congé* or formal farewell, and an epic, *La Chanson des Saxons*, as well as this play. The clerks who worked for the city government apparently had a guild of their own, dedicated to Saint Nicholas, whose feast they celebrated with wine paid for by their employers and, perhaps, with entertainments such as Bodel's play. The Prologue says that the performance is on the evening before Saint Nicholas' Day (i.e. on December 5). However, the odd and rather wordy Prologue spoken by the 'preacher' may be apocryphal and added some years after the play's composition.

Saint Nicolas has survived in one manuscript (*c.* 1300), which contains many other works in Picard dialect written mainly by Arras poets, one of them being Adam de la Halle. The manuscript text is good and the difficulties are mainly ones of interpretation. Some passages are obscure because of the richness of Bodel's language, his use of slang words and puns, and because he assumes a detailed knowledge of contemporary Arras tavern customs and dice games. Although the text is clear, the rubrics of the original are obviously faulty in places and some speeches are assigned to the wrong character. In our translation we are indebted to the many scholars who have contributed to the establishing of a satisfactory text. We have principally followed F. J. Warne's edition (Blackwell, 1951), because it is the one most likely to be used by English readers. We have abandoned Warne's division into scenes but followed his line-numbering. We have also received considerable help from Albert Henry's edition (P.U.F. 1962). On several occasions we have preferred Henry's ascription of the speeches or his interpretation and these instances are recorded in the notes. In providing stage-directions for the dicing we have gone slightly beyond the strict requirements of staging in order to make the stage action comprehensible to a reader. An explanatory note on *Hazard* is given in the Notes (1111).

Bodel is both a master of word-play and of verse-forms. *Saint Nicolas* is composed chiefly in octosyllabics, but Bodel changes the rhyme pattern constantly, alternating rhymed couplets with sextets and octets. The octosyllabics are rendered here in our staple four-stress line, with rhyme used only occasionally for the most formal speeches. Bodel's alexandrines, grouped in quatrains with a single rhyme (e.g. 239–50, 384–411), and his similarly grouped decasyllabics are translated into pentameters, with alternate rhymes where greater formality was required.

Staging

The text is not specific about the staging originally intended and gives only some hints of production detail. The story requires five distinct locales where action occurs: the Saracen King's palace, the tavern, the prison, the distant lands of the Emirs, the battlefield. Characters move freely from one to another without the action stopping, and the delightful interweaving of high and low plots is accompanied by corresponding shifts of locale. Although the play could be produced according to the conventions of modern staging with a changeable set, a great deal would be lost. Ideally the action should be presented as continuous on a 'simultaneous', all-embracing set. (Thus Auberon goes at the King's command to summon pagan armies and on his way is tempted into the tavern (251). Later, as the thieves fall asleep in the tavern over their stolen goods, the King wakes at the palace to find his treasure gone (1187).)

Only three actual 'houses' are necessary. At the back of the 'place' there are the Tavern, the King's Palace, the Prison. (The Prologue mentions a *manoque* (18)—a hut or possibly an oratory, where the Christian is found, but this is not important in the play itself.)

The Tavern should be a porch-like structure opening into the 'place' (the Taverner invites the passing Auberon to sit *en ceste achinte*—'in this corner' or perhaps even 'on this terrace'); it has a doorway at the back through which wine is brought to the tables and dicing board. Outside there is a barrel-hoop tavern sign (254).

The Palace may be simply an ornamental arch with the King's throne beneath it. Adjoining it to one side is the Temple, which need not be a separate 'house', but merely a flight of steps leading up to an altar where the idol Tervagan is enshrined. Tervagan could be a gilded body-mask which is occupied for the purpose of the lamentation (1517). The actor slips away before the 'empty bladder' is toppled down the steps (1530). The mask may also be animated for the smiling and weeping prophecy (182).

The Prison could be modelled on the Hell described in the rubrics of *Adam*, having barred gates and visible means of torture.

The Emirs may be located anywhere at the perimeter of the 'place' and may have standards proclaiming the names of their realms.

The dead Christians and the Angel present something of a problem which may be solved by the inclusion of a fourth 'house', an open-topped tower representing Heaven. The Angel standing on the top appears and disappears with ease, and he addresses the Christian Knights and, later, the Christian in prison, from a position of eminence. After encouraging the Christians to die gladly, he could descend into the 'place' to lead the bodies from the battlefield into the tower of Heaven.[1]

---

[1] Cf. the Latin liturgical play, *Ordo Rachelis*, from the Fleury MS., in which an angel summons the slain innocents to rise; they enter the angelic choir singing joyfully.

The dialogue suggests some of the costumes and properties needed. The image of Saint Nicholas should be a small portable statue or even a painted icon, which shows Nicholas' cloven mitre—the subject of the jokes about his 'horns' (458, 505). Its keeper, the Christian, is poorly dressed and has a hood which makes him look monkish (506). The crier of wine, Raoul, carries a stick and tankard, which he beats together to attract customers.

Although humour is by no means confined to the 'low' plot, the distinctive tone of the play depends upon the differences and contrasts between the world of the palace and that of the tavern. Consequently, two distinct styles of acting should be employed, one exaggeratedly formal, the other free and naturalistic.

LE JEU DE SAINT NICOLAS

The Prologue

PREACHER   Oyez, Oyez, lords and ladies,
God's blessing be upon you all,
To keep you free from every harm!
We want to talk to you this evening
About Saint Nicholas, the Confessor,
Who did so many miracles.
The truth of the matter is, they say,
Exactly as we read in his Life.
There used to be a pagan king,
Whose country bordered on Christendom;   10
War raged all the time between them.
One day this pagan set upon
The Christians at the very moment
When they were least expecting it.
They were caught completely unawares
And many of them were killed or captured;
The pagans routed them easily.
At last they saw, inside a hovel,
A worthy man down on his knees
Saying his prayers before a statue   20
Of Nicholas, that valiant saint.
Those wicked bastards fell upon him
And shamefully maltreated him;
Seized both him and Nicholas's image,
Took firm hold and held him prisoner,
Until they came before the king,
Who was greatly elated at his triumph.
The soldiers told the king the story,
Shortly and briefly, about the Christian.

G

'You lout,' the king said to his prisoner,   30
'Do you believe in this piece of wood?'
'But, sir, it's made in the very likeness
Of holy Nicholas, whom I love.
I pray and call upon his name,
Because no one who from his heart
Calls him will ever be abandoned.
And he is such an excellent guard
That he gives back with interest
Anything one entrusts to him.'
'You wretch, I'll fry you to a turn,   40
If Nicholas doesn't return my treasure
With profits; I'll entrust it to him,
To test the truth of what you say.'
The king committed him to prison,
An iron collar round his neck;
Then he got his treasure-chests unlocked
And had the statue laid on top.
He said, if anyone harmed his treasure
And Nicholas didn't make it good,
The Christian would be drawn and quartered.   50
And so he left his treasure in trust.
Some robbers came to know of it
And one night three of them got together,
Approached the treasure and carried it off;
And when they'd carried it away,
God made them feel a strong desire
To sleep; they felt so drowsy
They fell asleep right in their tracks
Somewhere or other, in a house.
But, so as to cut this miracle short,   60
I will pass on, as the good book does.
Now when the king became aware
That he had let his treasure go,
Then he considered that he'd been duped.
He had the fellow brought before him
And seeing him asked him this question:
'Fellow, why did you deceive me?'

The Christian was hardly allowed to speak
A word; the soldiers led him off
Holding him by both his arms, 70
The one pushing, the other pulling.
The king ordered he should be put
To an ugly and ignominious death.
'For God's sake, Sir, give me respite
For just one night', the Christian said,
'To know for sure if Nicholas
Will bring me freedom from my chains.'
Grudgingly the king agreed.
But—this is what the story tells—
He had the man put back in jail. 80
The Christian, captive once again,
Spent the whole of the night in prayer;
His crying never stopped a moment.
Saint Nicholas then took to the road,
Not once forgetting his disciple.
He went to the robbers with all speed
And woke them up (they were still asleep)
And straight away, as soon as they saw him,
They were suddenly full of eagerness
To do exactly what he wished. 90
So Nicholas, without delay,
Made them carry back the treasure
Without wasting a single moment
And place his image on the top,
Just exactly as they'd found it.
When in this way the king had tested
The Saint and his great miracle,
He gave command for them to bring
The Christian in and not to harm him.
He had himself baptized at the font, 100
Not only himself but the other pagans;
He became an honest and decent Christian,
And never wanted to sin again.
Gentlemen, we find it in the Life
Of the Saint whose vigil we keep tonight;

So don't be overmuch astonished
If you see some curious business here,
For whatever you see us doing
Will be a faithful attempt, it's certain,
At stage-depiction of the miracle   110
Just as I've recounted it.
The legend of Saint Nicholas
Is the theme and story of our play:
Give us some peace and you will hear it!   (*Exit*)

(*Enter the King, Seneschal, Connart, attendants. Enter separately Auberon.*)

AUBERON   O King, Mahomet who begot you
  Save and keep you and all your barons!
  And give you strength to defend yourself
  From those who are attacking you,
  Ravaging and ruining your land.
  Our gods they neither invoke nor honour   120
  For they are Christians, a stinking tribe.

KING   Away from me, by great Apollo!
  Are Christians in my land, you say?
  And have they mounted an attack?
  Are they so impudent and bold?

AUBERON   King, never, since Noah built the ark,
  Was such an army, such a force,
  As the one which has invaded us.
  Their foragers run all over the place
  Whores, and bawds, and lecherous brutes   130
  Go burning your kingdom down to ashes.
  King, unless you plan defence,
  The land will go to rack and ruin.

KING *to Tervagan*   Tervagan, son of a whore!
  Have you permitted this to happen?
  How I regret the gold with which
  I cover your filthy face and body!

I swear, if my magic doesn't teach me
How to destroy every single Christian,
I'll have you burnt and melted down   140
And handed out around my people;
For you are worth far more than silver—
You're finest gold of Araby.

to Seneschal   Seneschal, I'm almost mad—
Spite and anger are killing me.

SENESCHAL *to King*
Ah King, you never should have uttered
Such blasphemous and senseless things.
It doesn't become a count or a king
To pour such scorn upon his gods;
In doing so, you're much to blame.   150
But since I'm bound to give you counsel,
Let's go to Tervagan together
On our bare elbows, and bare knees—
To pray that he will give us pardon,
To pray that through his holy power
The Christians may be overcome,
And, if we are to win the day,
That he will clearly let us have
Some utterance, some kind of sign
By which we may be reassured.   160
There's no deceit in this advice;
You'd better promise Tervagan
Ten pounds of gold to fatten his face.

KING *to Seneschal*
Let's go then, since that's your advice.

(*The King prostrates himself on the steps of Tervagan's altar.*)

Tervagan, in a wicked mood,
I said many stupid things today—
Better for me they'd been unsaid!

But I was drunker than a coot.
I pray you mercy, confessing my sin
On naked elbows and naked knees.   170
Lord, support and succour me;
This day recall to mind our Faith
Which Christians think to take away;
Already they're spread through my vast realm.
By oracle and by prophecy
Show me how they can be dislodged.
Lord, show it clearly to your friend
By oracle or by magic art—
Shall I succeed in my defence?
This is the way to let me know: 180
If victory is mine, then smile;
But if I am to lose, then weep.
Seneschal, what's your opinion?
Tervagan has both wept *and* smiled:
Here's some deep significance.

SENESCHAL   Your Majesty, you speak the truth;
    From Tervagan's smile you can take
    Great certainty and great confidence.

KING   Seneschal, in Mahomet's name
    As you are my loyal servant,   190
    Plainly expound me this oracle.

SENESCHAL   Your Highness, by my loyal bond,
    If this prediction were declared,
    I think it wouldn't please you at all.

KING   Seneschal, don't be afraid:
    I swear to you by all my gods,
    Just let it be a game, a joke!

SENESCHAL   Sir, I believe your godly oath;
    But I'd believe you very much more,
    If you'd tap your finger-nail on your tooth.   200

KING   Seneschal, you've no need to fear
Look! the sign of highest trust!
If you had killed my very father
You'd have no further call for fear.

SENESCHAL   Now I can let my tongue run freely;
The oracles shall be expounded:—
That Tervagan smiled first—it's good;
You'll be victorious over the Christians
At the moment you attack them.
And it was right that, next, he wept;   210
For it's a matter for grief and pity,
That in the end you'll give him up:
And this is what the future holds.

KING   A hundred times cursed be he
Who uttered this, or even thought it!
But, by the faith I owe my friends,
If I hadn't placed finger on tooth,
Mahomet himself could not have saved you.
I would have had you done to death.
But what's the use? Now to our business: 220
Go now, and have the army summoned.
All are to come upon my business
From the Orient right to Catalonia.

SENESCHAL   Connart, where are you? Cry this at once!

(*Connart runs through the 'place'.*)

CONNART   Oyez, oyez, oyez, good men,
Your honour and your interest!
Summons from the King of Africa:
That all men come, both poor and rich,
Furnished with arms, as is required.
Let no man dally, from the land   230
Of Prester John to Caramania,

Alexandrians, Babylonians,
The Canaanites, the Achoparts,
Let all come armed, in this direction
And every other savage nation.
If anyone remains behind
Be sure the king will have him killed.
That's all; now you can yell again. (*Exit*)

KING *to Auberon*
Hallo, there, messenger! Are you around?

(*Enter Auberon*)

AUBERON   Yes, here, your Highness! Always dutiful.   240

KING   Auberon, give your whole mind to courier-work!
Go all around, call Giants and Canaanites,
Display my letters patent, show my seal,
Tell how my Faith through Christians is destroyed.
Those who remain at home can be quite sure
They and their heirs will live as slaves for ever.
Be off! You should be miles away by now.

AUBERON   My Lord, take heart! The fastest camel could run
A mile, and I would still have passed him by
And left him well behind at the halfway mark.   250

(*Auberon leaves the palace and crosses the 'place' by the
tavern. Cliquet sits inside the tavern, drinking. The Taverner
comes out of the tavern to attract Auberon's attention.*)

TAVERNER   Dine well, inside! Dine well, inside!
We've got hot bread! Hot herring, too,
And wine of Auxerre by the barrel.

AUBERON   Ah, holy Bene't, your ring-sign—

(*he points to the tavern sign*)

I'd like to meet it every day.
What are you selling?

TAVERNER   What am I selling?
My friend, a wine as thick as cream.

AUBERON   How much do you charge?

TAVERNER   The local rate.
I'm never like to be in trouble
For over-charging or short-measure.   260
Take a seat in the bower here.

AUBERON   Taverner, you can draw me a pint.
And I'll despatch it standing up.
I don't intend to stay here long.
I have to see to my own affairs.

TAVERNER   Who is your boss?

AUBERON   I'm the King's man.
I carry his seal and his authority.

TAVERNER   Take this, you'll feel the effects of it.
Drink up, the best is at the bottom.

AUBERON   This tankard isn't very deep—   270
Only adequate for a taster.
But tell me, how much do I owe you?
I'm a fool to hang about so long.

TAVERNER   Pay me a penny, and then next time
You'll have a pint for a halfpenny—
It sells at a shilling, and no mistake.
Pay me a penny, or have another!

AUBERON   No, you shall have the halfpenny now—
And the penny next time that I come.

TAVERNER   Are you trying to pull a fast one?   280
   You owe me, at the least, three farthings.
   Before you slip away from here,
   I'm going to know just how I stand.

AUBERON   But, Landlord, when I'm back again,
   You'll get a penny for the pint.

TAVERNER   Yes, that'll be when the cows come home—
   You've nothing to gain by trying it on!

AUBERON   I'll never be able to settle with you,
   Unless I cut a halfpenny in two.

CLIQUET   Who wants to gamble on the cut,   290
   A little game, to keep us amused?

TAVERNER   Did you hear, you courier?
   Come and settle your affair.

AUBERON   Well, for one farthing, to keep the peace!

CLIQUET   One farthing! No, for all you owe.

AUBERON   You must consult the taverner first.

CLIQUET   That wouldn't be a bad idea.
   Tell me, sir, will you settle at that?

TAVERNER   Yes, before anyone makes off.

AUBERON   Play 'Highest Points'! No cheating, now.   300

(*Cliquet throws three dice.*)

CLIQUET   There they go! I haven't touched them.

AUBERON   Good heavens, you haven't a five or a six,
   Double-three, only, and a one.

CLIQUET   That only makes seven, bad luck!
　　The dice will never run right for me.

AUBERON   At any rate, I'm still to throw—   (*he throws*)
　　Well, my good friend, whatever you've got,
　　You're paying for what you never tasted!
　　I've got two fours for my worst throw.

CLIQUET   Damnation to all messengers,   310
　　They're always slippery customers.

AUBERON   Sir, this young gentleman pays the bill.
　　He insulted me—but let that pass.

TAVERNER   Get out! I wish we'd never seen you.

(*Auberon leaves the tavern and runs to the far edge of the
'place', where he salutes the Emirs in turn.*)

AUBERON   In the King's name—Mahomet save
　　The Emir of Coine! The King commands
　　You come to his aid without default.

COINE   Auberon, greet the King from me!
　　I shall bring him a mighty army;
　　There's nothing that can hold me back.   320

AUBERON   Mahomet save and bless your honour,
　　Great Emir of Orkenie land!
　　In the King's name, who asks your aid.

ORKENIE   Auberon, Mahomet keep him safe!
　　Go! I'll set off this very day,
　　Since that is what the King commands.

AUBERON   Mahomet, ruler of all things,
　　Save you, great King of Oliferne!
　　In the King's name, who summons you.

OLIFERNE   Auberon, you can tell the King   330
   That I will bring my total power:
   I would not fail for all the world.

AUBERON   Emir of lands beyond the Withered Tree,
   The King of Aïr, Tranle, Araby,
   In the struggle against the Christians
   Asks you for your immediate aid.

WITHERED TREE   Auberon, in the morning early
   I'll bring a hundred thousand pagans.

(*Auberon returns through the 'place' to the palace.*)

AUBERON   O King, Mahomet save and keep
   You and your people.   340

KING   And bless you too,
   Auberon! How have you fared?

AUBERON   Truly, sir, I've spurred so fast
   Through Araby and pagan lands
   That never the tenth of such an army
   Was ever assembled by pagan King
   As is coming to you, I do believe,
   Counts and kings and princes and barons.

KING   Go and rest now, Auberon

(*Exit Auberon. The Emirs proceed separately through the 'place' and arrive in turn at the King's palace.*)

COINE   King, from Apollo and Mahound,
   I greet you, as your loyal subject,   350
   For I am come at your command:
   I do so, as my bounden duty.

KING   My good friend, you've acted wisely;
   Always come, when I send for you.

COINE   From far beyond the Fields of Nero,
  The country where the gardens flourish,
  I've come to save you from this threat.
  You will do wrong ever to hate me;
  I've travelled in my iron-shod shoes
  For thirty days' across the ice.   360

KING   Say, who are these men drawn up here?

ORKENIE   Your Highness, from beyond Galatia,
  Where the dogs excrete pure gold.
  You ought to love me best of all,
  For I have brought you over the sea
  A hundred ship-loads of my treasure.

KING   Your trials have earned my sympathy,
  My lords.—Where are *you* from?

OLIFERNE   Abroad,
  My lord—a land of burning heat.
  Nor am I grudging in my gift: 370
  I'm bringing to you thirty wagons,
  Full of rubies and emeralds.

KING   And you there, looking at me, where
  Are you from?

WITHERED TREE   Beyond the Withered Tree.
  I cannot make a fitting gift,
  For in our land we have no coinage
  Apart from money made of millstones.

KING   Away, in Lord Mahomet's name!
  What wealth this fellow promises!
  I see that I shall never be poor.   380

WITHERED TREE   My lord, I shall not lie to you—
  In our country one man alone
  Will carry a hundred in his purse.

(*Enter the King's Saracen knights.*)

SENESCHAL   My lord, your knights have come at your command.
Mount an attack at once against the Christians.

KING   Seneschal, by Mahound, they won't lack war—
They'll either be killed or captured or put to flight.
Go on, good man, and give them my command
To put themselves at once in battle-order.

SENESCHAL   My lords, in the King's name I speak to you: 390
Go and exterminate the Christian faith.
To ruin the Christians you were summoned here;
The harm they've done to us must be put right.
Advance! At once! It is the King's command.

ALL *together*   Forward! And may Mahomet be our guard.

(*The Emirs and Saracen knights advance to meet the Christian knights who enter from the opposite side of the 'place'.*)

CHRISTIANS   The Holy Sepulchre aid us! Now for great deeds.
Pagans and Saracens come to destroy us;
Look, how their weapons shine! My heart lights up.
We'll do such deeds, our prowess will be seen;
Each one of us, it seems, must fight a hundred.   400

FIRST CHRISTIAN   Comrades, fear not! This is your judgment day:
I know we must all die here, serving God;
But I'll exact a price, while my sword holds.
Their turbans won't protect them, nor their mail.
Comrades, let each man vow himself today
To God; Heaven is for us, Hell for the pagans.
Manage the attack that they may meet our swords!

YOUNG CHRISTIAN KNIGHT   Comrades, if I am young, despise
    me not!
  Each day we see great hearts in little bodies.
  I'll strike this brigand—I chose him long ago.   410
  Be sure I'll kill him, unless he kills me first.

(*Enter the Angel, in a high place.*)

ANGEL   Good men, be easy in your minds—
  Do not fear, nor hesitate!
  I am the messenger of our Lord:
  He will deliver you from pain.
  Commit your brave and faithful hearts
  To God! Don't let these infidels,
  Who charge against you in a rabble,
  Intimidate your sturdy hearts!
  Boldly entrust your lives entire   420
  To God; the death you'll meet today
  Is one all people ought to die
  Who love God and have faith in him.

FIRST CHRISTIAN   Who are you, sir, who give us comfort thus
  And bring so lofty a message to us from God?
  Be sure, if this is true that you relate,
  In fullest trust we'll face our mortal foes.

ANGEL   Good friend, I am an angel of God.
  He sent me here to comfort you.
  Be firm, for in the skies above   430
  God has appointed thrones for you.
  Fight on now, you have started well!
  For God you'll all be massacred,
  But you shall have the highest crown.
  I leave you now: God bless you all!   (*Exit*)

COINE   My friends, I am the eldest here
  And have given much good advice before.
  Believe me—it'll be best for you.

We are battle-tested warriors;
So if we come across the Christians,   440
Make sure no single one escapes.

ORKENIE   Escape, you say! Those sons of whores!
I'll strike the first that comes—you'll see!
But take care no one gets away!

COINE   My lords, you needn't be in doubt
That I shall mow the Christians down
Like Berengiers at the barley-harvest.

OLIFERNE   You wholesale murderers, between you
Will you make such a total slaughter
There won't be a single one left for me?   450

WITHERED TREE   Look, here they are, the loathsome crowd.
Knights of Mahomet, into battle!
Strike them, strike them all together.

*Now the Saracens kill all the Christians. (The Emirs discover
the one live Christian kneeling before the image of Saint
Nicholas.)*

ORKENIE   Comrades in arms, come here quickly!
The marvels of the Christian army
Are all a joke compared with this—
Look at the wretch, white-haired old rogue,
Praying to an idol with horns.
Shall we kill him here, or take him alive?

OLIFERNE   Let's not kill him for goodness sake!   460
We'll take him for the King to see:
He'll be dumbfounded, I promise you.
Get up, fellow and stir yourself!

WITHERED TREE   My friends, you hold the prisoner fast
And I will carry this idol here.

(The Emirs lead the Christian to the palace. Their knights leave the 'place'. The Angel re-enters.)

ANGEL   O Christian Knighthood, fallen here,
　　　How fortunate your lot has been!
　　　How worthily at this present time
　　　You scorn the world where you endured!
　　　But, to reward the pain you've suffered,   470
　　　You know for sure, I have no doubt,
　　　The joys that are in Paradise,
　　　Where God puts all those whom he loves.
　　　On you the whole world now is bound
　　　To turn its gaze, and die like you;
　　　For God receives with tenderness
　　　All those who wish to come to Him.
　　　The man who serves Him with good heart
　　　Will never find his labour lost,
　　　But, rather, crowned in heaven above   480
　　　With such a crown as you now wear.

(The fallen Christian knights stand up and may either leave the 'place' or ascend to 'Heaven' to join the Angel. Meanwhile, the Good Man has been brought before the King.)

GOOD MAN   Saint Nicholas, worthy Confessor,
　　　Have pity now upon your servant!
　　　Grant me your help and your protection!
　　　Good friend of God, true counsellor,
　　　Keep watchful guard over your man,
　　　Protect my life against these tyrants!

ANGEL   Good man, cowering here in fright,
　　　Be brave and wise, in the power of God!
　　　And, if these traitors take you off,   490
　　　Don't let that cause you any fear!
　　　Put all your confidence in God;
　　　Trust also, in Saint Nicholas,
　　　For he will give you strength and comfort
　　　Seeing you firm and strong in faith.

H

COINE   O King, be gladder now than ever,
For we have turned your war to peace
Through our power and through our wisdom.
Dead are those villains, dead the cowards;
The battlefield is covered with them   500
For thirty miles in each direction.

KING   My lords, you all have served me well . . . (*he sees
the prisoner with the image of Nicholas*)
But never was there such a ruffian
As I see over on the right:
That scarecrow in a cap with horns—
This villain in the hood right here!
Tell me, what on earth is up!

SENESCHAL   Your Majesty, just for the wonder of it,
We've brought him live for you to see.
Now, listen how he spends his time.   510
I found him on his knees, praying,
Clasping his hands together, weeping,
Before his idol with its horns.

KING   Fellow, do you believe in *this*?

GOOD MAN   Yes, sir, I do! By the holy cross!
The whole world ought to worship him.

KING   Tell me why, you horrid creature.

GOOD MAN   My lord, this is Saint Nicholas,
Who helps all those who are distressed
His miracles are widely known: 520
He's able to retrieve all losses,
He puts lost travellers on their road,
He calls the faithless back to God,
He gives a light to those who are blind,
He brings the drowned to life again.
Nothing entrusted to his care,

Can ever be lost or badly damaged,
However long it is left unguarded—
Not even this palace, if filled with gold,
Provided his image lay on the treasure: 530
Such is the power that God has given him.

KING   Fellow, that's what I'll soon discover:
Before I go away from here,
Your Nicholas will have his test.
I'll leave my treasure in his keeping.
But, if I lose a thimble-full,
I'll have you burnt, or broken on a wheel.
Seneschal, take him to Durant,
My torturer and executioner;
But see that he is safely guarded.   540

(*The Seneschal leads the Good Man to the prison.*)

SENESCHAL   Durant, Durant, open the prison;
I have a martyr's skin for you.

DURANT (*to the Good Man*)
By God, I'll give you a wicked welcome.

GOOD MAN   Sir, what a massive club you have!

DURANT   Come in, fellow, down in that pit!
The prison was completely empty.
So long as you are in my keeping,
My pincers won't be lying idle—
Not while there's still a tooth in your head.

(*The Good Man is chained.*)

ANGEL   Good man, rejoice and cast away all fear!   550
Sustain your firm belief in Christ your Saviour,
And in Saint Nicholas.
I know it for a truth

That you will have his aid:
You will convert the King
And all his baronage
Out of their foolish faith;
And they will then believe
As Christians do, I know.

GOOD MAN   I believe in Nicholas with all my heart.   560

(*The Seneschal returns to the palace.*)

SENESCHAL   Your Majesty, he's in the prison.

KING   Now Seneschal, my dear old friend,
All my treasures, whatever I have,
I want them all to be displayed,
The treasure-chests and boxes opened;
And put the 'Nicholas' on top.

(*The Seneschal brings out the King's treasure chests, sets them
in full view of the audience and places the image of Saint
Nicholas on top of the largest chest.*)

SENESCHAL   Your orders, sir, are carried out;
I've left no watchmen there at all.
Now you can sleep in confidence!

KING   Right! By the faith I owe Apollo,   570
If I lose as much as a single farthing,
That ruffian can tremble for his life.
He's very trusting in his God.
Now, quickly, send my criers out!
I want it known throughout the land.

(*Enter Connart.*)

SENESCHAL   Here, you, Connart, proclaim to all,
The treasure's left without a guard.
That's a piece of luck for thieves!

(*Connart runs through the 'place'.*)

CONNART Oyez, oyez, gentlemen all,
　　Come along, give me a hearing!　　　　　　　　580
　　On the King's behalf I have to tell you
　　That as from now his treasure hoard
　　Will not be under lock and key.
　　You'll find it all laid out, as if
　　On open ground, it seems to me;
　　Anyone can help themselves at will.
　　No one's left on guard at all
　　Except a single 'horned Mahomet',
　　Quite dead, he doesn't move a muscle.
　　Shame on the man who keeps it quiet!　　　　590

(*Raoul enters the 'place' and passes the tavern.*)

TAVERNER Caignet, our sales have fallen off.
　　Go and tell Raoul to advertise
　　'Wine for sale'. They've had a glut.

CAIGNET Hi, there! Raoul, go round and shout,
　　We've opened up a new supply—
　　Wine of Auxerre, a barrelful.

CONNART What's this, you lout? What're you doing?
　　Are you trying to steal my trade away?
　　You just pack up! It isn't right.

RAOUL Now who are you, to give me orders?　　　600
　　God help you, tell me what you're called.

CONNART Connart is my name, my friend.
　　I'm the crier—like my father—
　　I work for the City magistrates.
　　I reckon it's sixty years and more
　　That I've got my living by this trade.
　　And who are you, if I may ask?

RAOUL   Raoul—I advertise the wine;
    The folk of the Town are my employers.

CONNART   Clear off, you clown! Drop this act: 610
    You haven't the real authentic 'cry'.
    Throw away that stick and tankard!
    I don't give a fig for you . . .

RAOUL   What's this, what's this? Who are you shoving?

CONNART   You! For twopence I'd set about you.
    I tell you to throw away your pots;
    Give up your claim to compete with me!

RAOUL   Just hear that! What a filthy speech!
    He thinks I'll say goodbye to 'crying'!
    Connart, don't preach that line to me   620
    Or you'll be getting beaten up.
    Cuckolds like you, just ask for it—
    Not happy unless you're being beaten.

CAIGNET   Sir, sir, Raoul's in a fight—
    Him and Connart, about their job.

TAVERNER   Hey, hey, you there! No need for that.
    Calm down, Raoul! And you, Connart!
    Let me decide the issue for you.
    You'll both be better off for it.

RAOUL   All right by me.

CONNART   Yes, I agree too.   630
    Even if it means I lose the lot.

TAVERNER   Don't be anxious; I'll judge it fairly.
    Each one must have his rights in town:
    Connart, you shall be town-crier
    Under the King and the magistrates;

Raoul shall advertise the wines
So he at least can make a living.
And if Raoul happens to get drunk,
No one ought to hold it against him.
Go on, Raoul, make up the quarrel;   640
I don't want any disturbance here.

RAOUL   Shake on it, Connart, in the name of friendship!
We really ought to trust each other.

CONNART   It's peace, then! Go and 'cry' your wine!

RAOUL   New wine, just freshly broached,
Wine in gallons, wine in barrels,
Smooth and tasty, pure, full-bodied,
Leaps to the head like a squirrel up a tree.
No tang of must in it, or mould—
Fresh and strong, full, rich-flavoured,   650
As limpid as a sinner's tears;
It lingers on a gourmet's tongue—
Other folk ought not to touch it!

(*Pincedé enters the 'place'.*)

PINCEDÉ   Well, this is one I ought to sample;
It's clearly tailor-made for me—
Mere common drinkers will be at it!
—And I'm a proper devotee.

RAOUL   Look how it swallows up its froth!
And leaps and sparkles, bubbles too!
Just hold it on the tongue a minute,   660
I tell you, you'll taste a super-wine.

PINCEDÉ   By God! This is the real thing!
Just the stuff to set one up.

CLIQUET   Ah, Pincedé, make yourself at home;
It happens I was quite alone.

PINCEDÉ   With pleasure, Cliquet, it won't be
The first time we have drunk together!

(Pincedé joins Cliquet in the tavern.)

CLIQUET   Pincedé, what do you think of the wine?
I've got my clothes in pawn already.

PINCEDÉ   So long as the wine's above halfway   670
I shan't want to pass the door.

CLIQUET   Let's drink a pennyworth, anyway.
Draw us a couple of quarts, Caignet!

CAIGNET   Sir, could you draw up Cliquet's bill,
Before he starts to run up another?

TAVERNER   Cliquet you owed for half a gallon,
And then a penny on your gamble,
And for the messenger, three farthings.
That makes it fivepence, more or less.

CLIQUET   Call it five! I don't care.   680
No taverner ever found me mean.

TAVERNER   Caignet, now draw it off quite clear
For Pincedé who's just arrived.

CAIGNET   Heavens! There's not much profit there:
We shall make nothing out of this.

CLIQUET   Caignet, God damn you and your drawing,
And anyone else who draws short measure!
Why does he call on heaven so much,
This fellow who's always fleecing people?

PINCEDÉ   You, bring us in some candle-light   690
If you've enough intelligence . . .

CAIGNET   There you are, sir! Right by your hand;
   Take it—that'll cost you twopence.

CLIQUET   You're quick enough when it comes to counting—
   Or to *mis*-counting, if we trusted you!

PINCEDÉ   Pour out, Cliquet. Give me a drink!
   My lips are dry enough to split.

CLIQUET   All right, drink up! Who's stopping you?
   Drink, for God sake! And good health with it!

PINCEDÉ   Whew! What a wine! And ice-cold too!   700
   Drink up, Cliquet—we're doing well.
   He doesn't realize what he's selling:
   It could be sold at twice the price.

CLIQUET   Quiet, now—or the boss will hear,
   Or his flunky who's sucking him dry!

PINCEDÉ   True—and he cheats him of many a barrel
   By drawing wine he hasn't paid for.

CAIGNET   Cliquet, for heaven's sake, be quiet!
   Keep your mouth shut—not another word.

CLIQUET   Well, let's drink in peace and comfort.   710
   There's still some wine left in the pot
   From the first quart we had brought up;
   And still some candle left to burn.

(*Rasoir enters the tavern.*)

RASOIR   Good day to you, officers of the watch!
   Now I have all I could desire—
   Cliquet and Pincedé for company.
   I've been longing to see them both.

CLIQUET   Well, well! Come and sit down, Rasoir;
   You'll get some of our first round.

RASOIR   A pleasure, gentlemen. I put myself   720
   Absolutely at your disposal:
   We three are old acquaintances.

PINCEDÉ   Come on, give him a drink, Cliquet.

CLIQUET   Rasoir and his velvet tongue!
   Drink up, Rasoir; you're in luck:
   We've only ordered what you see.
   You've caught us up on the first lap.

RASOIR   The merest trifle, gentlemen.
   If they had fetched you ten gallons out,
   I wouldn't sneak off to avoid the bill.
   Aren't the three of us old friends?   730
   Caignet! Draw us a full gallon—
   Lord knows, you'll get your money for it.

CLIQUET   Rasoir must have sold his donkey,
   Ordering drinks so generously.

RASOIR   But this is the way I always am.
   Let's drink what we want—all will be paid.
   If we owed them twenty shillings here
   I wouldn't be the least disturbed
   About the taverner getting his money   740
   Before the dawn—if he'll take a risk.

PINCEDÉ   He has some thieving plan in mind
   When he talks boastfully like that.

RASOIR   Stow it, stow it! Drink like men—
   Not chicken-hearts and draggle-tails!

CLIQUET   Rasoir, we have drunk so much
   Our clothes will have to stay in pawn.

(*Caignet brings more wine.*)

CAIGNET   Take this, Cliquet. That makes fivepence:
   Three for this wine and two from before.

PINCEDÉ   Will you swear it isn't watered?   750

CAIGNET   Of course it isn't—Christ almighty!

CLIQUET   Unwatered, is it, you old ram?
   Drink some (*offering the wine*)—know what it is you sell.
   Take some, Rasoir, I bet you haven't
   Tasted wine like this all year.

RASOIR   Cliquet, pour the wine in a flood!
   Let's try some of this new draught—
   There's some left in the barrel still—
   And then we'll settle what we owe.

PINCEDÉ   Have you been eating salted herrings,   760
   Rasoir? You've certainly drunk your share

CLIQUET   He's had a windfall, Pincedé;
   I can see it with my own two eyes.

RASOIR   Stow it, stow it! Farewell to our cares!
   Pour it out like the cheapest beer.

PINCEDÉ   We're paying for your extravagance,
   Rasoir. We're not all well off.
   You must have been on the prowl last night,
   And now you're well and truly loaded.

RASOIR   I'm not. I have some news for you   770
   Through which some good might come to us.

PINCEDÉ   Then maybe you would come to some good
   If we could lay our hands on the stuff.

RASOIR   Let's drink some more and chatter less,
          Now all our losses are recovered:
          The garners of the Lord are open
          And nothing can stop us being rich,
          For the King of Africa's treasure hoard,
          His plates and cups and drinking bowls,
          Are lying without lock or bolt—   780
          No soldiers guarding night or day!
          An old 'Mahomet' lies on top,
          Of stone or wood—I don't know which.
          The King won't hear as much as a whisper
          From him if somebody steals the lot,
          Or takes it off. Let's go today
          When we've made sure the time is right.

PINCEDÉ   But is this true, so help you God?

RASOIR   Is it true? For heaven's sake,
          I heard the crier shouting it out: 790
          There won't be anyone on guard,
          Whoever wants the stuff can have it.
          Let's see if we can get credit on that.

CLIQUET   Go on, Pincedé, pour him a drink.
          Good news deserves a tankard full.

PINCEDÉ   There you are, Rasoir. You can collect
          The pool next time you see me gambling.
          I never like to break my word:
          My first winnings shall all be yours—
          Take them, no matter when it is.   800
          I shan't try to dodge my promise.
          That reminds me, who's for a game?

CLIQUET   Shall we toss for heads or tails?

PINCEDÉ   No, let's throw dice, the three of us,
          With the loot as credit—it'll bring us luck.

CLIQUET Landlord, lend me elevenpence.
I'll owe you seventeen in all.

TAVERNER You're wrong.

CLIQUET   How much?

TAVERNER   It's more than that;
I'm afraid you're not so lucky

CLIQUET Count up every item then.   810

TAVERNER Your first gallon cost you threepence.

CLIQUET All right.

TAVERNER   A penny hire of dice,
Three farthings you already lost—
Have I got it right so far?

CLIQUET Fivepence, if I still want to keep my word.
You're going to lend me elevenpence now,
That's seventeen. That add up right?

TAVERNER Look after what you borrow, Cliquet.
You know perfectly well by now
That I shall want a guarantee.   820
You're rather cramped inside that coat—
I'm afraid it must part company
With you, before you leave the house.

PINCEDÉ Look, Landlord, we've heard all that.
The foot is on the other shoe—
We've drunk *five pennyworth* of your wine!
So first, let's toss for that, at dice.

CLIQUET Who's got some dice?

PINCEDÉ   I have, square cut,
   Regular, and standard size.

CLIQUET   No dice of yours was ever square!   830

RASOIR   That shouldn't worry you, Cliquet.

CLIQUET   No, not at all. Caignet, come here.
   You know what you can do for us?
   Look here, lend your dice to us
   And take your usual share of the stakes.
   It could be we'll have a bit of luck
   And you'll benefit, I swear you will.

CAIGNET   I can shift for myself, Cliquet.

PINCEDÉ   Hey, you—Cliquet and Rasoir, say
   If you want to settle your share of the wine,   840
   Or shall we gamble for who's to pay?

RASOIR   The one with most points takes the stakes,
   The one with least shall pay the drinks.

CLIQUET   Caignet. I hope you choke unless
   You lend your dice to us at once!

CAIGNET   (*handing over his dice*)
   Look after them for me, Rasoir—
   I have had them officially tested.

RASOIR   This throw will settle who shall pay
   For the wine we down before the morning.

PINCEDÉ   Everyone throw with an open palm.   850

RASOIR   That's right.

CLIQUET   I agree to that.

PINCEDÉ Throw, by Christ! No cheating now!

(*Rasoir throws three fives.*)

RASOIR Fellows, look—it's fives all round!

PINCEDÉ May God send me so many sixes
That I can sell them by the dozen!

(*Pincedé throws a total of five points.*)

RASOIR Ha! That's a pretty feeble throw,
Pincedé,—what you just put down.
He's hardly got a single point.
That one's going to cost you your jacket.
Five *pence*—so he throws five *points*!   860
That's his rule, you can count on it!

PINCEDÉ (*to Cliquet*)
I defy you to do worse!

RASOIR (*to Pincedé*)
Right, it's an insult to ask him to throw.

(*Pincedé admits defeat and Cliquet puts the dice aside without throwing.*)

CLIQUET Just put it down to your account—
That's how decent folk behave.

PINCEDÉ Do you want to play for ready cash?

RASOIR Yes, all right.

PINCEDÉ   That's what I like.
Now, everybody turn his pockets out
And put down threepence beside the board,
And then the winner takes the lot.   870

I reckon there's no cheating then.
If you haven't any money, get some!

CLIQUET　What game is it?

PINCEDÉ　　　　　　　Whatever you like.

CLIQUET　Highest Points?

PINCEDÉ　　　　　　So be it. Amen.

RASOIR　I'll throw. God make it profitable!

(*Caignet interrupts, bringing a fresh candle.*)

CAIGNET　Wait. You can't see much over there.
Let's have a bit of candle-light.

PINCEDÉ　Treat us well and take your fee;
We shan't quarrel over that.

(*Rasoir throws quickly, before the light is set down.*)

RASOIR　Good Lord! Twelve to start us off!　　　880

CLIQUET　Two fours and a two—that gives you *ten*.

(*Pincedé picks up the dice.*)

RASOIR　There's some that hold the dice who throw
Much worse. I'll let you count mine for nine.

PINCEDÉ　Pox anyone so *asinine*
To be afraid of losing to ten.

CAIGNET　Are we supposed to light you for nothing?

(*He takes a penny from the stakes.*)

This one is mine, whatever happens.
(*Aside*) They'd not have asked for the bill for hours—
God blast the way they carry on!

CLIQUET   Caignet, put our money down,   890
Until we've given you permission.

CAIGNET   It's not a matter for your permission,
Cliquet. You're wasting this fat candle
And all our staff are staying up
Throughout the house, for the sake of your game.

PINCEDÉ   I'm throwing. Gentlemen, he's right.

(*He throws eleven.*)

Aren't you interested, Rasoir?

RASOIR   No, you've beaten me by one.

CLIQUET   Now there's only me to throw.
I shall beat your eleven in two: 900
The third one needn't be counted at all.

(*Cliquet throws.*)

PINCEDÉ   Hey! That throw doesn't count—
That was a bit of jiggery-pokery!

CLIQUET   Well, anyway I get the beans:
I have two fours and a six.

(*He attempts to pick up the stake money.*)

PINCEDÉ   Put that money down—or else—
You'll regret it! You're provoking me.

CLIQUET   What right have you to contradict?
Haven't I three more than you?

I

PINCEDÉ Put down the cash, I'm asking you—　　910
　　Before you make me flaming mad.

CLIQUET Damn your eyes! You shut your mouth—
　　You can see it come up on the dice!

PINCEDÉ Didn't I say that was no throw?
　　Do you want to run off with the lot?

(*He grabs Cliquet*).

CLIQUET What the devil . . .? He's pulling so hard
　　He's almost ripping off my coat.

PINCEDÉ Here are your winnings—a poke in the face!
　　I'm glad to begin—I'm stronger than you.

CLIQUET I'll pay you back for that . . . so there!　　920
　　Now you see how scared I am.

(*They fight, upsetting the tables etc.*)

CAIGNET Landlord, you're losing everything!
　　Run quick! They're ruining the clothes for pawn.
　　These bastards are ripping each other to shreds—
　　There's not a rag worth anything.

(*The Taverner runs out from inside.*)

TAVERNER What's this, Cliquet? Is it a fight?
　　Let go of him! You too, leave off!
　　Go and sit down, the pair of you,
　　And each will get what he deserves.
　　Rasoir, tell us the cause of this—　　930
　　You must know who was in the wrong.

RASOIR It's better to have them make it up;
　　This rough-house doesn't agree with me.

Ask Caignet whose fault it was;
Get him to tell it truthfully.

CLIQUET   He leaves it all to you, Caignet.

PINCEDÉ   I won't quarrel with his judgment.

CAIGNET   Put all the money that there is
Down on top of the dicing board.

CLIQUET   All right. There—all eight pennies.   940
And now, decide for us like a friend.

CAIGNET   Gentlemen, since it's up to me,
You know I can't afford to lose.
Twopence is mine for candles and wine,—
The other six divide between you.
If one man were to get it all
There'd always be someone with a grudge.
Now Cliquet, you pour out some wine
And offer Pincedé a drink.
I want you two to make it up,   950
Since the problem is in my hands.

CLIQUET   Pincedé I apologize;
I give you this wine a a sign of peace.

(*Cliquet pours wine for Pincedé and they drink in turn from the same tankard.*)

PINCEDÉ   I'll let you off for quarrelling, Cliquet.
I know it was wine that made you do it.

CLIQUET   Let's talk about some other business,
So everyone here can pay his debts.
Most of the night is gone already—
High time to go prowling in the dark,
Because the moon has set by now.   960
We're earning nothing sitting here!

RASOIR   Landlord, do a favour for us.
  We owe you a matter of some pence,
  But we know where there's a heap of stuff
  And we can make a massive haul.
  We'll take the whole lot in one go.
  This place we know is a treasure hoard,
  With platters made of gold and silver—
  Each man loaded till he bends.
  I want to make a deal with you,   970
  The like of which you've never had:
  You shall harbour what we get
  And so you'll become one of the gang.
  You'll divide up and draw the lots
  And out of that get what we owe.
  No worries about getting paid!

TAVERNER   Can I be absolutely sure
  Of what Rasoir has promised me?

CLIQUET   If God almighty keeps me free   980
  From failure, infamy and jail—
  And provided no one catches us
  In the act and we all get hanged—
  Then you'll be lavishly repaid:
  You'll have a barrel full of gold.
  But first, make us the loan of a sack
  So we can put the stuff away.

TAVERNER   Caignet, go and get them a sack.
  It's going to pay for its way, by Christ!

(*Caignet fetches a sack.*)

CAIGNET   Here you are, Cliquet. It holds four bushels. 990
  Off you go—God speed you back!

PINCEDÉ   Goodbye, landlord. Pray for us.
  Wish our enterprise success.

TAVERNER   God bless you, lads! Good luck to you!

(*The three thieves leave the tavern and go towards the King's palace.*)

RASOIR   Pincedé, you've made an art of it;
    Sneak very quietly through that way
    And spy out if the King's asleep.

(*Pincedé goes into the palace and returns.*)

PINCEDÉ   Come on, quick, you thieving bastards!
    The King's asleep, and all his lords—
    So sound, they might as well be dead.   1000

(*They enter the palace. Rasoir picks up the image of Saint Nicholas.*)

RASOIR   He didn't set much store by his goods
    If he left this horny tramp in charge
    Guarding such a priceless treasure!

CLIQUET   Rasoir, help lift this heavy chest.
    Look, it's full of golden coins.

RASOIR   The devil it is! What a weight!
    Move the sack closer, Pincedé.
    This coffer's heavy as a flagstone;
    One ounce more would rupture me.

PINCEDÉ   Tip everything into a heap!   1010
    I don't want to leave the chest behind—
    I'd rather break my back with it.
    Watch me while I try my strength!
    No one else is going to take it.

(*Pincedé picks up the largest chest.*)

    Load me up then, if you will.

(*Rasoir and Cliquet lift the sack on to his shoulders.*)

RASOIR   Here you are. We'll help you anyway.

CLIQUET   Let's get on the road, my lads,
  While our luck is holding out.

(*They return to the tavern.*)

RASOIR   Landlord, landlord, open the door!
  We haven't brought your sack back empty—   1020
  We don't want to swindle you.

TAVERNER   Welcome, welcome, gentlemen!
  Quickly, Caignet, give them a hand.
  A pleasure to welcome such a guest!

PINCEDÉ (*setting down the sack*)
  Fellows, what a load that was!
  I don't think it would be amiss
  For me to have a drink at this point.

CLIQUET   Blow anyone who'd begrudge you that.
  Good wine helps all *my* aches and pains.

TAVERNER   Gentlemen, you shall have a fire   1030
  And comfortable chairs, don't you worry,
  And wine that's not the least bit ropy—
  A vintage from a mountain-side.

(*Caignet starts to draw the wine.*)

RASOIR   Caignet, lean it so the tap is lower—
  Let's taste the rich stuff at the bottom.

CLIQUET   Landlord, my friend, have him bring
  A candle of the double size.

TAVERNER   He won't come back empty-handed,
   I can guarantee you that.

CAIGNET   There's candle-light, and wine that's better   1040
   Than what is higher up the cask.

RASOIR   Ah! Dear God, blessed be the hour
   This wine descended into the tun!

CLIQUET   Give us some now, Pincedé.
   Now our pawn shall be redeemed.
   Ah. God! How wine restores the soul!
   At last we're well provided for.
   Curse anyone who doesn't drink
   A lot. Our tankard's big enough.

PINCEDÉ   Come on, let it circulate.   1050
   I want to have a crack at it.

(*They pass the tankard round.*)

CLIQUET   Drink then—but not the tankard too!
   No one's standing over you.

PINCEDÉ   Goodness, this is real vintage!
   I can't drink enough of it.

CAIGNET   Do you want me to fetch my dice?

RASOIR   Oh yes. Let them be put in their place.

PINCEDÉ   Now you're talking. Let's have a game.

CLIQUET   There's plenty to draw on now, Pincedé.

(*He points to the treasure.*)

RASOIR   Right! For our gambling and our spending   1060
We'll take a risk on the hangman's rope.

PINCEDÉ   Rasoir, shall we play Hazard?
I've a fistful of halfpennies tucked away.

RASOIR   All right. I never let a chance go by.
Everyone put his stake, and good luck!

CLIQUET   It's Hazard then, on the dicing plate.
I'll take my share. All do the same.

(*Cliquet takes a fistful of coins from the treasure sack and the other two follow suit.*)

PINCEDÉ   My handful's about the same as yours.

RASOIR   And mine, as close as I could judge.

TAVERNER   May I take a fistful, gentlemen?   1070

(*They restrain him.*)

But it's only what is due to me.

CLIQUET   When it's time for sharing out
We'll protect your interests.

PINCEDÉ   Rasoir, throw for who plays first,
And don't let anyone jog the board!

(*Rasoir and Pincedé go to one side of the dicing board, Cliquet to the other. The board slopes down towards Cliquet's side.*

RASOIR   (*noticing his advantage*)
God damn anyone who tips it!
It's the flattest, truest board on earth.

CLIQUET   Hey, no! I'll have to throw up hill:
It's resting higher on your side.

PINCEDÉ   By heavens, Cliquet, that's a lie!   *1080
I'll bet you one of those gold bits.

RASOIR   Put a pea in the centre of the board
And it will roll straight over here.

CLIQUET   Get on and throw, I'll take a chance.

(*Rasoir throws.*)

RASOIR   They're off! Watch what happens now.

CLIQUET   There you are. Seven.

RASOIR   Watch it! Watch it!
Those last two dice are loaded ones.

PINCEDÉ   No, Rasoir, your hand's too sweaty;
Rub it in the dust a bit.
This is how I make them roll . . .   1090

(*Pincedé throws.*)

Two sixes and five, that's seventeen!

CLIQUET   I'm blowed if I will take my turn.
Let's stake, Rasoir; he gets first throw.

RASOIR   Good Lord, Cliquet, you should wake up!
He's expert at laying the dice.

(*Caignet brings a fresh candle over to the dicing table.*)

CAIGNET   You must see clearly for this game;
They're not glass marbles you're playing for.
Cliquet, put this candle there,
Then you'll have a better view.

CLIQUET   Caignet, when this game is over,   1100
  You'll get a penny from each of us.

CAIGNET   But why not give me some from the bank—
  Three of them, made of shiny red gold?

PINCEDÉ   Did you hear this greedy magpie?
  When would there be an end of his grabbing?

TAVERNER   Caignet, let them gamble in peace.
  I'm expecting more than that from them.

RASOIR   You'll lose nothing by it, landlord;
  I'll look after things for you.

TAVERNER   Carry on.

PINCEDÉ   Gentlemen, my throw.   1110
  I have first dice; I throw for the pool.

CLIQUET   I hope the first two give you seven.

PINCEDÉ   God forbid! Hazard or sixteen!
  Hazard, O God!

(*Pincedé throws thirteen points.*)

RASOIR   That thirteen's ours.
  Now we'll gladly give you Hazard.

PINCEDÉ   No you won't. God forbid it!

(*Pincedé prepares to throw again and lets one dice slip.
Noticing that it turns up a three, he tries to claim it as a throw.*)

  A runaway! Look, for Pete's sake!

CLIQUET   That's no throw! Shake them properly
  In your palm—never mind what it was.

PINCEDÉ   Are you trying to cut me short?   1120
  At least you ought to let me finish.

CLIQUET   Go on, throw—with an open hand.
  I hope you damn well get Hazard!

PINCEDÉ   On the contrary, my count is eight;
  That's better than Hazard anyway.

CLIQUET   You covered yourself with that fallen three:
  The other two are ace and four.

PINCEDÉ   So now my eight fights your thirteen.
  Come on, this game will soon be over.

CLIQUET   Well, I'm damned! Blast those fingers   1130
  That keep on fiddling all the time!

(*Pincedé throws again, trying to repeat his eight. The others watch for a thirteen. First he throws a seven.*)

PINCEDÉ   Ah, Christ! One more! That would have been
  Well thrown. I shouldn't have made that seven.

CLIQUET   Now thirteen is what we want,
  If it will turn up for us again.

PINCEDÉ   No, Saint Leonard, send the lower chance
  And then the matter will be settled.

(*Pincedé throws fourteen.*)

CLIQUET   Holy Nicholas, send one point less!

(*Pincedé throws his eight again.*)

PINCEDÉ   That's it! Eight old friends again.

(*He goes to pick up the bank.*)

May I pick this lot up now?   1140
That's quite a handsome brood of chicks.

(*Rasoir forestalls him.*)

RASOIR   Thanks, Pincedé, I'll take the winnings
You promised me some time ago.
You definitely swore an oath
That I would get the first game's stakes.

PINCEDÉ   What are you talking about, you devil?
This lift is worth a hundred pounds!
Do you think that I was drunk enough
To promise you the evening's coup?
That was the game with Paris pence.   1150
Now when we play to get more wine . . .

RASOIR   Shout your head off! I wouldn't give
Two rotten eggs for your promises!

PINCEDÉ   But, Rasoir, you'll be better off.

CLIQUET   Oh, sure, sure! We can believe that!

PINCEDÉ   God damn and blast you, Rasoir,
For trying to pocket our money!

RASOIR   Well, whatever's on the board,
You're going to have to give it up.

PINCEDÉ   Then you'll have to take me too: 1160
You won't get it otherwise.

(*Rasoir and Pincedé fight over the stake money.*)

RASOIR   Leave 'em alone!

PINCEDÉ   Get your hands off,
Before I smash out both your eyes!

CAIGNET   Landlord! They're tearing each other's hair!
   Can't you hear the row they're making?

(*The taverner comes running.*)

TAVERNER   What's up? Pincedé, are you mad?
   Let go at once—you too, Rasoir.
   Come over here and sit down quiet.
   I know how the quarrel arose.
   Now bind yourselves over to me on oath—   1170
   I don't want to victimize.

PINCEDÉ   All right, I won't touch the gold.

RASOIR   Nor me—can't say I'm happy though.

TAVERNER   Caignet, pick up all these coins
   And put them back into the chest.

CLIQUET   You won't get less than we offered you.
   That's the lot. I can't see more.

TAVERNER   Good. Now we're quits. Everything
   As it was before, in the common pile.
   And now, let everyone take his share.   1180
   What's up? What are you waiting for?

RASOIR   Listen, landlord, wait a bit.
   We're all of us worn out because
   We've stayed awake the whole night through.
   Of course we'll share it out like friends,
   But first, why don't we get some sleep?

(*The thieves sleep. At the King's palace the Seneschal wakes.*)

SENESCHAL   O gods! Apollo and Mahomet!
   I had a curious dream in which
   I saw the King's own mighty treasure

Lost beyond recovery: 1190
The earth was caving in beneath it,
So that it plunged down into hell.
I shan't be happy till I've seen it.

(*He discovers the theft and runs to wake the King.*)

Your Majesty—a dreadful thing—
It would be treason not to tell you!
Get up, you most unhappy King!
Your priceless treasure has been stolen.

KING   What's that? The devil! Who wakes me up?
Seneschal, what's that you say?

SENESCHAL   Oh, King, you're poor—you're made a
    beggar! 1200
You can't blame anyone for this,
Because you entrusted the greatest treasure
That ever was known, to a wooden man.
Look at him—lying on the ground!

KING   Seneschal, are you telling the truth?
Have I really lost my treasure?
That white-haired fool, he made me do it,
Coming here preaching the other day.
Have him brought to me at once.
His day of judgment is at hand. 1210

(*The Seneschal goes to the prison.*)

SENESCHAL   Hey, you, Durant, jailer! Come here!
Is your prisoner still alive?
The King would like to look at him.

DURANT   Oh, yes. Here, wretch! For your disgrace
Today I'll make you take three steps
Along the road of no return!

(*He takes the Good Man to the King.*)

Your Majesty, he's here. Please God
No one else be allowed to put him to death
But me: I ask it as my reward.

KING   Fraudulent wretch! A poor return   1220
Of yours for my colossal hoard!
What a price I've paid for hearing you preach.
Your god cannot protect you now:
Durant, now we must make our plans
For a cruel death to shatter his bones.

DURANT   My lord, I am overjoyed to have him;
I'll keep him at death's door, alive,
For two whole days before he dies.

GOOD MAN   Oh, King! Don't act so spitefully!
Give me one more day of freedom,   1230
So they don't kill or torture me!
God is still where he always is,
He'll help me if it is his will.
A day's grace is worth a hundred pounds
And often has turned a war to peace.

KING   Why not? Durant, leave him alone,
But bring him back to me tomorrow.

(*Durant drives the Good Man back to the prison.*)

DURANT   In front—you beast! Back to the chains!
Oh, how I wish all Christians
Had just begun their Passion Week!   1240

GOOD MAN   Saint Nicholas, may you be blessed!
Help me now in my distress,
For I have reached my life's last hour:
My enemies hold me in their power.
In time of need one finds one's friends—
Master, to your servant send

Help against this threatening pagan king!
He longs for my death; in the morning
My time runs out. I stand condemned
Unless the treasure is returned. 1250
O Lord, deliver me from these fears,
From perishing in pain and tears!

DURANT   You swine! By all the gods, we shall see
The day when you must learn to serve
Your gruelling apprenticeship!
I don't care for your god and your prayers.
I am going to make you a scarf
Out of a rope tied full of knots.

GOOD MAN   Saint Nicholas, help me, oh help!
The time of grace allowed to me 1260
By my enemy is running out.
Saint Nicholas, look down on me!
I have trusted myself to your charge—
Where nothing can ever come to harm.

(*The Angel enters.*)

ANGEL   Come, good Christian, comfort! Do not weep.
You shall conquer those that now oppress you.
Pray to Saint Nicholas to succour you,
And in a little while he will send help.
    'God will deliver you; pray ceaselessly to the Saint.
    God will never fail his servant.' 1270

Suffer affliction with bravery and with patience
And keep Saint Nicholas always in your heart.
You must not doubt that he will do his part,
He will effect your safe deliverance.

If you have served and loved him as your lord,
Do not renounce your faith, but serve him still!
Cease not your prayers nor dry your tears until
God grants you for your pains his great reward.

(*At the tavern, Saint Nicholas appears to the sleeping thieves.*)

ST NICHOLAS   Criminals, enemies of God,
  Arise, for you have slept too long!   1280
  You shall be hanged without reprieve!
  Woe to those who stole the treasure,
  And woe the taverner who received it!

PINCEDÉ   What was that? Who woke us up?
  Good Lord, how heavily I slept!

ST NICHOLAS   Sons of whores, you're as good as dead:
  This minute the gallows are prepared.
  And you shall forfeit your three lives
  If you do not obey my voice.

PINCEDÉ   Your Honour, you have frightened us—   1290
  Who are you? You terrify us all.

ST NICHOLAS   You wretches, I am Saint Nicholas,
  I who put wanderers back on the road.
  Retrace your steps along the way
  And carry this treasure back to the King!
  You have done something criminal
  In daring even to think of theft.
  The treasure should have been well guarded
  By my statue laid on top:
  Make sure it is put there again   1300
  When you have put the treasure back.
  If your lives are worth anything to you,
  Return the statue to its place!
  I shall leave you now, at once.

(*Exit*)

PINCEDÉ (*crossing himself*)   Per signum sancte cruchefis!
  Cliquet, what do you think of that?
  And Rasoir, what have you to say?

      K

RASOIR   Jesus, I think the religious fellow
  Spoke the truth. It's shaken me.

CLIQUET   I'm miserable; I've never been   1310
  So scared of a man in all my life.

TAVERNER   I have nothing to do with this,
  If you men have overstepped the law.
  Go on—get out! Out of my house!
  I won't harbour stolen goods.

PINCEDÉ   Just now you were our accomplice—
  Since we're going to tell home truths.
  Each must take his proper share
  Of the profits and the loss.

TAVERNER   Get out, you bastards! Greedy swine!   1320
  Do you want to heap the blame on *me*?
  Collect the pawn for what they owe,
  Caignet, and throw them out of my house.

CAIGNET   Now then, Cliquet, no way out—
  Just you rid yourself of that cape!
  What can we expect but trouble
  From harbouring the likes of you?

(*Caignet starts to strip off Cliquet's cape. Rasoir and Pincedé
pick up the treasure and slip unobtrusively out of the tavern
into the 'place', where they wait for Cliquet.*)

CLIQUET   How much do I owe?

CAIGNET   Seventeen pence:
  Five for the wine and twelve for the loan.
  Where have Rasoir and Pincedé gone?   1330
  Well, leave your cloak for everything.

CLIQUET   You've turned very nasty, Caignet.

CAIGNET   What's that? Didn't I count up right?
In fact, I'm doing you a favour
By troubling to take your cloak in pawn.

CLIQUET   For taking pawn and giving short
There's no one to match you from here to the coast!

CAIGNET   Now go to hell, the lot of you!

(*Caignet turns Cliquet into the 'place', where he rejoins Rasoir and Pincedé.*)

PINCEDÉ   We're worse off than we were before—
The devil's casting a spell on us,   1340
He wants to bring us all to ruin.
Wealth can come and wealth can go,
But if we're destroyed and torn to pieces
No one can put us together again!

(*to Rasoir*)

Damn and blast you for your deals!

RASOIR   Here, take hold. Pincedé, load up.
You carried it here, you carry it back.

(*They load up Pincedé with the treasure.*)

CLIQUET   The landlord will be glum today—
He reckoned up worse than he ever thought:
He never charged us for the sack!   1350

PINCEDÉ   Lads, now take a risk with me!
Everyone grab himself a fistful
Of these gold coins—it wouldn't show.

CLIQUET   Shut up, you fool! It'd ruin us
If we were ever caught with it.

(*They enter the palace.*)

RASOIR   Put it here—that's where we got it.
    And put the image back on top.

PINCEDÉ   Down you go! God blast the hour
    I ever picked you up last night!

CLIQUET   Don't get so upset, Pincedé.   1360
    Take the advice of a fool like me
    That we all go our separate ways,
    Then one of us is sure to get a break.

PINCEDÉ   All right.

RASOIR   Agreed. Nothing good
    Will happen while we stick together.
    I've got my eye on a bedroom wall,
    Which I shall soon have drilled right through
    To get my hands on a bride's fine clothes,
    That are packed away in a chest of oak.

CLIQUET   And I shall go to Fresnes, my lads,   1370
    A little way beyond Gavrelle.
    If I conduct my business right
    The mayor of Fresnes will feel the pinch.

PINCEDÉ   The mayor's wife is pretty sharp,
    She'll know you if you pass the house.
    I shan't bother to go so far:
    Just a stone's throw away from here
    I caught sight of a line of washing.
    I think I'll lend a hand with the rinse.

RASOIR   Well, Pincedé, have good pinching!   1380

PINCEDÉ   God lead us all in the paths of wealth!

RASOIR   Adieu, Cliquet!

CLIQUET   Adieu, Rasoir!

(*They part and disappear from the 'place'.*)

(*At the palace the King wakes.*)

KING Mahomet, make everything I saw
In my dream come true in life!
May Tervagan expound it favourably!
I had just called my noblest lords
To come and attend me at my court,
And I had had a new crown made . . .
Seneschal, are you awake or asleep?

SENESCHAL Sir, neither: I had a marvellous dream.   1390
I hope it may be interpreted
As good. It soothed me as I slept.
The treasure was brought back again
And the thieves who had stolen it were hanged.

KING What? Seneschal, at least go and look!

(*The Seneschal discovers the treasure and returns to the King.*)

SENESCHAL Your Majesty, my dream's explained.
Your treasure has come back again—
It's greater than before the theft!
I reckon it's twice the size it was,
And Saint Nicholas is still on top.   1400

KING Seneschal, are you mocking me?

SENESCHAL Your Majesty, I never heard
Of such a hoard—it's greater than that
Of Octavian, or Caesar, or Herakles!

KING My word! What a miracle!
Go quickly for the Christian.

(The Emirs and the King's court assemble while the Seneschal goes to the prison.)

SENESCHAL   Durant, bring the Christian out;
　　He needn't fear you any more.
　　(*Aside*)   Why should I conceal the news?

DURANT   You miserable wretch! I was a fool   1410
　　Not to have hanged you by your thumbs
　　And pulled out all your molar teeth!

(They lead the Good Man to the King.)

SENESCHAL   I've brought the man, Your Majesty.
　　It lies within your power and will
　　Whether he's to live or die.

GOOD MAN   Saint Nicholas, in whom I trust,
　　And whom I'll never cease to serve,
　　Shield my body, send me rescue!
　　Take care of your own man today,
　　And temper the anger of this king   1420
　　Who threatens to tear me limb from limb—
　　His hatred of me is so great.

KING   Tell me, Christian, my friend,
　　Do you believe he could do that?
　　Do you think he could make me change my faith?
　　Do you think he could send my treasure back?
　　Is your belief in him so strong?

GOOD MAN   Ah, King! Why should he not do that?
　　He helped the three young girls in need,
　　And once revived three clerks from death.   1430
　　I'm sure that he could vanquish you
　　And make you leave your pagan faith
　　Which you should be called a fool to hold.
　　In him are all the seeds of good.

KING Good Christian, he has started well:
My treasure has returned to me.
His miracles are evident,
Since he brings lost things to light again.
I'd not have believed it of anyone.
Seneschal, what good would lying be? 1440
My heart is so utterly convinced,
I'll never seek another god.

SENESCHAL My lord, I have not dared to speak,
But I have reproached you in my heart
For not telling me your mind before,
Because I have the same desire.

KING Good man, go fetch Saint Nicholas;
I shall serve him without question.

(*The Good Man fetches the statue of Saint Nicholas.*)

GOOD MAN O God, may you be thus adored,
For you have filled with heavenly grace 1450
This king who fought against your word.
The man who disbelieves is as false
As he who slackens in your service.
Your power shines forth in every place.
King, cast your pagan folly out,
Lift up your hands and heart to God,
Asking him for his forgiveness,
And pray to our lord Saint Nicholas.

DURANT (*Aside*) You Christian, you Christian!
I'm sorry I have spared you so long! 1460

KING Saint Nicholas, I give myself
To your protection, and ask your mercy,
Without deceit or treachery.
Master, I swear that I am your man.
I renounce Apollo and Mahomet
And this pagan bastard Tervagan.

SENESCHAL   My King, exactly as you've done,
  I bind myself, body and soul,
  To our new master, Nicholas.
  I spurn Mahomet and Apollo   1470
  And all their pagan race of Gods,
  And Tervagan—that filthy fiend.

COINE   Your Highness, as you've been converted,
  We emirs, who hold our fiefs from you,
  Will also change our faith with yours.
  My lords, get down upon your knees,
  And all of you do as I do.

ORKENIE   Most willingly.

OLIFERNE   And I shall too.
  Now let us be good Christians,
  Obedient to Saint Nicholas—   1480
  His virtues are so excellent!

WITHERED TREE   Do not count me in, my lords:
  I am quite deaf to this Christian tale.
  Cursed be the man who counsels me
  That I become a renegade.
  Wretched King, you should be drowned
  Like a traitor and a recreant
  For turning into an infidel!
  You should be burned or flayed alive!
  You and your wisdom and your power   1490
  Aren't worth an empty ear of corn.
  Beware! I defy you and give back
  Your homage and the fief I hold.

KING   Quickly, my lords! By my crown
  I shall force him against his will
  To obey my pleasure and commands.
  Hurl him to the ground by force!

(*The emirs struggle with him.*)

ORKENIE   Here, help, my lords! He's very strong,
  You must take him from behind.

WITHERED TREE   Damn you—devils! Do you think
    you'll take me   1500
  As long as Mahomet gives me strength?
  Fly, you knights, you hypocrites!
  I don't care for you and your tricks.

OLIFERNE   You will come here . . . I've got you now.

(*They force him to his knees before the King.*)

ORKENIE   Your Majesty, behold your traitor.

WITHERED TREE   Oh, King, mercy for Mahomet's sake!
  Do not make me renounce my gods—
  I'd rather have my head cut off,
  Or my body torn apart by horses.

KING   Upon my life, I swear you shall   1510
  Do what I do; you must learn that.

WITHERED TREE   Saint Nicholas, against my will
  I have been forced to worship you,
  You'll get nothing but my skin.
  By my words I become your servant,
  But my faith is in the god Mahomet.

(*The idol of Tervagan speaks.*)

TERVAGAN   Palas aron ozinomas
  Baske bano tudan donas
  Geheamel cla orlaÿ
  Berec-he-pantaras taÿ.   1520

GOOD MAN   King, what is he trying to say?

KING   My friend, he's dying of grief and anger,
   Because I renounced him and turned to God.
   I take no notice of his preaching.
   Seneschal, go for me and hurl
   His statue from the synagogue.

(*The Seneschal carries the statue of Tervagan to the steps of the temple.*)

SENESCHAL   Tervagan, in your misery,
   You'll soon see the prophetic truth
   Of the smiles and tears that you have shown.
   Prophesy how many steps!   1530

(*He hurls the statue down.*)

Down! Curse you if you're ever raised!
   You're empty as a bladder of wind!

(*He returns to the King.*)

   My King, I've smashed him into pieces.

KING   Christian, we shall be baptized.
   As soon as it is possible.
   I long to prove myself God's servant.

GOOD MAN   (*to the converts and to the audience*)
   Let us sing to God for evermore
   'Te Deum laudamus'.

Here ends the play of Saint Nicholas that Jean Bodel made. Amen.

Texts

Jean Bodel, *Le Jeu de Saint Nicolas*, ed. F. J. Warne, Oxford (Basil Blackwell) 1951.

Le Jeu de Saint Nicolas de Jehan Bodel, éd. Albert Henry (with translation into modern French), Paris (Presses Universitaires de France) and Bruxelles (Presses Universitaires de Bruxelles), 1962.

T. B. W. Reid, 'On the Text of the Jeu de Saint Nicolas', in *Studies in Medieval French Presented to Alfred Ewert*, Oxford, 1961, pp. 96–120.

Staging and interpretation

Charles Foulon, 'La représentation et les sources du *Jeu de Saint Nicolas*', *Mélanges d'histoire du théâtre du Moyen-Age et de la Renaissance offerts à G. Cohen*, Paris, 1950, pp. 55–66.

Grace Frank, 'Wine reckonings in Bodel's *Jeu de Saint Nicolas*', *Modern Language Notes*, L (1935), pp. 9–13.

C. A. Knudson, 'Hasard, et les autres jeux de dés dans le *Jeu de Saint Nicolas*', *Romania*, LXIII (1937), pp. 248–53.

Patrick R. Vincent, *The Jeu de Saint Nicolas of Jean Bodel of Arras*, Johns Hopkins Studies in Romance Literatures and Languages, XLIX, Baltimore, 1954.

COURTOIS D'ARRAS

PERSONS OF THE PLAY

COURTOIS, the prodigal son
his FATHER
his BROTHER
POT-BOY
TAVERNER
LEKET, barman
POURETTE ⎫ women of
MANCEVAIRE ⎭ the town
a BURGHER

COURTOIS D'ARRAS

Text

This dramatization of the parable of the prodigal son was made in the late twelfth or early thirteenth century, probably before 1228 (see line 81), by an anonymous contemporary of Jean Bodel's in Arras.

Four manuscripts of *Courtois* have survived, three from the thirteenth, one from the early fourteenth century. The manuscripts give three different versions of the text (one of them adds a scene in which Courtois' sister begs her father not to send him away). None of the manuscripts names the speakers or divides the dialogue. This fact, together with the occurrence in all texts of some lines which are plainly narrative (91–5, 102), has led to the theory that *Courtois* was a dramatic monologue which could have been performed by a single *jongleur* using different voices and costumes and perhaps puppets. But this assumption is not necessary. The narrative lines, unlike those of the *Resureccion*, are few in number and may be explained as intended for manuscript readers rather than performers. The play clearly belongs to an Arras tradition of tavern realism which lasted at least from Bodel's *Saint Nicolas* (*c.* 1200) to the time of Adam de la Halle, three generations later.

The anonymous poet uses the two favourite metres of the Arras dramatists—octosyllabic couplets or sometimes, as in 1–90, *sixaines* for the dialogue and narrative lines, and alexandrine monorhymed quatrains for Courtois' lament (431–50), translated here in pentametric quatrains with alternating rhymes.

We have translated Edmond Faral's edition, first printed

in 1911 (CFMA) and reprinted in 1961, in preference to his
revised edition of 1922. We have followed Faral's division of
the dialogue, his naming of speakers and his line-numbering.
At one point (after 147) we have inserted as stage-directions
three lines of metrical narrative from the 'A' text not printed
in Faral's 1911/61 edition.

Staging
The action of the play is in four parts, taking place at
Courtois' home, at the tavern, at the Burgher's swine field,
and back home again. The staging can be extremely simple.
Only two 'houses' are necessary: Courtois' Father's house
and the tavern. The 'place' between the 'houses' serves for
Courtois' wanderings and for his swine-herding. Both
'houses' should be porch-like structures, open to the 'place'
and with entrances at the back so that characters can enter
from off-stage and retire through the 'houses' when not
needed.

Details of the tavern 'house' are suggested by the dialogue.
The tavern seeems to be visualized as an open terrace or
courtyard with tables and possibly also potted plants. (As he
sets off Courtois longs for a *raverdie* (100)—a tavern green
or garden; the Pot-boy invites customers to sit 'on the grass
or on rush mats' (104).) The tavern 'house' may also, at the
producer's discretion, have a separate curtained alcove into
which Pourette leads Courtois (after 235).

"A comic version of the Prodigal Son story"
(Tydeman)

COURTOIS D'ARRAS

(At his 'house' the Father wakens Courtois' elder Brother.)

FATHER   It's time you drove the animals out:
 Bullocks and cows, and sheep and pigs
 Should have been in the fields long since—
 The turf is moist and fresh with dew,
 The skylark and the nightingale
 Began their singing hours ago.
 Get up, my lad, you've slept too long:
 Your little lambs already should
 Have cropped the tender springing grass.

BROTHER   Father, you're pushing me too far.   10
 Late to bed and up at dawn
 My life has been, day after day.
 Each day I work as hard as I can
 And you treat me as if I were your slave.
 I have to cope with everything—
 You've always put the load on me.
 My brother has the best of the deal,
 He's your favourite—for doing nothing!
 He's younger than I am and not so strong,
 But couldn't you have sent him with me   20
 To do some job you wanted done,
 Or to keep the cattle in the field?
 I know you're my father, but I must say
 He should do something—it's only fair.
 Lucky fellow, he spends his time
 Drinking and gambling at draughts and dice—
 Spending all that we two earn!

L

FATHER   My son, what would you have me do?
  If I were to beat him and throw him out,
  He'd be in very serious straits,   30
  Because he never learned a trade
  Which might be of use to him
  In any country where he went.
  I don't know what's the best advice.
  I always hope that he'll reform
  Before I strike him or give him a thrashing—
  I'm afraid of turning him against me.

(*Exit Brother. Enter Courtois.*)

COURTOIS   To the devil with this slavery!
  Damn anyone who'd suffer it.
  I've decided I'm going to leave,   40
  But before I set out on my way
  I'll have whatever is due to me.
  I know the better part of your wealth
  Is in livestock and in cattle,
  But I've no use for cattle-skins—
  They're not on a par with ready money.
  So give me mine in good hard cash,
  And not less than my share is worth!

FATHER   Calm yourself, Courtois, dear boy.
  Get on and eat your bread and peas,   50
  And just forget this stupid plan.

COURTOIS   Father, this is a wretched place—
  There's nowhere on earth I could do worse.
  God couldn't grudge me 'bread and peas'!

FATHER   My boy, you're talking like a fool.
  All the same, I've sixty shillings,
  And since you're set on going away,
  You shall have them—on one condition:
  Give up your right to anything else
  And call it quits between us two.   60

COURTOIS Here, Father, hand me the purse.
  My God, I never felt one lighter!
  I'm not tempted to look inside.
  I'll take it on the terms you said
  And stick to my part of the agreement,
  However it turns out for me.

FATHER Take it, dear boy; it's counted out.
  God give you health and happiness.
  I hope we hear good news of you.
  You haven't any means of help   70
  To get you on your feet again
  If you should lose the money you have.
  The world's so full of craft and cunning!

COURTOIS Oh, I know all the tricks of gambling,
  Dicing at 'Highest Points' and 'Hazard'.
  I swear by the love I have for you
  I'll never want for food and drink
  As long as I find someone to play with.
  These sixty shillings shall earn me more
  Than the hundred pounds that are stowed away   80
  In Gerart Lenoir's treasure chest—
  And that's kept under lock and key
  So he can never divide it out
  For himself or for his legal heirs.
  There's no point in having money tied up.
  I reckon money's well employed
  When you please yourself with it.
  I know what I'm doing with this purse.
  Goodbye, dear Father, I'm on my way.

FATHER Go, my son; and God be with you.   90

(*The Father goes into his 'house'. Courtois walks across the 'place'.*)

Now Courtois has gone on his way,
Making merry as he goes,

And carrying his heavy purse
Fat and stuffed to overflowing:
He thinks the money will never be spent.

COURTOIS   My God, what a store of silver and copper!
    Where shall I ever spend all this?
    If there was a salted ham and a pot
    Brimful of good wine, and clear of dregs,
    And a little spot of tavern green,   100
    A fellow might stretch out pleasantly!

(*The Pot-Boy enters the 'place' from the tavern 'house'*.)

Then he hears a pot-boy shout.

POT-BOY   This way, inside for Soissons wine!
    Sit on the grass or on rush mats—
    Wonderful drinking from silver tankards!
    Credit extends to everyone,
    Fools and wise men drinking inside—
    And no one has to leave a pledge!
    There's nothing to do but chalk it up.
    Mancevaire and Pourette will tell you—   110
    They eat and drink here all the time
    And take on credit all they need,
    And never pay a farthing for it.

COURTOIS   Almighty God be blessed and praised
    For leading me to find this place
    Where I have stumbled on such plenty!
    One sees a lot if one roams the country—
    My father was a proper fool
    To have frightened me so much,
    When everywhere there's such abundance   120
    That one has lots to eat and drink
    By writing the landlord a credit note!
    Only a fool wouldn't drink on credit.
    May God bless and preserve this place—
    It's better than a monastery!

(Courtois follows the Pot-boy into the tavern porch and sits down at a table by himself. Further inside the tavern are the Taverner and Leket, Mancevaire and Pourette. The Taverner comes forward.)

Landlord, how much is it for a pint?
And when did you broach this barrel of wine?

TAVERNER   Tapped and broached early this morning—
We sell it at sixpence for a gallon,
But no one drinks unless he likes it.   130
If there's anything that takes your fancy,
Just say the word and it will be done.
We have every comfort here:
Decorated rooms, soft beds
Piled with covers, soft with feathers,
Made in the fashionable French way
With blankets beautiful and clean
And pillows scented with violets;
Finally, to crown your comfort,
Fragrant lotions and rose water   140
With which to freshen your mouth and face.

COURTOIS   Goodness, what a delightful inn!
They've got whatever one could want.
Well, landlord, draw me half a gallon,
I love it when it's freshly tapped.

TAVERNER   Leket, draw from the cask that's full,
As clear as you know it ought to be.

While the wine is being drawn,
Pourette and Mancevaire come in
And sit down side by side, and say:

POURETTE   Drink up there, young gentleman!
Now God bless your beautiful eyes!
The rest will be much tastier   150

   After your lovely teeth and lips
   Have kissed the wine in *our* tankard.

(*She offers him their tankard and he drinks.*)

   Already you are one of us.

(*Leket brings wine in a silver tankard.*)

   Here, now drink from the silver one—
   This gallon's not been started yet.

COURTOIS   I'm glad of your company, *ma dame*;
   I've never been a woman-hater.

POURETTE   Now darling, don't get up for me.
   Where are you from?

COURTOIS   I'm from Artois.

POURETTE   And tell me, what's your name?

COURTOIS   Courtois   160
   By name and by nature, dear.

POURETTE   I can see you're not a common man.
   You know, something tells me in my heart
   You're clever—and a gentleman.
   I wish to God and Saint Rémi
   I had a lover just like you!
   I bet there was never a king or count
   Ever had half the money he will
   Without ever doing a hand's turn—
   Don't you think so, Mancevaire?   170

MANCEVAIRE   Oh, yes. I'm sure you're right, Pourette.
   You could pay his debts and get
   His clothes and horses out of pawn—
   But he must keep himself from gambling.
   I won't make a song and dance,

But really, Pourette, you and Courtois
Are quite a match for one another.

COURTOIS   Come, Mancevaire, let's have some fun—
But I'm still sitting by myself!
Can't I come between you two?   (*He moves.*)   180
A man would be a fool to think
That I would boast on an empty purse—
I've got a tidy bit in here.

MANCEVAIRE   She's not deceiving you, Courtois.
I know her and her little ways:
She really is in love with you—
I don't know if she's being wise.
But if you're looking for a girl,
I can tell you absolutely
That you've struck really lucky here.   190
She's nice girl, shapely, pretty,
Hard-working—and her wits are sharp.
She won't just love you for a lark.
Courtois, pour some wine in the bowl—
It's not made out of Judas wood.

COURTOIS   Leket, we three will drink together,
One tankard for the three of us.
We'll reckon everything together,
Mancevaire, Pourette and me,
When it comes to closing time   200
And we have to pay the final bill.

POURETTE   Courtois, let's all test what sort
Of wine it is that we are drinking.
We never ought to trust Leket—
There's not a bigger crook on earth.

(*Leket brings more wine to their table.*)

LEKET   Just look at it—strong as a lion.
It's from Auxerre.

POURETTE   It's Paris stuff.

COURTOIS   Taste it.

POURETTE   You must drink it first.

COURTOIS   I'll like it better after you.

POURETTE   Here, take hold, see how it feels—   210
   You'll find it strong and smooth and fresh.
   I'll tell you something—and I'm not lying—
   These grapes were never grown in Rochelle.

(*Pourette holds out the drinking-bowl in a formal loving toast.*)

   I'm your sweetheart and your mistress;
   I love you truly with all my heart.
   I give you this wine as a token of love—
   Believe me, dear, I won't deceive you.

COURTOIS   My sweetest lady, I accept
   With all my heart and fondest love.

(*He takes the bowl and drinks.*)

POURETTE   And now I ask for a loving advance   220
   Upon our ripening amour.

(*She takes back the bowl and drinks.*)

MANCEVAIRE   Hush, now! Be careful what you say—
   You're talking like a stupid girl.

POURETTE   (*to Courtois*)
   We'll reap whatever the plot will yield,
   If you can find the place tonight.

(*Aside to Mancevaire*)

> Look, you slut! What a lark this is!
> Did a woman ever have such a chance?

(*Aloud*)

> Oh, Lord! Why doesn't he kiss me now?
> I think he's most unkind to me.

COURTOIS Hush, darling. Time enough for that.　　230
　I'm behaving so no one will notice.

MANCEVAIRE That's wise. Give us some more to drink.

COURTOIS I think that's best, Mancevaire, don't you?

MANCEVAIRE Just pour me out a tiny drop.

COURTOIS Drink up, there's plenty. Good luck to you!

POURETTE As long as no one disturbs us here
　You needn't be ashamed, Courtois;
　This is a very secluded place.
　If you want to step outside a moment
　Into the garden, for a pee,　　　　　　240
　You needn't be uncomfortable.
　You can do harm by holding it back.
　Don't mind about leaving us alone.

COURTOIS Thank you for reminding me,
　I'll just go out to ease myself.

(*Courtois steps out into the 'place' and walks behind the tavern.*)

POURETTE Now my old whore we'll get him drunk!
　We've found a proper Sir Gawain here!
　Pah! he's just a labourer putting it on.

He thinks he's found wild strawberries,
But before he's paid his wedding debt   250
He's going to lighten that purse a bit
That's bulging there so fat on his arse.
I know how to trim his sides.

(*to the Taverner*)

Why don't you talk to us a bit,
Landlord, make us some company?

TAVERNER   What's doing, ladies? Is he rich?
You ought to let me in on this.

POURETTE   We've stumbled on an idiot.
I've promised he can make love to me,
But first I plan to take a cut   260
Of that purse of his that's stuffed so full.

TAVERNER   Have you found where he keeps his purse?
Good Lord, just think of draining it!

POURETTE   No one's going to help him now
Or stop me finishing my game.
We'll leave him here in place of us
To pay our bills and all our debts.
And don't you stand there like a fool,
Don't be afraid to ask for pawn.
Just reach your hand out for the pennies!   270
There's plenty there—I don't know
How much. Then strip him of his cloak
And jacket—he won't put up a fight—
And make him put on one much worse.
And when he's left all that he owns,
Throw him out into the street;
We shan't have any fuss from him.

(*Courtois returns through the 'place' and re-enters the tavern.*)

TAVERNER   Shsh! Good riddance to him, too!

COURTOIS How pretty the garden out there is!
    It's charming and so nicely kept;   280
    No flower on earth that doesn't grow there.

POURETTE Leket, bring us a towel, please,
    Warm water, and some washing bowls.

LEKET Here you are, all fresh and clean.
    The water is just the proper heat.

(*Courtois, Pourette and Mancevaire wash their hands and faces.*)

COURTOIS I must try not to give offence
    Or break the customs of the house;
    The service here is admirable.
    Whatever delights the bodies of men
    Is here in Maltese opulence,   290
    As far as I can judge these things.

POURETTE Mancevaire, pour out some wine;
    One ought to drink when one has washed.

COURTOIS I shan't be stingy with the wine.
    Drink it down by the tankardful.
    Pourri, why don't you dip your bread—
    It'll give you an appetite for supper.

POURETTE I've never liked soaking bread in wine.
    But you drink up, my dearest love,
    And then we want to talk to you,   300
    If you will give us some good advice.

COURTOIS Why, you can ask whatever you like:
    No question but I'll answer it.

POURETTE Can you guess what I will say?
    Whoever likes good food and wine

Needs to keep his eyes wide open
And to use his wits to enjoy himself.
Well, now we're off to do some business
For a little while, if you don't mind.
We'll make ourselves a bit of cash—   310
'A penny is a good companion'!
You stay here and drink the profits,
But watch that you don't gamble here,
And don't you budge from where you are,
Or that might ruin our affair.

COURTOIS   Hush, hush, you needn't worry at all
That I shall gamble, if you'll come back.

POURETTE   You'll find it very hard to resist—
You've got such very clever fingers,
I fear for the safety of your money;   320
Someone will lead you astray at dice.

COURTOIS   Take it, look after it for me.
You don't think I need the money?
I'd rather have it in your bosom
Than wasted in some stupid cause.

(*Pourette takes Courtois' purse. The women move out of his hearing.*)

POURETTE   Leket, just a word with you:
This one must settle the score for all.
We shall go off and about our business
Where we know of something good—
You know how it is with us,   330
With all our old debts and the new.
Before my friend here goes away
You'll have everything you want.

LEKET   I trust I will, I guarantee
I'll keep close to him all the time.

COURTOIS   Well, that's fine. Till she comes back
   I shall not want to stir from here.

POURETTE   (*aloud*)
   Leket, have them kill two capons
   And get them ready for our return.

COURTOIS   Well, off you go. That suits me fine.   340

(*Exeunt Mancevaire and Pourette. Leket takes the Taverner aside*.)

LEKET   Sir, do you want to hear the news?
   You've no idea how much this fool
   Is intoxicated with Pourette.
   He's been left behind to wait for them—
   That's how far they took him in!

TAVERNER   Let's go and take a pledge off him;
   I don't want to chase after *her*.
   What's up, Courtois? Where's Pourette
   And her girl-friend Mancevaire?

COURTOIS   They had to go off on some business,   350
   So I'm left here as a hostage!

TAVERNER   By Christ, I've got a lousy pledge
   Through having trusted the pair of them!
   You took a bit of bad advice
   To let Pourette leave you here in pawn.
   She's the shiftiest, most deceitful
   Woman that ever plied the trade.
   Pourette has more of Renard's cunning
   Than you have strength of Isengrin's.
   She made a fool of Damagrin   360
   And of Baudet; when they went away
   They hadn't a stitch of their own between them;
   Oh, yes, she really caught that pair,

And one of them had to leave his horse.
However, that's no concern of mine.
I must have security for my bills
So that I'm sure of getting paid.

COURTOIS   You needn't worry about that—
  They're sure to come back presently.
  If you're afraid of anything,   370
  Take my cloak. Here you are, take hold!

(*The Taverner takes Courtois' cloak from him.*)

TAVERNER   Why, that's fine talk—now you owe less,
  But I must have your jacket too.

COURTOIS   How can I go away without?
  I never heard of such a thing.

TAVERNER   You've got no choice, Courtois, by Christ!
  And your breeches, if they're clean.
  Hurry up, unfasten your sleeves;
  We've got other things to do.

(*Courtois takes off his outer clothes and hands them to the Taverner.*)

COURTOIS   Here you are.   380

TAVERNER   There's nothing more to take—
  No pennies, no silver of any kind?

COURTOIS   I swear by common decency,
  I don't know if I was a fool or not,
  But I had sixty shillings on me,
  Fastened into my breeches here;
  But Pourette didn't want to leave them—
  She took the money and wallet too.

TAVERNER   I tell you what, you're better off
   Without your wallet and your mistress.
   You know she never loved you a bit—   390
   You'll find out for yourself in time.
   But if you ever want to get in touch,
   Or hear the latest news of her,
   Take the road straight to Béthune.
   You're travelling light—you'll get there fast!

COURTOIS   Well, that's poor comfort to me now—
   Running in the storm and wind.
   My father often used to say
   I should stay quietly at home;
   I never had any common sense.   400
   I closed my ears to good advice.
   Now, of necessity, I must seek
   Some means of mending my broken life,
   Unless I want to die of hunger.
   I never wanted to learn a trade
   Or undertake an honest job—
   It's only right I pay for it now.
   I can't fall back on my father again,
   Nor to relations, nor to my friends.

TAVERNER   My word, Courtois, it worries me   410
   That you have ended up like this—
   And that I've scarcely half the pawn
   That you owed me for those two girls.
   There's an ancient smock inside,
   That long ago we used to lend
   To good-for-nothings passing by.
   You can have it if you like,
   So you won't be quite undressed—
   For that's a shameful thing for a man.
   You go and fetch it here, Leket,   420
   So he'll be more respectable.

(*Leket brings out the smock, which Courtois puts on.*)

There, Courtois, you are in luck.
I have plenty coming in,
But you will lose that coat tomorrow,
When you come to another foreign place.

COURTOIS What a wretched change in my luck!
I've been tricked by everyone.
God bless and keep you safe, Landlord!
It's no good here without some money.

TAVERNER God guide you, Courtois—and so,
goodbye.   430

(*The Taverner and Leket retire inside the tavern. Courtois
leaves the tavern and wanders about the 'place'.*)

COURTOIS O Lord, what a desperate state I am in,
When you seem to sleep and are so slow to send
Me aid. I've lost the help of parents and kin—
My father rightly predicted how it would end.

Often he warned me—if only I had listened!
Hardship I never knew; and now I learn
Because I must. I don't know where to turn.
I cannot beg and I have nothing to spend.

I've crushed myself through foolishness. I'm barred
For ever from my father's will. O Lord,   440
If for my good you punish me, I'll say
That wisdom's best for which one has to pay.

I took my father's words for an idle tale
And now go hungry while he sits at table.
Too late I see that I have been a fool:
The horse has gone, and *now* I shut the stable!

I'm far from my country, far from every friend;
I deserve to suffer this ordeal. O God,

This poverty has wrung me to repent—
Direct me somewhere that I may find food!   450

(*The Burgher enters the 'place'.*)

BURGHER   Hey you, fellow, why are you so sad?
What is it you want so desperately?
Who brought you into such a state?

COURTOIS   Sir, I could spin you quite a tale,
But I'll just tell the simple truth;
I am the wretchedest man on earth
And the most unfortunate of all.

BURGHER   Come, my friend, you never know
What God is keeping for you later.
One year does not last for ever;   460
One year's a father, another a step-father.
If this one treats you like a step-son,
You must be sensible and brave—
To be the true son of the next!
Now, you are fit and tall and strong;
You shall learn to keep a herd of pigs.
Tell me, friend, what is your name?

COURTOIS   Everyone calls me Courtois, sir.

BURGHER   Courtois, I don't think you're a liar;
You shall have fourpence and your footwear   470
Until the feast of Saint Rémi,
If you want to stay with me
And be the herdsman of my pigs.

COURTOIS   Oh, yes, sir, I will willingly—
If I could have some bread as well?

BURGHER   By Christ, you shall not go without.
You can have a whole large loaf

M

In your dinner basket every day.
And now be quiet and rest yourself.

COURTOIS   No, I'll chase my hogs from their sty   480
     And drive them to their feeding ground
     In that meadow over there,
     So they can stuff themselves to bursting.

BURGHER   Then take your herder's stick in your hand—
     It'll make you look more used to the job.

(*The Burgher leaves the 'place'. Courtois moves about the 'place' as if driving pigs.*)

COURTOIS   Now I've everything I need.
     Get up there! Thanks be to God
     That things are turning out all right.
     As far as I can judge, this flesh
     Was never fattened up on acorns: 490
     Her rump is thick with solid meat,
     Her back is broad and fat as well.
     Good luck to the man who's kept you!
     My master will very soon be able
     To cut you into joints and rashers!

     Oh, God! What time can it be now?
     I know I should have eaten something,
     But my bread is baked as hard as biscuit;
     It's full of ears of rye and tares.
     Such filth I hardly could have eaten   500
     When I was at my father's house.
     How my brother would mock me now,
     If he knew that I was tending pigs!
     I've changed so much in my condition
     As well as in the life I lead.
     They'd be revenged upon my pride
     If they just knew of my disgrace.
     Oh, God! This bread is so revolting,

It must be made of oats or barley.
My throat must be stuck full of holes   510
From bits of chaff and long, sharp straws.
I would rather die of hunger—
I would never stoop to eat it!
Now I shall be forced to cheat
My master, to whom I've been attached.
I won't return to his house, nor will
The pigs, unless driven by someone else.
This has been a Lenten week;
Nothing good can happen to me in it.
As long as I can recall I've not   520
Eaten anything worth a farthing.
Now I'm so hungry it makes me groan,
But when I even look at that crust
I marvel that anyone could bite it,
It's made out of such mouldy grain.
Already past three in the afternoon!
I'm not used to fasting at this hour.
Oh, oh! How my guts are griping!
We used to breakfast at six o'clock.
Through the bargain I made myself   530
I've plunged my life in misery.
I didn't merely cut a branch
To whip myself in punishment,
I made a club to smash me down,
So now I die at my own hands!
One thing is certain: I don't dare
Ever return to my father again.
I must settle somewhere else,
I don't know where or in what part.
Hunger is wrenching my heart in two.   540
God has forgotten and cast me off.
I wonder about those peas in the shell
That the pigs are trampling in the mud;
Perhaps they would comfort me a bit
And help to ease this awful pain.
There's no help left except to try—

One should not allow oneself to die.
If only God would grow me some peas—
New ones—these are shrivelled up.
Bah! Sour and rotten, every one!   550
I shan't get very fat on them.
They would have tasted better hot—
Shelled and mashed, and cooked in lard.
Now I know I shall die of hunger.
I need God's guidance desperately.
Oh, God! If only father knew
That I was living in such filth,
It would move such pity in his heart
He'd love to have me in his sight.
It would be best to go to him;   560
I know now that's what I must do—
I hope that it is possible:
Instead of dying here, it would
Be better to ask for his forgiveness.

I know the way back home quite well,
But I fear my father may not look
At me, or allow me any wealth,
When he sees me in such a wretched state.
I've fallen as low as I can get.
If I'd gone riding a horse,   570
Gorgeously dressed in a cloak of fur,
I could be sure of a warmer welcome.
But now there won't be any rejoicing:
My brother's such a vicious brute
I know how he will reproach me
With having fallen on hard times.
But, though my brother is like that,
My father is kind and merciful;
He'll hear my tale with sympathy.

(*Courtois' wanderings about the 'place' have now brought him
back near his father's 'house'.*)

Thank God. Now I can see the house,   580

The very windows and the doors—
I was a fool to run away.
I see my father sitting inside,
But dare not look upon him now,
Nor go any way that he will see me.
I've wronged him too much; all the same,
I'll have to go and show myself.
I am his son, and he my father—
But I was too proud to work for him.

(*Courtois goes round to the front of the 'house'. His Father sits inside.*)

He's seen me. He doesn't know me   590
Because he's never seen me before
In clothes like these and such a state—
It makes me feel ashamed to go in.
What good does all his staring do
When he cannot recognize who I am?
I must struggle to put down
This sense of shame and bitterness
And do something that he'll recognize.
I'll never be proud with him again.

Gentle father, your wretched son,   600
Who foolishly departed from you,
Who never believed the warnings you gave,
Nor ever carried out your wishes,
Has come to ask for Christian mercy,
Repentant for the wrong he's done.

(*His Father comes forward, out of the 'house'.*)

FATHER   Who are you? Come now, you're mistaken
In setting upon me with your prayers.
Explain what is this grievous fault
That you are asking me to pardon?

COURTOIS   Oh, my dear Father, look at me!   610

I am your son, Courtois the wretch;
The one who quarrelled so with you
And went against your strict command.

FATHER   My dearest boy, you're welcome home,
Welcome a hundred thousand times!
Come, wrap yourself about—you're naked.
I never would have known you, boy.
Dear son, if I'd known yesterday
That you'd come home in such a state,
I would have found you another coat.   620
Your wrong-doing doesn't matter two pins,
Since you have come to know yourself
And left off doing wicked things.
We'll kill the fattest calf I have
To celebrate your coming home,
And then we'll have a splendid feast
At home, for family and servants,
And we'll invite the neighbours in.
You've had enough of poverty,
So till you're properly recovered   630
I think you should be bathed and spoiled.

(*Enter Courtois' Brother from inside the 'house'.*)

BROTHER   What's this? I'm coming back for dinner
And find the house is crowded out.
Who is this wretched new arrival
You're making such a fuss about?

FATHER   My son, it's Courtois—your own brother.

BROTHER   Brother? The devil! Is this a joke?
Come back so he can leave again?
He went off with the ready cash
But I see he found his time was dear—   640
It shows in his face and on his cheeks.

FATHER   He has no fur-lined mantle now!
   Indeed, as you may well believe,
   He's not had much to eat or drink.
   Let's have a new coat made for him.
   For a young man who ends up so well
   We ought to do the best we can,
   And kill and flay our fatted calf.
   We all should show him sympathy.

BROTHER   But I must pull off your boots, and slave   650
   Day and night at that fellow's work—
   For me you wouldn't kill a chicken!
   The worst is always loved the most.

FATHER   Don't say that, son, for love of God!
   He's turned out decent in the end.
   He was lost and now he is found,
   And surely it's a miracle?
   Almighty God, the scriptures say,
   Has greater joy about one sinner
   Who turns, repenting, back to him,   660
   Than over the other ninety-nine.
   And so ought we to kill our calf
   For happiness that he's come home.

(*to the actors and to the audience*)

   Let us sing *Te Deum laudamus*.

Texts

Courtois d'Arras, éd. Edmond Faral, Classiques Français du Moyen Age, Paris (Librairie Ancienne Honoré Champion), 2nd ed. (1911, reprinted 1961) and also revised ed. 1922.

Staging and interpretation
Grace Frank, *The Medieval French Drama*, pp. 217–21.
Marie Ungureaunu, *La bourgeoisie naissante*, pp. 178ff.

LE MIRACLE
DE THÉOPHILE

by Rutebeuf

PERSONS OF THE PLAY

THÉOPHILE, previously priest and seneschal (officer of justice) in the Bishop's household, but stripped of his office and ecclesiastical dignities by the new Bishop.

SALATIN, a Jewish magician, conversant with the Devil

THE DEVIL, Satan

THE BISHOP

PINCEGUERRE, a clerk in the Bishop's household

PIERRE, a priest, colleague of Théophile's

THOMAS, seneschal until Théophile is reappointed

OUR LADY

The Bishop's congregation

LE MIRACLE DE THÉOPHILE

Text
Le Miracle de Théophile was composed *c.* 1261 by the Parisian trouvère known simply as 'Rutebeuf'. The author also wrote a number of equally polished poems, *diz* and *complaintes*, and left behind him a legend of poverty. Nothing is known about the circumstances of the play's performance; it may have been composed for the clercs in the university in Paris. The text has survived complete in one late thirteenth-century manuscript, written in the dialect of the Ile-de-France. Théophile's 'repentance' (384–431) and his 'prayer' (432–539) occur also in a second manuscript of Rutebeuf's poems. The play manuscript names the speakers and gives several prose 'stage-directions'. Our translation follows Grace Frank's edition (CFMA, 1949).

The play is remarkable for its richness of imagery and metrical variety. In addition to the octosyllabic couplet, Rutebeuf uses linked couplets and tercets (101–229, 540–639, 656–63), which we have reproduced as closely as was possible in English. Rutebeuf's complicated twelve-line stanza (the *douzaine*, used for the prayer) properly has only two rhymes, although we have sometimes, for the sake of fluency, introduced a third. For the monorhymed alexandrine quatrains (384–431, 640–55) we have used pentameters with two rhyme words.

Staging
The rubrics in the manuscript are chiefly narrative links and do not give much indication of the staging intended. When Théophile repents, he goes 'to the Chapel of Our Lady', but

the 'house' is not described. Nor is the dialogue more informative: we only learn that the Bishop's 'house' is next to Théophile's, when Théophile is invited to look inside his new lodgings (339–40).

'Simultaneous' staging is appropriate and was probably intended. Supposing that each of the main characters has a 'house', then five of these are necessary: Théophile's is central; to the audience's left of him are the Bishop's palace and Our Lady's Chapel; to the right, Salatin's 'house' and Hell's Mouth. This arrangement, either in a straight line or an arc, has the advantage of symmetry and readily visualizes the opposition of good and evil forces in their struggle for Théophile's soul. The 'houses' may simply be doorways distinguished by their shape and the ornament of their portals; thus Salatin's could have a gilded oriental dome. They have curtains through which the characters enter and exit. The production of Gustave Cohen's modernised text of the play in Paris in 1933 used blue and gold curtains for the Virgin's Chapel, red for the Bishop's palace, green for Théophile's 'house' and yellow for Salatin's.

Hints of the contemporary costuming of the actors are given by medieval iconography of the legend. Miss M. D. Anderson notes that the thirteenth-century glass at Lincoln cathedral may well show the influence of a play of the miracle:

Four scenes from the legend are shown, in two circular medallions. In the first we see Theophilus consulting the Jewish wizard, who introduces him to the Devil in the second. Satan sits on a green hillock, with one foot cocked high in what is generally recognized as a lordly attitude in medieval art, and his head is red, with horns and a ferocious beak and is large enough to suggest the possibility that the glazier copied a theatrical 'devil's head'. He has green and white winglets attached to his elbows and ankles, an unconventional fashion among medieval devils, but one very easily represented in stage dress. Theophilus kneels before him and hands over a white scroll while behind him stands a Jew, wearing a conical pink hat, and resting his hand upon his client's shoulder. ... The next pair of scenes show the Blessed Virgin snatching from the devil's claws a scroll inscribed with mysterious symbols, and Theophilus showing this to his Bishop when confessing his sin.[1]

The medieval legend tells that Theophilus of Cilicia prayed to a *statue* of the Virgin, fell asleep in her church and dreamed that she appeared to him, finding the covenant in fact returned when he awoke; the Virgin of the play may appropriately be shown as a statue, blue-robed and bearing a cross, who 'comes alive' at line 540 in response to Théophile's prayer.

According to Théophile himself (404), seven years pass between his pact with the Devil and his repentance. The passage of time may be suggested by the use of music after line 383, during which there might be a mime of the spiritual conflict which leads Théophile eventually to the Virgin's Chapel.

[1] M.D. Anderson, *Drama and Imagery in English Medieval Churches* (Cambridge University Press, 1963), p.187.

LE MIRACLE DE THÉOPHILE

(Théophile enters from his 'house'.)

THÉOPHILE   O God, almighty, glorious Lord!
  I have always kept your word
  In mind; I've given away my goods
  And offered beggars all I could:
  What's left is not worth a sack.
  Like chess, the Bishop told me, 'Check!'
  He'd cornered me—I was fool's mate.
  He's left me poor and desolate,
  And I'm compelled to starve to death
  Unless I pawn my robe for bread.   10
  But what will all my household do?
  Will God feed them? I don't know.
  God? Yes, him? What does he care?
  They will have to go elsewhere,
  For in this place God's ears are deaf;
  He thinks my prayers are so much chaff.
  I shall turn him a mocking face:
  Curse all those who enjoy his grace!
  There's nothing one would not undertake
  For the sake of wealth. I scorn God's threats.   20
  Shall I go drown myself, or hang?
  I can't reproach God for this thing,
  Because one cannot ever reach
  Him there. If man could only catch
  A hold of him to strike him back—
  That would be a good day's work.
  But he has placed himself so high
  To avoid his many enemies
  That one can't pull or hurl him down.
  If I could only threaten him,

Struggle with him, fight and slash,   30
I'd make him tremble in his flesh!
He lives in happiness up there
While I, poor wretch, am caught in the snare
Of poverty and suffering.
My fiddle's broken and unstrung—
They'll say I'm senile and they'll mock;
And make me into a laughing stock.
I shall not dare see anyone
Nor sit in company again   40
Without someone pointing a finger
At me. I don't know any longer
What to do: God has cheated me.

*Here Théophile comes to Salatin, who was able to speak with
the devil whenever he liked.*

(Salatin enters from his 'house'.)

SALATIN   What's the matter, Théophile?
For God's sake, what misfortune
Has made you so unhappy, man?
You always used to be so happy.

THÉOPHILE   They used to call me 'Monsignor'
And 'Father of the Town'—as you know well.
Now they've not left me anything!   50
I'm more distressed, Salatin,
Because I've never ceased to pray
Both in Latin and in French
To the God who wants to punish me
And who has had me stripped so bare
I've nothing left to call my own.
There's nothing now so desperate,
No practice so irregular,
I would not gladly undertake
To get my reputation back.   60
The loss has shamed and wounded me.

SALATIN   My dear sir, you're talking commonsense.
    If a man has learned what wealth can be,
    It is a sad and painful thing
    When he declines and must depend
    On others for his food and drink—
    And has to hear so much abuse!

THÉOPHILE   That's what distresses me so much,
    Salatin, my dear, good friend—
    To have to bear servility: 70
    It's almost enough to break my heart.

SALATIN   I understand how much it hurts
    And how embarrassing it is.
    For a man as eminent as you
    It surely is a cruel blow.

THÉOPHILE   To come to the point, Salatin:
    If you know any means at all
    By which I might regain my post,
    My influence and self-respect,
    There's nothing that I would not do.   80

SALATIN   Would you be willing to renounce
    The God to whom you've always prayed,
    His holy things and all his saints?
    And, with clasped hands, would you become
    The loyal servant of a lord
    Who could restore your dignities,
    So that you would have greater honours
    (If you always worshipped him)
    Than otherwise you'd ever have?
    Trust me; leave your present master.   90
    Well? Tell me what you wish to do?

THÉOPHILE   I should like that very much—
    I'll do anything you ask.

SALATIN Then you can go home quite secure;
 Whatever they may do to you,
 I shall get back your post again.
 Return tomorrow in the morning.

THÉOPHILE I will indeed, friend Salatin.
 May the god you worship and believe
 Bless you, if you achieve this plan.   100

Now Théophile departs from Salatin and thinks that re-
nouncing God is too dreadful a thing, and he says:

THÉOPHILE Alas! What will become of me?
 My reason must have left my body
 If this is my extremity.
   Oh, what, alas,
 Shall I do? If I renounce Saint Nicholas,
 The Apostle John and Saint Thomas,
   Our Blessed Lady,
 What will my wretched soul do then?
 It shall be burned up in the flame
   Of blackest hell!   110
 There for ever it must remain,
 Lingering in hideous pain—
   No children's tale.
 And in that everlasting blaze,
 No people who know love or grace,
 But only evil—they are devils
   Their nature's foul!
 The darkness there is so intense
 One never sees the radiance
 Of the sun—a pit of excrements!   120
   I shall go there?
 The die is irrevocably cast
 If I should ever choose to waste
 My soul, and God would surely blast
   Me from his gate.
 And he would have good cause to hate.

N

No man was ever tormented so
  As I am now.
He promises that he can bring
My wealth and power back again,   130
And no one shall know anything—
  It shall be done!
God has wronged me—I'll do him wrong;
I will not serve him any more—
  I cause him pain.
I shall be rich as I am poor;
If he hates me, I shall hate him.
  Now let him choose
Where he likes to wage his wars,
Since heaven and earth are in his palm.   140
  I break my bond—
If Salatin can now perform
  What he's promised me.

(*Salatin goes to Hell's Mouth.*)

Here Salatin shall speak with the Devil and say:

SALATIN   A Christian has come to me,
  I've waited on him busily,
For you are not my enemy,
  Satan, do you hear?
If you'll receive him, he comes at dawn;
I've promised him four times and sworn.
  Wait for him then,   150
For he has been a powerful man,
A priceless gift for us to own;
So lavish your riches upon him.
  Give me your ear!
I think that I shall make you come
  Running quick.
You shall come now, while it is dark
For your delay destroys my work.
  I've longed for this!

Here Salatin shall conjure up the devil.

Bagahi laca bachahé   160
Lamac cahi achabahé
   Karrelyos
Lamac lamec bachalyos
Cabahagi sabalyos
   Baryolas
Lagozatha cabyolas
Samahac et famyolas
   Harrahya.

Now the devil shall come, having been conjured, and he shall say:

THE DEVIL   You spoke the proper formula well—
   Your teacher forgot no part of the spell.   170
     You pester me!

SALATIN   There's no reason you should fail
   To help me, or oppose my will,
     When I command.
   I can make your hide run with sweat!
   You want to hear the latest sport?
     We've got a clerk,
   A splendid prize, as we've long known—
   We've often been distressed by him
     In our affairs.   180
   What do you think should be done
   With this clerk so willing to be won?

THE DEVIL   What is he called?

SALATIN   Théophile's his proper name;
   He's been a person of some fame
     Throughout this land.

THE DEVIL   Ha! Every day I fought with him
   And not one battle could I win.

Since he's decided to give in,
    Let him come down,   190
Without a friend, without a horse;
That will not trouble him, of course,
    Since it is close.
Satan will freely give him grace,
So will the devils in this place.
    He must not pray
To Jesus, Holy Mary's Son;
No kindness could we show him then.
    I go my way.
Now you must pay me more respect.   200
Don't bother me for several weeks!
No Hebrew prayers and none in Latin!
    Go Salatin!

(*Salatin returns to his 'house'.*)

Now Théophile shall return to Salatin.

THÉOPHILE   Am I too early in the morning?
    What have you done?

SALATIN   I've dealt so quickly with your case
    That the Bishop, cause of your disgrace,
        Will now restore
    Your office, with a large reward.
    You'll be Monsignor and a greater lord   210
        Than ever before.
    Instead of being poor, despised,
    You shall be happy, rich and praised.
        Don't be afraid.
    You must go down without delay;
    It will not help for you to pray
        Or ask God's aid,
    If you want to help your interests.
    In the love of your God you'd too much trust
        And he has failed.   220

You came out of it unhappily:
He would have hurt you cruelly
   Had I not helped.
The devils wait and you must pass
   This way at once.
Stifle all thoughts of repentance.

THÉOPHILE   I'll go. God cannot harm me now
   Nor help my need.
I can no longer pray or plead.

Here Théophile shall go to the devil in great fear, and the devil shall say to him:

THE DEVIL   Come this way! Get moving there!   230
   Don't imitate some peasant oaf
   Creeping to the offertory!
   What is it your master has commanded
   And forces you to do? He's a tyrant!

THÉOPHILE   He is, my lord. He was the chancellor
   And thinks to drive me out to seek
   For food. And so, I've come to pray
   That you will help my desperate need.

THE DEVIL   You ask me?

THÉOPHILE   Yes.

THE DEVIL   Then clasp your hands
   Together, and do me proper homage,   240
   And I shall help you all I can.

(Théophile kneels in feudal submission. The devil takes his offered hands between his own, accepting Théophile into his service.)

THÉOPHILE   Witness the homage I make to you.

If I could just get back my loss,
Great Master, for the rest of my life.

THE DEVIL   In return, I make this pact with you:
I'll set you up in such great power—
They'll not have seen a greater lord
Than you. And now, since we're agreed,
You ought to know that for your part
I must have deeds of covenant,   250
Sealed and unequivocal.
Many folk have cheated me
Because I did not take their deeds—
That's why I like things cut and dried.

(*Théophile makes his deed, writing in his own blood and sealing the document with his ring.*)

THÉOPHILE   Here they are—signed sealed and delivered.

Théophile hands his deed to the devil, and the devil orders him to behave like this:

THE DEVIL   Théophile, my dearest friend,
Now that you've made yourself my man,
I'll tell you what you have to do:
You mustn't have pity on the poor.
If a poor, decrepit man should beg,   260
Turn a deaf ear and go your way.
If anyone bows reverently,
Treat him with pride and cruelty.
If a beggar comes knocking at your door,
Make sure he goes away with nothing.
Gentleness, humility,
Pity, love and charity,
Keeping fasts and penitence,
Strike a pain into my guts.
Giving alms and prayers to God—   270
These things grieve and anger me.

Loving God and living chastely
Make me feel a snake or viper
Tears at my heart inside my chest.
When anyone goes to the hospital
To visit a sick person there,
My heart feels dead and beats so feebly
I scarcely know that I am alive.
Doing good is pain to me.
Go back; you shall be seneschal.   280
Leave doing good; do wickedness.
Be sure you never give fair judgement,
For that would be great foolishness
And contrary to my command.

THÉOPHILE   I'll carry out what I must do.
  It's only right to try and please,
  Since that's the way to regain favour.

(*The Devil goes into Hell's Mouth.*)

Now the Bishop sends someone to look for Théophile.

THE BISHOP   Pinceguerre, go quickly now
  And search out Théophile for me.
  I shall restore him to his post.   290
  I did a very foolish thing
  In taking it away from him.
  He's the finest man I've ever seen,
  I must admit that honestly.

PINCEGUERRE   What you say is true, my lord.

Then Pinceguerre shall speak to Théophile and Théophile shall reply:

PINCEGUERRE   Who is there?

THÉOPHILE   Who are you?

PINCEGUERRE   I am a clerk.

THÉOPHILE   And *I* am a priest.

PINCEGUERRE   Théophile, my dearest friend,
   Do not be so harsh with me.
   My lord the Bishop asks for you: 300
   You're going to have your living back
   And all the powers that go with it.
   So cheer up, now! Smile and be happy
   For that is only right and proper.

THÉOPHILE   May the devils take care of him!
   I should have had the bishopric,
   But I put him there—that was a sin.
   He was invested, then we fought
   And he thought to drive me out for food.
   Hang and blast him for his spite,   310
   His bickering that never ends!
   I'll go and hear what he will say.

PINCEGUERRE   When he sees you he will laugh
   And say it was to test your faith
   He did it. Now he wants to recompense,
   And you'll be friends just as you were.

THÉOPHILE   The canons have told quite enough
   Gossip and lies about me now.
   I'll send them all to a pack of devils!

The Bishop rises to meet Théophile and reinvests him in his
clothes of office, saying:

THE BISHOP   You have done well in coming back.   320

THÉOPHILE   I have. I could look after myself.
   I've not fallen by the wayside.

THE BISHOP   Good father, whatever I have done
    To injure you, I make amends
    And in good faith I give you back
    Your offices. Accept them, please.
    You are a wise and worthy man;
    Whatever I own shall be yours as well.

THÉOPHILE   What a splendid pater noster—
    You never said it quite so smoothly!   330
    Now I suppose the wretched peasants
    Will come in hundreds paying homage,
    But I shall make them sweat for it.
    No man's important unless he is feared.
    Do they think I haven't eyes in my head?
    I'll treat them with anger and cruelty.

THE BISHOP   Théophile, what do you mean?
    My friend, think about doing good.
    Have a look inside your residence—
    Here are your lodgings, next to mine.   340
    Our belongings and our wealth
    From this day onwards shall be shared.
    I think we ought to be firm friends;
    All that is mine shall be yours too.

THÉOPHILE   Really, my lord? That pleases me.

(*Exit Bishop.*)

*Now Théophile goes to pick a quarrel with his colleagues,
first to one whose name is Pierre.*

THÉOPHILE   Pierre, do you want to hear the news?

(*Enter Pierre from the Bishop's 'house'.*)

    Fortune's wheel has turned for you—
    You've thrown the worst two dice at last!
    So now hold on to what you have,

Because you've failed to keep my job!   350
The Bishop's reappointed me;
I don't owe you any thanks.

PIERRE   Théophile, are you threatening me?
Only yesterday I begged
The reverend Bishop to give back
Your office—that was only fair.

THÉOPHILE   That was a nasty piece of work—
Condemning and defrocking me.
In spite of you, I'm reinvested.
You had forgotten my suffering.   360

PIERRE   But my dear sir, it was my wish
That you should be appointed bishop
After our old bishop died.
You didn't want to be—you were
So much in awe of God in heaven.

(*Exit Pierre, Thomas enters from the Bishop's 'house'.*)

Then Théophile picks a quarrel with another.

THÉOPHILE   Thomas! Thomas, bad luck for you
That I'm made seneschal again:
You'll have to get in harness now,
Leave wrangling and chicanery.
You won't have a harsher colleague than I.   370

THOMAS   Théophile, I swear to you,
It looks to me as if you're drunk.

THÉOPHILE   Well, I shall be rid of you
Tomorrow. A curse upon your face!

THOMAS   Good Lord! You're not in your proper mind—
I love you and respect you so!

THÉOPHILE   Thomas, I'm not a prisoner,
  I can make or mar you now.

THOMAS   It seems you're looking for a quarrel,
  Théophile; leave me in peace.   380

(*Exit Thomas.*)

THÉOPHILE   Thomas, what shall I do to you?
  You shall groan with remorse in time;
  That is my purpose and my plan.

(*Seven years pass.*) *Now Théophile repents and shall come to a chapel of Our Lady and say:*

THÉOPHILE   Pathetic wretch! What will become of me?
  How can the earth support my sinful weight,
  When I've renounced my God and venerate
  A fiend as lord, who causes sin and misery?

  God I denied—the secret can't be kept.
  I've lost the balm of life; I'm caught
  Upon the Judas tree. The devil bought   390
  My title deeds: my soul must pay the debt.

  What will you do with this unhappy fool,
  O God, whose spirit will go to the boiling heat
  Of hell, there to be trampled by devils' feet?
  Break open, earth, and swallow up my soul!

  Lord God, what will this desperate outcast do?
  Despised by God, exposed to ridicule
  By men, betrayed and trapped by fiends in hell—
  Shall I be hounded by all creation too?

  I was puffed up with ignorance and pride,   400
  When I rejected God for that small gain.
  The worldly wealth I wanted to obtain
  Has drowned me here; I can't escape the tide.

Satan, I walked your way for seven years;
Your evil music tempted me to spill
My store of life; the price I pay is cruel—
My flesh sliced through by fiendish slaughterers!

A man's soul must be loved, but mine was not.
Our Lady might save it—I dare not ask. Bad seeds
Were sown at seeding time; and choked with weeds   410
My soul sprang up, to droop in hell and rot.

A fiendish master—oh, what slavery!
Tormented in my soul and in my body!
If I dared to trust the sweet grace of Our Lady,
My soul might now be saved from purgatory.

Filthy I am; I must go to filth beneath.
In filthiness I've lived; God must know—
He lives for ever. My dying will be slow,
Poisoned by the bite of devils' teeth.

No refuge on the earth nor in the skies—   420
What place could shelter me? I loathe the thought
Of offering myself in hell. I fought
My Lord and cannot claim his paradise.

I dare not call God's saints, nor beg again
For grace. I served the fiend; hands clasped, I kneeled.
The devil has the bond my ring has sealed.
I curse the riches that will cause me pain!

I dare not call on saints, nor say God's name,
Nor hers, whom all should love, our sweet,
Our Lady. But since no harshness or deceit—   430
Is in her, in begging grace I cannot be to blame.

This is the prayer that Théophile shall say before Our Lady:

Holy, lovely Queen,
Glorious heavenly virgin,
Full of grace indeed,
In whom all virtues shine,
Delivering from sin
Those who call in need;
Those whose hearts shall turn
To your everlasting realm,
They shall have joy again.   440
O fountain, ever springing,
Full of joy and healing,
Call me to your Son.

Your sweet and loving service—
My longing and my solace—
I left. I was seduced
By one who stirs up evil
And crushes good: the devil
Enchanted me with vice.
Ah, break the evil spell!   450
For in your holy will
Are liberty and grace;
Or else in pain and torment
My body shall be sent
Before the harshest justice.

Blessed Lady Mary,
Change my heart entirely,
Make me serve and love;
Or else my grief shall never
Slack nor mend; rather   460
My soul shall be your slave.
Harsh judgment it deserves
When Death comes and unnerves
Me then, unless you clasp
My aspiring soul to you.
Torment is the body's due
That the soul may not be lost!

Queen of charity,
In your humility
You once bore our salvation.   470
You have rescued us
From pain and filthiness—
The pit of hell's damnation.
I bless and praise you, Lady,
Your healing power has saved me;
I know that this is true.
Guard me, lest the devil
With Tantalus in Hell
Snatch soul and body too.

The open gates entice   480
Me to hell, to sacrifice
Myself for my offence.
It will be dreadful loss
And open foolishness
To stay for ever there.
Lady, I bow my knee,
Turn your sweet face to me!
Despite my guiltiness,
For the sake of your wise son,
Let not the wages of sin   490
Be paid in wretchedness.

Glass in a window,
When sunlight passes through,
Does not shatter or divide:
So you stayed a perfect virgin,
Though God came from heaven
To make you mother and bride.
Jewel, brightly shining,
Woman, tender, loving,
Hear my prayer through.   500
From fires that always burn
Keep my vile flesh and turn
My spirit back to you.

Queen of grace and charm,
Brighten this hellish gloom,
Lighten the eyes of my soul!
Grant me heavenly favour
So that I may labour
To please you and do your will.
I have walked too long   510
The darkened paths of wrong;
The devil's filthy spawn
Plan to seize me still;
May it never be your will
To let them do me harm!

In filthiness and sin,
A wretched life of gloom
I have followed for too long.
O Queen, spotless, pure,
Take me in your care,   520
Heal me, make me strong.
Pour your heavenly power
In an everlasting shower
Of light into my heart;
Brightness pure and lovely
Dazzle my eyes, lest I
Be ever led apart.

The fiend who robbed and stole
Caught me for his fool;
I shall be seized and torn!
He has racked me bitterly.   530
Pray I may be utterly
Released—implore your Son!
Lady, you know my sins;
Defend me from their hands,
Forestall their hellish toll!
You, who rule the air,
Protect me, hide me where
No fiend may see my soul!

Here Our Lady shall speak to Théophile and say:

OUR LADY   Who are you, walking in this place?   540

THÉOPHILE   Have mercy, Mother, full of grace!
   It is the wretched
Théophile, who is shunned
By men, by devils caught and bound.
   I come to pray
To you, Lady, and to ask your power
That I may never see the hour
   Of torment come
With him who has thrust me in such pain.
Once you embraced me as your son,   550
   O lovely Queen!

OUR LADY   I will not hear your hypocrite's babble.
   Go! Go! Get out of my chapel!

THÉOPHILE   I dare not go.
   Rose, eglantine, lily flower,
Whom God's own Son has made his bower,
   What shall I do?
I feel myself cruelly pledged
To serve a fiend that is enraged
   I do not know.   560
I shall never cease to cry
To you, Virgin, meek and holy,
   Highly favoured.
I know my soul will be devoured
Completely, if it is immured
   With pagan gods.

OUR LADY   Théophile, I once knew you,
   When you served me—long ago.
     Now, in your need,
Trust me to reclaim the deed   570
That ignorance made you concede.
   I'll fetch it back.

Now Our Lady shall go for Théophile's covenant.

OUR LADY   Satan, where are you concealed?

(*The Devil enters from Hell's Mouth.*)

OUR LADY   If you've come to the battlefield
   Hoping to make my servant yield,
     That thought's a curse!
   Give me the deed you took from the clerk;
   You have gone too far in your hellish work.

THE DEVIL   I—give it back?
   I'd rather they would hang me first   580
   Once I gave him back his post,
   And in return he sacrificed
     Quite readily
   All his substance, soul and body.

OUR LADY   Then I shall trample on your belly.

(*Our Lady raises her cross, the Devil falls and she treads him
underfoot. She takes the covenant. The Devil crawls back into
Hell's Mouth.*)

Now Our Lady shall carry the covenant back to Théophile.

   My friend, I bring the charter back.
   Your soul's ship was almost wrecked
   Without hope of better luck.
     Now hear my words:
   Go to the Bishop, do not wait;   590
   Give him the charter that you made,
     To read aloud
   Inside the church, before a crowd,
   So that good men are not seduced
     By such deceit—
   The man who sells his soul for greed
   Shall be downtrodden and abused.

   O

THÉOPHILE   I will! Body and soul
     Should have withered to the root:
     The seeds of evil bear no fruit—   600
       I see that now.

(*Enter the Bishop, his court and congregation.*)

Now Théophile shall go to the Bishop and give him his covenant and say:

THÉOPHILE   My lord, for God's mercy, listen:
     Despite my sins, I kneel here chastened.
       Soon you shall know
     By what I have been so oppressed;
     I was poor and naked, cold, diseased
       Through poverty.
     The devil, who assaults good men,
     Made my soul commit a sin
       For which I should die;   610
     But Our Lady, who directs her own,
     Turned me from the path of wrong,
       Where I had strayed
     And lost my way. Without her aid
     I would by now have been conveyed
       By the devil to hell.
     The devil made me turn from God,
     The father of hope; all works of good
       He made me leave.
     What he dictated formed my deed;   620
     Whatever he required, I sealed.
       The dreadful pain
     Almost split my heart and brain.
     Then the Virgin brought my deed again—
       God's own Mother,
     Whose goodness shines bright and clear.
     I beg you as my reverend father
       That this be read
     So others may not be deceived,

If they have not yet perceived   630
  The devil's treachery.

Now the Bishop shall read the charter and say:

THE BISHOP   For Jesus' sake, Mary's Son,
  Good people, listen; you shall learn
    Of Théophile,
  Whom the devil cheated by his guile.
  This miracle is as true a tale
    As the gospel.
  It ought to be told to you in full.
  Now listen carefully to what I shall tell:

  'To all who shall see this charter publicly   640
  Satan makes known that Fortune turned her wheel;
  The Bishop was abhorred by Théophile
  Because he'd left him no authority.

  When thus insulted, Théophile despaired;
  He came to Salatin, in a passionate rage,
  And said that he would willingly do homage
  To Satan, if his wealth and honour were repaired.

  Throughout his saintly life I battled hard,
  But I was never victor of the field.
  When he came to beg, I longed to make him yield;   650
  He worshipped me and his power was restored.

  This deed was sealed with the ring upon his hand.
  There was no ink—he wrote it in his blood
  And signed before I promised that I would
  Restore him to his dignities and land.'

  And that is what this good man did.
  The blessed maid has freed his soul
    From chains of sin.

Our Lady Mary, holy Virgin,
Snatched the devil's reckoning.   660
To celebrate this miracle
    Arise and sing
Te Deum laudamus!

Thus ends the miracle of Théophile.

Texts

Rutebeuf, *Le Miracle de Théophile*, éd. Grace Frank, Classiques Français du Moyen Age, Paris (Librairie Ancienne Honoré Champion), 2e. éd. 1949.

— *Oeuvres complètes de Rutebeuf*, éd. Edmond Faral & Julia Bastin, 2 vols., Société des Anciens Textes Français, Paris, 1959.

— *Le Miracle de Théophile*, transposition de G. Cohen, Paris (Delagrave), 6e éd., 1935.

Staging and interpretation
See the modernized French edition of Gustave Cohen.

LE GARÇON ET L'AVEUGLE

PERSONS OF THE PLAY

THE BLIND MAN   THE BOY

LE GARÇON ET L'AVEUGLE

Text

This play of a Blind Man and his Boy is the oldest surviving farce in French. Its rather savagely comic theme is that of the famous sixteenth-century Spanish *Lazarillo de Tormes* and many other European fabliaux. The play was composed in the vicinity of Tournai (cf. line 30) in the second half of the thirteenth century. The song that the two rogues sing (57–64, 83–90) refers to the King of Sicily and his levy of troops against the Saracen enemy. This would have been topical at any time after 1265, but perhaps the song is deliberately old fashioned.

The text is found in a single thirteenth-century manuscript. Only about half the speeches are headed by an indication of the speaker's identity, and most of these headings were added by a scribe in the fifteenth century. Apart from the rubric 'They sing together' at lines 57 and 83, there are no stage directions. We have translated Mario Roques's edition (CFMA, 1921), following his line-numbering, and have added a few stage directions to his.

Staging

The play may have been performed under almost any auspices—in a market place, after a banquet or in a tavern. It needs no special stage conditions. Since the play depends chiefly on the cruel deceptions practised by the Boy on the Blind Man, its effect is heightened if there are no stage properties: thus the real-life objects the Boy describes to his master will have no visual reality for the audience. The audience serve also as bystanders in the action of the play.

The Blind Man and the Boy appeal directly to them for alms, while the Boy asks them to approve his trickery. Since the play presumably belonged originally in the repertoire of travelling entertainers, the begging from the audience, which takes up a good proportion of the action, probably was 'a game in earnest'.

LE GARÇON ET L'AVEUGLE

BLIND MAN   Give us something, gentlemen;
   And God, the Son of Mary
Bring you all safe home to heaven,
   Safe to his company.
   I can't see you at all;
May Jesus see you on my behalf
And bring all those to Paradise
   Who help me in my need!
Ah, Mother of God, Holy Mary,
Queen of Heaven, what's the time?   10
I don't hear anyone; I'm badly off
Not having even a boy to help me,
Who could take me to my home—
For even if he couldn't sing
At least he'd know how to ask for food,
And lead me to the bigger houses.

BOY   Oh, life's a bore! (*sees the Blind Man*)
                  —Or it was till now.
   Now I've got just what I need.

(*to the Blind Man*)

   Excuse me, sir, you've missed your way.
   There's a basement here—You may fall down.   20

BLIND MAN   Ah, Mother of God, help me, please!
   But who's this guiding me so well?

BOY   Noble sir—as I hope for heaven!—
   It's just another down-and-out.

BLIND MAN   By God, I think he's a splendid fellow.
Come here! I want to talk to you.

BOY   Here I am!

BLIND MAN   Do you want a job?

BOY   Sir, what would I have to do?

BLIND MAN   Guide me, and keep me out of danger
Down through the city of Tournai.   30
You will beg, and I shall sing;
And we'll get lots of money and food.

BOY   Well! By the belly of St. Gilain,
You must think me a perfect fool!
I tell you frankly, I must have
At least a fiver every day,
As long as I look after you.
On these terms I'll do everything.

BLIND MAN   Come now, my friend! Don't bicker so!
What is your name?

BOY   Little John.   40

BLIND MAN   Then, Little John, a pox on you
If you don't have your fee, and welcome!
If you show promise in my trade,
In time you'll be a millionaire!

BOY   Let's go! (aside) I'm not at all worried
At suddenly becoming rich.
I pray to God he'll send a plague
On those who give this poor blind man
Even a single contribution;
They'll just be throwing it away!   50

BLIND MAN   Now, dear Johnny, what are you saying?
   You're going to make me lose my temper.

BOY   Sir! Sir! Don't get upset!
   It's only to deceive those louts.
   Sing up! And I will help you, honest.
   Then everyone will give me food.

Now they sing together.

   Whoever serves you, Mother of God,
      Will always live in joy;
   And he shall have a rich reward,
      For in your company,   60
      Sweet lady, he will be.
   I pray to you for all my patrons
   And soldiers with the king's own son
      Serving faithfully.

BOY *(to passers-by)*
   Hey, for God's sake, don't pass us by
   Without giving us something to eat!

(to Blind Man)

   Sir, just wait a moment here:
   I'm going to beg at this big house.

(to passers-by)

   Gentlemen, by God in heaven,
   Be generous to a poor blind man.   70

(to Blind Man)

   I see we're doing no good here,
   Let's get along! God blast them all!

BLIND MAN   They've nothing to *give*—but, tell me, Johnny,
   Isn't anyone answering?

BOY   Not a soul! But I could see
   That they were jeering nastily.

BLIND MAN   John, you should have persevered—
   Then you'd have got something at least.

BOY   Sir, Christ himself couldn't—there!
   I am an expert in this trade.   80
   Sing, so we'll get something to eat,
   For I shall manage to talk them round.

Now they sing both together.

   The King of Sicily I'll sing—
     May God be on his side!—
   Who every day is put on trial
     Against the heretics!
   And now from coast to coast
     His summons has gone out;
     All who are destitute
   Will go, to join his host.   90

BOY   Well, by Saint Sophia's orifice!
   If we're able to live on air
   This evening we shall be quite drunk.
   Just look how they are rolling up!
   God's arse, I've not seen a single gate,
   Or door, opening to us tonight,
   We could starve to death right here
   Before they brought us anything.
   By the faith I owe St. Vast, I'll never
   Ask to be a blind man's dog.   100

BLIND MAN   Not one single bit of luck!
   John, by the promise I owe your guts,
   'A single stroke won't fell the oak.'
   If I never begged for bread again,
   I could still enjoy myself;
   I've got a tidy pile laid up.

BOY   You seem a miserable chap to me,
   Because if *I* had lots of money,
   I'd give us both an easy life.
   And, for as long as it lasted out,   110
   You wouldn't have to beg for bread;
   It would be yours without any question.

BLIND MAN   Johnny, now for saying that,
   You'll have a share in all I've got
   From this time on, I give you my word.
   And if today we've taken nothing,
   We're pretty well provided for
   With what we need to eat and drink.

BOY   Sir, God help me! that's a decent thing.
   Good God, we'll have a celebration!   120
   I tell you, I know a tale or two
   To sing, and that'll keep you happy.
   And if you feel the urge, I'll have
   Some pretty young wench brought in at once.
   Not one of those with a wrinkled paunch
   But nice and pale, with a youthful face.
   No-one could draw a girl like her
   With paint-brush or an artist's pencil.
   Don Juan himself has no apprentice
   Prettier or with a nicer figure.   130
   And she'll have such a fine little what's-it,
   We'll thrust inside it at full tilt.

BLIND MAN   Ugh, you're setting my teeth on edge,
   Johnny, with your disgusting talk.
   I don't want you to talk to *me*
   Of having women. I've got a beauty!
   And when I turn her on her back,
   Then you shall come and stuff her for me;
   And the bottoms of her feet will be
   So level you could dice upon 'em.   140

BOY   Sir, your talk is quite obscene;
    Don't speak so filthily again!

BLIND MAN   No one can hear me apart from you,
    Johnny, old friend, so far as I know.

BOY   Wait here for a moment, sir;
    I must just go and relieve myself.

(*disguising his voice*)

    You dirty tramp, God curse your luck
    For speaking such obscenities.
    You'll have to pay for it, you know

(*strikes the Blind Man*)

    Just take that!   150

BLIND MAN   Johnny, tell me, am I wounded?

BOY   Wounded? How could you be wounded?

BLIND MAN   Just this moment, someone or other
    Gave me such a nasty packet.

BOY   God's arse! I was just standing by.
    Tell me—why didn't you shout out?

BLIND MAN   Ah, Johnny, friend, my very good friend,
    If I'd uttered a word of protest,
    He would have given me such a thump.
    I should have had the scars for life.   160

BOY   Sir, you've no need to get upset:
    One or two bruises are quickly healed.

BLIND MAN   True, Johnny! But every bone
    Inside my head aches horribly.

BOY   O master, sir, some people die
From blows like these. But you'll recover—
Tonight, you put a dressing on,
Made from the dung of a fat young foal;
Tomorrow you'll be fit again.
I'm telling you the gospel truth.   170
Sometime ago I made a pile
Simply from a single cure—
On a child who was about to die:
I made him drink a heavy dose
First, garlic cloves—a filthier mess
One couldn't have—I left the lot.

BLIND MAN   Heavens, Johnny, God's been kind;
He's given you the perfect home.
If you behave, you've found yourself
A patron who will keep your chin up.   180

BOY   Sir, you'll find you've got in me
A first-class servant, steady and smart.

(*aside*)

You'll see far whiter sheets than me
Hung out to die upon a line!

BLIND MAN   I'll love you for ever, Johnny my boy—
And now I'd like to go back home.
When you come to a flight of steps
Two houses on, you'll find my own.

BOY   Then, Hugh must live next door to you?—
Hugh Hontevuignies, to give him his   190
Full surname. Near Ramegnies
Is the village I am speaking of.

BLIND MAN   Johnny, I see you've been well schooled;
You'll get us to my house all right.

BOY   Here we are, sir! Just wait a moment,
      I'll open the door. Where is the key?

BLIND MAN   Do you see the periwinkle, John,
      Over the lintel? That's where it is.

BOY   You're home, sir. Now, if you don't mind,
      Deal straightly with me right away,   200
      And hand me over some of the cash,
      So I can go and buy the food.

BLIND MAN   John, my boy, in my big purse
      You'll find a lot of ready cash.
      Take out exactly what you want!
      If you haven't enough, then take some more.
      And now I wish my little girl
      Were here—I've got a sort of yearning.

BOY   My dear master, when I come in
      I'll bring her back.

BLIND MAN   Do you know where she works? 210

BOY   Yes, down in Comb Street. She's a wench
      Who works on young skins, fleecing them
      I've seen her working, down at the mills
      Rubbing off short hairs and fluff.
      Come on, let me go at once—
      The decent wine will soon be gone.
      And you take off your outdoor coat—
      It's absolutely torn to shreds;
      And look, sir, don't you see the buckle
      Has come unfastened from your belt?   220

BLIND MAN   Take them, buckle, belt and cash,
      And coat—and get them all replaced.
      I know that you won't bungle things.
      But take care how you spend your money.

For wine, for bread, for flour, and see
The meat you buy is really fresh.
These are my orders; and, remember,
Bring my mistress as you come.

BOY   I'll do it with the greatest pleausre.
I'm off now. Say a prayer for me!   230

BLIND MAN   Get off! You're a real friend, my boy.

BOY   Gentlemen, haven't I nicely managed
That blind old man, who hasn't got
A penny left, nor a coat to his name?
I've got the lot—no 'ifs' or 'buts'.
Good Lord! He really thought I was
So poor I hadn't got a bean.
But I shall drink away his pile
And pass it round amongst my friends
Until there isn't any left.   240
But (as I'm an honest man!) I wouldn't
Run off with all he has, no never,
Without informing him about it.
Damn me, if I won't let him know!

(*to the Blind Man*)

Sir, you must look for another servant.
Now, I don't want to play you false—
I'm going off to enjoy myself,
With what you gave me—quite right, too—
Haven't I been an excellent guide?
I needn't thank you for my *earnings*,   250
I'm sure of that. Nor for the money,
Nor for the coat. Well, now I'm off!

BLIND MAN   O God, I'm absolutely finished!
Why can't I die now? Death's too slow
In fetching me. But before that time,
I swear I'll wait for the rogue, tomorrow,

P

And then—I'll give him such a hiding
I swear it by my mistress, Margaret.

BOY   Pfui to you! I'm not for catching.
    I just don't care a crap for you—   260
    You nasty, miserly old man.
    If it weren't for your faithful friends,
    Like me, you'd be a millionaire!
    But for their sakes—you'll go without!
    If you don't like it—come and catch me!

Text
Le Garçon et l'Aveugle, éd. Mario Roques, Classiques Fran-
    çais du Moyen Age, Paris, 2e éd. 1921.

Staging and interpretation
Gustave Cohen, 'La scène de l'aveugle et de son valet dans
    le théâtre français du moyen âge', *Romania*, XLI (1912)
    pp. 346–72.

LE JEU DE LA FEUILLÉE

by Adam de la Halle

PERSONS OF THE PLAY

ADAM, the author
HENRI, his father
RIKIER, Rikier Auri, 'Rikeche', a rich merchant
HANE THE MERCHANT
GILLOS, Little Gillos
A DOCTOR
RAINELET
DAME DOUCE
A MONK, bearer of the relics of St. Acaire, patron of lunatics
WALET
THE IDIOT
THE IDIOT'S FATHER
CROKESOS, Messenger to Hellekin, King of Fairies
MORGAN LE FAY ⎫
MAGLORE   ⎬ fairies
ARSILE   ⎭
TAVERNER, Raoulet the Watchman
Walaincourt, various madmen and a crowd of spectators
FORTUNE

LE JEU DE LA FEUILLÉE

Text

Topical references suggest that Adam de la Halle's *Jeus de le fuellie* was probably composed soon after 1276 (see line 434), possibly as an entertainment for a meeting of the *Confrérie* or *Carité des Ardents*—the large guild of poets, entertainers and burghers of Arras. The manuscript title of the play has been interpreted in two ways. The *fuellie* is traditionally seen as a *feuillée* or canopy of green leaves, such as was constructed over the shrine of Notre Dame exhibited in one of two public squares in Arras in summer, between Pentecost and the Assumption. The alternative explanation is that *fuellie* means *folie*. The square in which the Confrerie held their summer festival on Assumption Eve was known in Arras as *la place de la folie* ('mad square'), the place of executions and public exhibition of sacred relics. Either interpretation enriches one's appreciation of the milieu in which the play was produced; both may have been apt for the pun-loving Arrageois.

One manuscript (*c.* 1300) gives the complete text with speakers' names. Two others contain the first section of the play (to line 174), showing that Adam's tour de force on the delusions of love was well known separately from the whole entertainment.

Apart from the opening twelve lines, which form three monorhymed quatrains in alexandrines, the play is composed in octosyllabic couplets, with some *sixains* (33–182, 837–92). Because of its mainly colloquial style, we have not used rhyme in the translation. The text includes three fragments of songs, one of which occurs with its musical notation (this melody must have been well known, since it also occurs in two contemporary motets, one of them by Adam himself).

Since none of the manuscripts contains any stage-directions, some entrances and exits which are not immediately obvious have been inferred from the text. We have translated the text of Ernest Langlois's second edition (CFMA, 1951) and followed his line-numbering.

Staging

The acting place is 'open' in every sense: characters appear to 'enter' from the street and to 'exit' to real places nearby in Arras (the Fairies go to meet the old women of the town at the Meadow Cross (873), the company of men go to light candles at the shrine of the Virgin (1080). At the end of the play the Monk finds himself in the street.

Two allusions in the dialogue suggest that the final 'tavern scene' was designed to take place in the open air, against a building: there is a handy window sill on which to put the wine jug (917); and the Idiot, in a final fit of violence, claims that someone is defiling him from above (1087–8), presumably from an upper window. A tavern yard or half-open terrace adjoining an open space or square is ideal for performing the play. There should be a door at the back for the Taverner to enter from 'inside' (905) and through which he brings wine to the tables outside, overlooking the 'place'. All the earlier action is performed in this playing 'place', which should be surrounded by the audience on three sides, leaving room for a few gangways. The 'place' contains seats for the actors and also a bower with a banquet table for the fairy feast. The bower should be to one side of the 'place' or, if it is central, it should be removed after the Fairies have left. The title of the play suggests that the bower should be constructed of green leaves (*feuillée*), suitable for the traditional summer tryst of the three fairy sisters of folk-lore.

The dialogue of the play gives a little help with production details. Adam wears a student's gown (422) to set him off from his friends. The Fairies were probably not only dressed as but played by women (587), although Dame Douce, like the 'dame' of the English mummers' plays, may have been acted by a man. Crokesos and the Fairies wear little bells on their costumes (580). The nature of Crokesos's *hurepiaus* is unclear (see note, 589); it is probably some kind of fantastic head-dress. The Monk's relics of Saint Acaire should be an ornamental chest with a bust or head of the Saint on its lid. Fortune is best impersonated; she is mute and blindfold. She carries a huge spoked wheel on the rim of which are painted figures of the men in varying fortunes mentioned. The device is realistic enough to occasion the question, *Sont che gens?* ('Are those real people?') (767).

A good deal of the curious and very sophisticated effect of the play comes from the continual shifting of the roles of performers and spectators. Many of the characters themselves become spectators as Adam, the Doctor, the Monk in turn provide the focus of attention. At the entrance of the Fairies (after 613) the whole company retires to form a stage audience, and to overlook the fairy feast unnoticed. After the fairy show the characters of the stage audience disperse, several of them to meet again at the tavern porch for the last 'scene'.

The action of the play takes place in a single night: the Fairies have to fulfil their obligation to the townswomen before dawn (841ff.), the Doctor chides the company for staying in the tavern so late (1006) and the Monk is finally left alone listening to the first morning bells from St. Nicolas' church.

The play is bizarre, a fantastic hotch-potch of characters and themes. The interweaving of formal set pieces or 'turns' with satirical comment on topical issues makes it closest in form and spirit to a modern revue-fantasy. The form of the play and its manner of staging provide a naturalistic setting, against which the 'turns' (Adam's, the

Doctor's, the Monk's, the Fairy feast, Fortune's Wheel)
should be played with stylistic exaggeration. The Idiot
provides a powerful note of midsummer madness and his
oblique, often obscene comments and antics, form a sort of
grotesque chorus to the 'black comedy'.

LE JEU DE LA FEUILLÉE

(In the course of the play Adam and Rikier prepare the bower for the fairy feast, setting the table with three places.)

ADAM My friends, you wonder at my change of clothes?
  I've been attached to a wife—now back to my books,
  To make my dream of long ago come true!
  Now none of my friends can say my plans to return
  To school in Paris have only been idle boasts.
  Any man could go—however deep the spell:
  'After sickness cometh perfect health.'
  But still, I haven't wasted the time spent here.
  Because I've learned the arts of a faithful lover: 10
  'The shape of a pot appears in the broken bits.'
  So I'm off to Paris.

RIKIER   What'll you do there, you lout?
  Not one good scholar has come from Arras
  And you want to make that your career!
  What grand delusions you suffer from!

ADAM What about Rikier Amions—
  He's a good student and clever at his books?

HANE Yes, 'twopence a book, twopence a book!'—
  That's as far as his knowledge goes.
  But no one dares find fault with you,   20
  You're always so mercurial.

RIKIER Adam's always talking about it—
  Do you fellows think he'll ever succeed?

ADAM   Everyone ridicules what I say,
It seems, tossing my words to the wind.
But since this is a critical time,
And I must do something to help myself,
Get this clear: I'm not so fond
Of life in Arras and all its pleasures
That I ought to neglect my studies for them.   30
Since God has given me a wit
It's time I turned it to good account.
I've emptied my pockets here often enough.

GILLOS   And what will become of your 'local girl'.
My neighbour—Madam Marie, Adam?

ADAM   She'll stay with my father here.

GILLOS   Adam, that will never be—
As long as she is fit to travel.
Sure as I know that wife of yours,
If she heard you were in Paris today,   40
She'd be off there tomorrow in a trice.

ADAM   And do you know what I would do?
To wean her of it I would put
A pinch of mustard on my prick.

GILLOS   Master, that's no good at all—
You don't understand the point of these things.
You can't go away like this, because
When Holy Church unites two people
There's nothing that can sever them.
You must keep putting grain in the mill!   50

ADAM   You're talking metaphysical nonsense—
Cut it out and stick to the point!
Who could have resisted taking her on?
Love caught me at just that moment—
A lover is kicking against the pricks

If once he tries to resist its force.
Oh, I was taken on the boil,
Flush in the greenest month of spring
And in the passion of my youth,
When 'that thing' has a fresher taste,   60
When no man hunts what's good for him
But only that which takes his fancy.
The summer then was sunny and fine,
Soft and green, cloudless, lovely,
Ringing with the song of birds.
High in the forest, close to a spring
That bubbled down on sparkling pebbles,
There came to me a vision once
Of the girl who is now my wedded wife
And seems so pasty and so dull.   70
But then she was all white and rosy,
Laughing, slender, made for loving.
Now I see her fat and shapeless,
Haggard and quarrelsome.

RIKIER   What a wonder!
    You really are inconstant then,
    If you've so easily forgotten
    The features that once delighted you!
    I know why you have had enough.

ADAM   Why's that?

RIKIER   She gave you too good a bargain,   80
    Sold you all her dainties cheap.

ADAM   Pooh! Richy, that's not the point—
    It's Love, who so anoints his people
    That he lights up every grace and feature,
    In a girl, and makes them seem the finer;
    So that you'd think a beggar woman
    As lovely as you would a queen.
    It seemed her hair shone like fine gold,

Glistening, thick with curls, but now
It's lank and dark and falling out.
Every part seems changed to me.   90
Her forehead was so sweetly shaped—
Broad and open, with smooth, clear skin;
But now I see it wrinkled and pinched.
Her eyebrows were so gracefully arched,
Delicate lines of dark brown hair,
Like strokes of a brush, drawn so fine,
To make her glance seem lovelier;
Now they straggle and stand on end
As if they wanted to fly in the air.
Her black eyes were brilliant blue to me,   100
Wide-set, bright and eager to love,
Large beneath their slender lids,
Which were twin walls encircling them,
Opening and closing as she willed
In a gaze passionate and frank.
And, perfectly dividing them,
The bridge of her nose was fine and straight,
Exquisite in each dimension,
To give her grace and comeliness;   110
It used to quiver when she was gay.
On either side, her cream-white cheeks—
Two dimples when she used to laugh,
And lightly blushing the colour of roses—
Peeped out from underneath her scarf.
God himself could not have formed
Another face as lovely as hers,
Or so it used to seem to me.
Then, to her mouth: fine at the corners,
While her lips were full and ripe,
Soft and fragrant, red as roses;   120
Her teeth were evenly-spaced and white.
Then, from beneath her dimpled chin,
The swelling whiteness of her throat
Flowed smooth and flawless down
To her shoulders, plump and sleek.

The nape of her neck was free of hair
And soft and white, and gently curving
Against the collar of her dress.
Her shoulders weren't the least bit stooped
And her long arms reaching down from them   130
Were plump and slender in the proper places.
  But all this was nothing to compare
With the sight of her delicate white hands;
Their slender fingers stretching out,
Flat knuckled, graceful to the tips,
Nails pink as flesh, prettily shaped,
Close to the skin, shiny and clear.
  Now let me think of her body in front,
From her neck and her throat going down:
First, to her breasts, placed up high,   140
Small and firm—perfectly appointed!
Smooth hills enclosing the valley of love
That plunged to the hollow of her stomach;
Jutting navel, arching loins,
Sculptured like the ivory
Upon the handle of a lady's knife.
Flat buttocks, and full, round thighs,
Plump calves, trim ankles, then
Feet high-arched, taut-skinned and lean.
  That was how she appeared to me.   150
I think that underneath her slip
The rest of her body wasn't too bad.
And she knew well enough, I know,
That I was beside myself with love,
So she behaved disdainfully.
The more aloof and proud she grew,
The more my love intensified
With passionate longing and desire;
With these were mingled jealousy,
Frenzied madness and despair.   160
The more feverish my passion grew,
The less I recognized myself,
Until I lost all peace of mind.

My master, Love, had become a tyrant.
Good people, that's how I was seized
By Love, who caught me unawares.
No woman's features were so fine
As Love made hers appear to me.
But Desire brought me to taste her charms
Through the spiciness of her Little Valleys,   170
And I must come to my senses again
In time, before my wife gets pregnant
And this 'thing' becomes expensive—
My appetite for that has cloyed.

RIKIER   Master, if you'll leave her to me
I think I'd find her tasty enough!

ADAM   I don't doubt it in the least.
Pray God I don't have trouble with her:
I don't need any more bad luck.
I only want to recover my losses,   180
So I'm running away to Paris to study.

HENRI   My dear boy, how I've regretted
Your hanging about here so long,
Squandering your time on women!
Now do the wise thing and go back.

GILLOS   Then you had better give him money—
A fellow can't stay in Paris for nothing.

HENRI   Alas! I'm poor. What will it cost?
Twenty-nine pounds is all I have.

HANE   Christ almighty! Are you drunk?   190

HENRI   No, I've not had a drop of wine all day.
I've stored it all away in a barrel.

(*He slaps his stomach.*)

Shame on you for suggesting it!

ADAM   Watch it! Watch it! Watch it! Watch it!
   I shall become a scholar on that!

HENRI   My son, you're vigorous and strong,
   You're quite able to help yourself.
   I am an old man with consumption,
   I'm plagued by chills and chronic illness.

DOCTOR   I know quite well why you are ill,   200
   Master Henri—with all due respect—
   I see your illness as plain as can be:
   You have the disease that's known as Greed.
   If you'd like me to cure your ailment
   You should come to me in private.
   I'm a doctor with plenty of custom;
   I've clients up and down the country
   Whom I shall cure of this disease.
   Right here, in this very town,
   I've more than a couple of thousand patients   210
   For whom there is no cure or comfort.
   Halois lies at the point of death,
   Yes, and so does Robert Cosel.
   The same thing crippled Faverel.
   Their families all suffer too.

GILLOS   By Christ, it wouldn't be much loss
   If all of them were dead and cold.

DOCTOR   Two by the name of Ermenfrois—
   The one from Paris and Crispin here—
   They do nothing but creep along   220
   Towards their deaths from this disease;
   Their children too, and relatives.
   But Halois is the most grotesque—
   He's a proper suicide;
   If he dies, he's only himself to blame
   For buying dead and stinking fish.
   I'm amazed he doesn't burst.

HENRI   But Doctor, what makes me swell up so?
   Are you expert in this disease?

DOCTOR   Have you brought a chamber pot?   230

HENRI   Yes, Doctor, I've one right here.

(*The Doctor examines Henri's urine.*)

DOCTOR   Did you pass water first thing today?

HENRI   I did.

DOCTOR   Let's have a look. Now, with luck—
   Sir, you have Saint Leonard's disease.
   I don't ever want to see it again.

HENRI   Doctor, must I go to bed?

DOCTOR   No. You needn't stay in bed for that.
   I have three patients in the town
   Who are taken with the same complaint.

HENRI   Who are they?

DOCTOR   Jehans d'Autevile,   240
   Willaumes Wagons, and the third
   Is known as Adam li Anstiers.
   All of them are sick because
   They filled their barrels far too full.
   That's why your belly's so blown up.

(*Dame Douce enters carrying a chamber-pot.*)

DAME DOUCE   Please, Doctor, give me some advice;
   And here, look, take my money too.
   My stomach is all swollen too—
   So much so that I can't walk.

I have come three leagues on foot   250
To bring this sample of my water.

DOCTOR   This comes from lying on your back,
Madam, that's what the urine says.

DAME DOUCE   You're lying, you filthy-minded lout!
I'm not that kind of ladyship—
Not for promise or reward
I never made a trade of *that*!

DOCTOR   I'll have to make the thumb-test first
To find out whether you are lying.
Rainelet, we must put some ointment   260
On your thumb. Lift it a bit.
We'd better clean it first. That's done.

(*The Doctor marks a cross on the anointed thumb. He addresses Rainelet.*)

Now look carefully at this cross
And tell us what you see in it.

DAME DOUCE   I certainly want him to speak out.

RAINELET   I see some one screwing you—
I shan't hide that from anyone.

DOCTOR   Ha, ha! By Heavens, I was sure
I knew how the case was going.
The urine didn't tell a lie.   270

DAME DOUCE   Take that! God damn your ruddy head!

(*She attacks Rainelet. The Doctor and others separate them.*)

RAINELET   Hey! This is not a free-for-all!

Q

DOCTOR   Don't get upset, Rainelet, old son.
   Now, madam, tell me, between friends,
   Who is the father of this child?

DAME DOUCE   Well, Doctor, since you know so much,
   I won't conceal the rest from you:
   That old robber spawned it, I swear.
   Oh, would that I were rid of it!

RIKIER   What does the woman say? Is she drunk?   280
   Is she blaming the brat on me?

DAME DOUCE   Yes, you.

RIKIER   I know nothing about it.
   When did this happen, anyhow?

DAME DOUCE   Good Lord! It wasn't so long ago—
   Just a short while before Lent.

GILLOS   That'll be good to tell your wife,
   Rikier. What else would you like her to know?

RIKIER   Hey, fellows, please! Let it rest!
   For Heaven's sake don't start a row.
   She's got such a nasty mind   290
   That she believes what never happens.

GILLOS   Lucky the one who's feared, I say.
   I reckon it's a splendid thing
   That the wives who live in Waranche Street
   Make themselves so feared and dreaded!

HANE   And what of Mahew L'Anstier's wife,
   Who was married to Ernoul de la Porte?
   She commands everyone's respect—
   Uses her nails to help her out
   Against the bailiff at Vermandois.   300

I think her husband's wise to keep
His mouth tight shut.

RIKIER   In that neighbourhood
  There are two other sweet young things:
  First, there's Margos aux Pommettes,
  And then the other, Aelis au Dragon.
  One scolds her husband constantly,
  The other talks nineteen to the dozen.

GILLOS   Bring a stole for exorcism!
  He's just named a pair of fiends.

HANE   Master Adam, don't be surprised   310
  If I must mention your wife too.

ADAM   I don't care, but she mustn't hear.
  I know plenty of scolds myself:
  Henri of Arjan's wife for one—
  She spits and scratches like a cat—
  And then the wife of Master Thomas
  Of Darnestal, who lives over there.

HANE   They're both possessed by a hundred devils—
  As I was ever my father's son!

ADAM   Dame Eve, your mother, is just the same.   320

HANE   And your wife, Adam, is not far short.

(*The Monk enters, bringing his relics of Saint Acaire.*)

MONK   My lords, my master Saint Acaire
  Has come to visit you tonight.
  Approach him with your intercessions
  And each of you offer him a gift.
  There's not a saint from here to Ireland
  Can do such splendid miracles;

He can chase the devil from a man
By his miraculous performance,
And cure all kinds of lunacy   330
In men and women who are mad.
I often see the craziest fools
Come to our monastery at Haspre,
And they're sane and well when they go home.
Saint Acaire is famous for his power,
And for a paltry halfpenny
The Saint shall benefit you all.

HENRI   I reckon someone ought to bring
Walet here, before he gets worse.

RIKIER   Walet, get up. Come over here.   340
There's no one here madder than you.

(*Walet approaches the relics, carrying a cheese in his hand.*)

WALET   May Saint Acaire—whom God crapped out—
Send me lots of pounded peas,
Because, see, I'm a well-known fool.
I'm very glad to see you, sir.
I'm bringing you a cheese, old son,
A fine, rich, tasty, creamy one,
So you can eat it right away:
That's the best feast I can make you.

HENRI   Now Walet, swear by Saint Acaire,   350
What gift would you be willing to give,
If you could be, from this day on,
As good a minstrel as your dad?

WALET   Old son, if I could be as good
A fiddler as he used to be,
Then they could string me up by my neck
Or maybe even cut off my head.

MONK   Oh, what a stupid ass he is!
 He ought to go to Saint Acaire.
 Walet, just kiss this chest of relics—   360
 Quick—the people are flocking in.

(*Walet kisses the chest of relics. A queue of suppliants forms.
Walet addresses one of them.*)

WALET   You kiss, Walaincourt, old son.

MONK   *Old son* Walet, now you sit down.

DAME DOUCE   Please God, sir, will you listen to me?
 Look, here's two pennies that are sent
 By Colart of Bailloel and Heuvins;
 They have great faith in the holy saint.

MONK   I've known them both since they were boys
 And used to go chasing butterflies.   370
 Put the money down in here
 And bring those two along tomorrow.

WALET   Here's something from Gautier-à-la-Main;
 Will you make the Saint pray for him too?
 He's very poorly nowadays
 With that disease inside his brain.

(*While the Monk is collecting the offerings, some of the
company devise a game to bait the Idiot.*)

HANE   Let's all go round mooing like cows—
 They say that gets him all worked up.

THE COMPANY   Moo! Moo!

(*They prance round the Idiot, provoking him, until line 418.*)

MONK   Has no one else an offering?
 Have you forgotten the holy saint?

HENRI   Yes, look, here's a bushel of wheat   380
From Jean le Keu, our policeman.
I commend his health to Saint Acaire—
He's been a devotee for ages.

MONK   Brother, you've spoken well for him.
How is it he didn't come himself?

HENRI   He's had a return of his complaint
And had to be put to bed for a while.
Tomorrow he'll be here on foot,
God willing, provided he is well.

IDIOT'S FATHER   Come on, get up now, my fine lad!   390
Come over here and adore the Saint.

IDIOT   What's going on? Do you want to kill me?
Heretic, robber, son of a bitch—
Do you believe these hypocrites?
Leave me alone, for I am a king!

IDIOT'S FATHER   Just you shut up and sit down there,
Or else I'll give you a few sharp knocks.

IDIOT   I won't sit down. Look, I'm a toad.
I won't eat anything but frogs.
Listen, I'll make a trumpet call—   400

(*He breaks wind.*)

Isn't that good? Shall I do some more?

IDIOT'S FATHER   Now you calm down, my fine lad!
And get down on your knees, or else
I'll get Robert Sommeillons,
The newly elected Prince of the Puy
To bash you!

IDIOT   He's a load of crap!
I'd be a better Prince than him.

In his Puy they've got to put on
The songs of Master Walter-aux-Paus
And one other of their fine friends   410
Who goes by the name of Thomas Clari.
I heard them boasting the other day:
Master Walter was practising
To play a tune on his instrument;
He reckons to get the winner's crown!

HENRI   That will be for playing dice—
They never think of anything else.

IDIOT   Listen how our heifer's mooing!
I'll mount her quick and make her pregnant.

(*He jumps on his Father's back.*)

IDIOT'S FATHER   You stinking fool! Get your hands   420
Off my breeches—or else I'll thrash you!

(*The Idiot stares at Adam.*)

IDIOT   Who's the scholar in the gown?

IDIOT'S FATHER   He's from Paris, my fine lad.

IDIOT   He looks like a dried pea boiled in water!
Bow wow!

IDIOT'S FATHER   What now? Shut up for the ladies' sake!

IDIOT   If he remembered the bigamists
He wouldn't be so high and mighty.

RIKIER   Oh ho! Master Adam, have you *two* wives?
I'm familiar with the first of them!

ADAM   Why does he presume to judge?   430
I take no notice of what he says;

I'm not a bigamist in any sense—
It's the more important ones who are.

HENRI   Now surely the Pope made a great mistake
And everyone blamed him for what he did
When he dismissed so many good clerks.
But it won't turn out as he intended,
For some of them are boasting now—
The richest influential ones—
That they've found lawyer's arguments   440
To plainly prove once and for all
That it's illegal to reduce a clerk
To a state of serfdom because of marriage.
Otherwise marriage is much worse
Than living together in fornication.
The prelates come out of it rather well:
They've wives and mistresses to spare,
Without forfeiting *their* exemptions;
Meanwhile a clerk must lose his franchise
By marrying, lawfully in the Church,   450
A woman whose previous husband is dead.
And yet, those sons of bitches, those crooks,
From whom we should take inspiration,
Carry on in sin and lechery
While still enjoying clerical status!
Rome has reduced a third of her clerks
To servitude and poverty.

GILLOS   Plumus is boasting openly
That, unless his clerical cunning fails,
He will get back all they take   460
As easy as grabbing a handful of stuffing.
The Pope who was to blame for this crime
Is dead now—luckily for him.
No matter how powerful he had been
He'd have been deposed by now!
It would have been too bad for him
If he'd dared take Plumus' privilege:

He'd have told *him* 'dung beetle'—
He'd have made him live on dung.

HANE   A wise man doesn't blather around.   470
    Yet Mados and Gilles de Sains
    Boast about it as much as he.
    Master Gilles will be the lawyer
    And will put forward both their cases
    For getting clerical privilege back.
    He says he'll give his services
    If Jehan Crespin puts up the money.
    And Jehan's sworn an oath to them
    That he will pay for all the costs,
    Because he'll be wretched if they tax him.   480
    Either way will be expensive.

HENRI   Two neighbours living close to me
    In the City are both good lawyers,
    And advertise that they will do
    Anyone's legal work for nothing,
    Because they think it's a filthy business
    To class them both as bigamists.

GILLOS   Who are they?

HENRI   Colars Fousedame
    And Gilles de Bouvignies.
    They'll run proceedings out of spite   490
    And two of them plead for the rest.

GILLOS   Master Henri, what about you?
    Ha ha! You've had more than one wife,
    And if you want to enlist their help
    You'll have to pay towards the cost!

HENRI   Gillos, are you making fun of me?
    By God, I swear I haven't a penny—

Not even enough to live decently,
So I don't need to make a petition.
There's no reason I should fear 500
The tax collectors for what I have.
Let them pick on Marie le Jaie—
She wrangles like an advocate.

GILLOS   Honestly though, you've made a pile.

HENRI   I've not; the drink runs away with it all.
I've worked a long time for the magistrates;
I don't want to side against them now.
I'd rather lose a hundred shillings
Than risk the loss of their good will.

GILLOS: You always side with influence— 510
You just watch your step, Henri!
My word, there's a crafty piece
Of good old fashioned twist for you!

IDIOT   Ow, ow! Gillos said that they should twist
Me by the throat. I'm going to kill him.

IDIOT'S FATHER   Oh, come on, son; leave him be.
He's talking about the bigamists.

IDIOT   Look—I'm the Pope standing here.
Make him come before me now.

MONK   O Lord! We shall do well to listen 520
To this fool! What marvellous nonsense!
Fellow, does he speak such gibberish
When's he's away from a crowd of folk?

IDIOT'S FATHER   It's never any different, sir;
Always raving or singing or braying.
He's no idea of what he does
And even less of what he says.

MONK   How long since he's been this way?

IDIOT'S FATHER   I reckon it is two years now.

MONK   Where are you from?

IDIOT'S FATHER   Duisans village.   530
  It's been misery to care for him.
  Just look at how he shakes his head:
  His body is never still for a moment.
  I bet he's broken two hundred pots—
  I'm the potter in our town.

IDIOT   The deeds of Anseïs and Marsile
  I often have heard Hesselin sing.
  Isn't that true? This punch is proof.

(*He strikes his Father.*)

  Have I used my thirty talents well?
  He beats me so, the great fat oaf   540
  I have become a croquet ball.

IDIOT'S FATHER   He doesn't know what he does, poor boy.
  You see it when he hits his dad.

MONK   Good man, for the sake of your mother's soul,
  Act sensibly and take him home,
  But first make your devotions here
  And offer something that you have.
  He's too worn out from staying up,
  So bring him back to me tomorrow,
  When he has had time to sleep a bit.   550
  All he does is repeat his nonsense.

IDIOT   Did the monk say that you were to beat me?

IDIOT'S FATHER   No, no. Come, let's go home, my son.

(*He gives the Monk an offering.*)

Take this, I haven't any more.
My boy, let's go and sleep a while.
Let's say goodbye to everyone.

IDIOT   Bow, wow!

(*The Idiot is led away by his Father amid the mockery and
horseplay of the company. Meanwhile, Adam and Rikier have
been preparing the table for the fairy feast. Rikier addresses
the company.*)

RIKIER   What's this? Shall we have brawling all day,
    Mad men, mad women, all day long?
    Now, Sir Monk, will you do me a favour?
    Stow your sack of relics away.   560
    I'm sure if it hadn't been for you
    The fairies with their magic spells
    Would have been at this spot long ago;
    Morgan le Fay and all her troupe
    Would now be sitting at this table,
    For it's their long established custom
    To come on this night every year.

MONK   Good fellow, please don't be annoyed;
    Since that's the case, I'll go away.
    I shan't take any more offerings tonight.   570
    But no—allow me to stay here
    And see these splendid miracles.
    I shan't believe them till I see them.

RIKIER   Shut up. Keep absolutely quiet.
    I don't think that she'll be much longer;
    It's just about the proper time.
    They must be on their way here now.

GILLOS   I can hear Hellekin's people;
    If I am right, he's their leader.

Lots of little bells are ringing—   580
I'm sure they must be close at hand.

FAT WOMAN   Will the fairies come right after him?

GILLOS   By heavens, yes, I think they will.

RAINELET   (*to Adam*)   Oh, Lord! This is dangerous, sir!
  I wish now I was safe at home!

ADAM   Shut up! Everything's going right.
  They're ladies, beautifully dressed.

RAINELET   In God's name sir, they're not; they're fairies.
  I'm going home.

ADAM   Sit down, you twit.

(*Rainelet runs away in terror, as Crokesos enters.*)

CROKESOS (*sings*)   'How does my fancy head-dress fit?' 590
  What's this? Is there no one else?
  I must say that I'm disappointed,
  Because I lingered on my way—
  Or else they haven't been here yet.

(*to Dame Douce*)

  Tell me, my old painted lady,
  Has Morgan le Fay been here tonight—
  Herself, or any of her troupe?

DAME DOUCE   Oh no. I haven't seen them at all.
  Are they supposed to come *this* way?

CROKESOS   Yes, to banquet at their pleasure,   600
  Or so I'm given to believe.
  I shall have to wait for them here.

(*Dame Douce goes off to look for the fairies.*)

RIKIERS   Tell us, who's your master, young fellow?

CROKESOS   Who? Me?

RIKIER   Yes, you.

CROKESOS   King Hellekin—
    He sent me here as messenger
    To Lady Morgan, the Knowing One.
    My master has fallen in love with her.
    I shall wait around for her here—
    The fairies gave me this rendez-vous.

RIKIER   Sit down then, Master Messenger.   610

CROKESOS   I will with pleasure, till they come.
    Ah, look! They're here!

RIKIER   You're right, they are.
    By heavens, we mustn't speak a word!

(*Morgan, Arsile and Maglore enter; they do not see the stage-audience. They are followed by Fortune who carries her Wheel.*)

MORGAN   You are most welcome, Crokesos.
    How fares your lord, King Hellekin?

CROKESOS   Madam, as your own true love
    He greets you. I left him yesterday.

MORGAN   God's blessing be on you and him.

CROKESOS   Madam, he charged me with this task,
    To speak with you on his behalf,   620
    When you will give me audience.

MORGAN   Sit down a moment, over there,
      And I will call you presently.
      Dame Maglore, come over here,
      And Arsile, you sit next to her.
      I myself shall take this place
      Between you, at the end of the table.

(*They sit down at the table prepared with three places.*)

MAGLORE   Look, I've got the lowest place:
      They haven't even given me a knife.

MORGAN   I think mine is a lovely one.   630

ARSILE   Mine too.

MAGLORE   Then what does it mean
      That I have none? Am I the worst?
      Heaven's above! They didn't think much
      Of me, whoever it was that planned
      That I alone go without a knife!

MORGAN   Maglore, don't distress yourself,
      Since we have two knives anyway.

MAGLORE   That makes me even more upset—
      That you have two and I have none!

ARSILE   Don't be angry; these things happen—   640
      I doubt if anyone gave it a thought.

MORGAN   My darling friends, do look and see
      How gay and lovely everything is!

ARSILE   I think it would be nice to give
      A present to the folk who troubled
      To decorate this place.

MORGAN   Yes, let's.
  We've no idea who it is.

CROKESOS   Madam, before all this was ready,
  I arrived and found them setting
  The table and making decorations.   650
  It was two clerks who did the work—
  I've heard their people call their names:
  Rikier Auri is one,
  The other Master Henri's son—
  And he was in a gown, that one.

ARSILE   It's proper to reward them for it—
  Each fairy should contribute a gift.
  Madam, what will you give to Richy?
  Begin the presents!

MORGAN   A handsome gift:
  I'd like him to have a heap of money.   660
  As for the other, I want him to be
  The most perfect lover there ever was
  In any country in the world.

ARSILE   I wish that he may be charming and gay
  And a wonderful writer of poems and songs.

MORGAN   You still have a gift for Rikier—
  Go on.

ARSILE   Great lady, I desire
  That all his goods and merchandise
  Shall multiply and make him rich.

MORGAN   Lady Maglore, don't bear malice.   670
  Let them have something nice from you.

MAGLORE   From me? They won't get a thing, I swear!
  They can do without a present,

Since I must do without a knife.
A curse on anyone who rewards them!

MORGAN   Oh, no! My dear, that must not be—
They must have something or other from you.

MAGLORE   If it please your ladyship,
Will you release me from this task?

MORGAN   You must do what we command,   680
Madam, if you love us at all.

MAGLORE   I say that Rikier shall go bald
And have no hair at all in front!
And Adam, who's been bragging around
About going off to study in Paris—
I hope that he becomes disgraced
By joining the riff-raff of Arras;
And that he so forgets himself
In the arms of his sweet and loving wife,
That he wastes his time, hates his studies,   690
Abandons his projected journey.

ARSILE   Heavens! Lady, what have you said?
Good God! Revoke this terrible wish!

MAGLORE   By the soul that gives my body rest,
I swear it shall happen just as I say.

MORGAN   Madam, that makes me very sad.
I'm sorry now—but it's too late—
I asked you for anything today.
I thought by these imploring hands
That they deserved at very least   700
Each one to have a precious gem.

MAGLORE   No! They'll pay for their mistake,
Forgetting to put a knife in my place!

R

MORGAN   Crokesos!

CROKESOS   Madam?

MORGAN   If you've a letter
Or message to give me from your master,
Step forward now.

CROKESOS   May God reward you!
I came in such a hurry too.
Take it.

MORGAN   (*after reading Hellekin's letter*)
                    Pah! What a waste of labour!
He writes to ask me for my love,
But I have set my heart elsewhere.   710
Tell him that he wastes his time.

CROKESOS   For pity's sake—I wouldn't dare.
He would throw me into the sea.
Madam, I know you could not love
A man more valiant than he.

MORGAN   I can indeed.

CROKESOS   Madam, who's that?

MORGAN   A young man in this city, worth
A hundred thousand Hellekins—
Or else we languish pointlessly.

CROKESOS   But who?

MORGAN   Robert Sommeillons,   720
Expert in arms and on a horse;
He jousts for my honour up and down
The country at Round Table lists.
There's no worthier knight in all the world
And none more expert at self-defence.

Everyone saw at Mondidier
How he jousted against all comers;
And he still suffers from the wounds
In his shoulders and his chest and arms.

CROKESOS   Isn't he the one in green   730
  With a single crimson stripe?

MORGAN   Yes, he's the one.

CROKESOS   Ah, I knew it.
  My master's been in a jealous rage
  Since he jousted the other day
  In town, right in the market square.
  He boasted of his affair with you,
  But as soon as he spurred his horse to charge,
  My master came in a cloud of dust
  And made his horse stumble and trip
  So that he tumbled the young man off   740
  Before he'd even struck his opponent.

MORGAN   People have jeered at him quite enough.
  In spite of that he's terribly brave
  And he isn't a boaster; he's quiet and shy;
  And no one talks more pleasantly.
  Everything about him thrills me
  So that I love him. (*to Arsile*) What do you think?

ARSILE   Madam, your pride must be in your boots
  If you consider a man like that.
  From the River Lys to the River Somme   750
  There's no man falser nor more deceitful.
  No matter where it is he goes
  He always wants to be cock of the walk.

MORGAN   Is that true?

ARSILE   Yes.

MORGAN   Then may the hand
Of God forgive and sanctify me!
I really do despise myself
For thinking about that bragging fool
For whom I've neglected the greatest prince
Of all that live in fairy land.

ARSILE   I think you're very well advised   760
Now to repent for what you've done.

MORGAN   Crokesos!

CROKESOS   My lady?

MORGAN   Convey
My friendly greetings to your lord.

CROKESOS   Madam, I thank you heartily
In the name of my great lord, the king.

(*He points to Fortune's wheel*)

   Tell me, what is that I see
Around the wheel? Are they real men?

MORGAN   Oh no, it's just a pretty show.
The woman who holds and guides the wheel
Is subject to the three of us.   770
And since the time that she was born
She has been dumb and deaf and blind.

CROKESOS   Tell us, what's her name?

MORGAN   Fortune.
Her power controls all things on earth:
She holds the world in her hand and makes
You poor today and rich tomorrow.
She does not know whom she advances;

That's why no one should ever trust her,
No matter how eminent he's become;
For, once her wheel begins to turn,   780
He must go crashing to the ground.

CROKESOS   Who are those two—high up there?
  Both of them look like noble lords.

MORGAN   It is not wise to explain all things;
  At this point I must excuse myself.

MAGLORE   I'll explain for you, Crokesos.
  As I have been so incensed
  I'll spare no one at all today,
  And speak no words except in spite.
  Those two are favourites of the Count's,   790
  Important gentlemen in the city.
  Fortune has set them up in honour:
  Each is a king in his own domain.

CROKESOS   Who are they then?

MAGLORE   Sir Ermenfrois
  Crespin and Jakemes Louchars.

CROKESOS   I know them well—a pair of misers!

MAGLORE   Well, anyway, they reign like kings,
  And their children are all thriving too,
  Hoping to lord it after them.

CROKESOS   Which ones?

MAGLORE   You see at least two up there: 800
  Each one follows his father's footsteps.
  I don't know who that is at the top.

CROKESOS   That one who's tumbling down head first—
  Has he been a thief or criminal?

MAGLORE   No. That's Thomas de Bourriane;
  He used to be in the Count's good books,
  But Fortune now is tumbling him down
  And sending those below on top.
  They turned against him and pursued him   810
  And quite unjustly injured him.
  Even the people at his shop
  Wanted to persecute the man.

ARSILE   They were wicked to sentence him to death,
  There wasn't even the slightest cause.
  He's left his trade of selling cloth
  To take up brewing ale and beer.

MORGAN   It's Fortune who has caused his fall.
  He'd not deserved it in the least.

CROKESOS   Madam, who's that other one,   820
  Bare-footed and completely nude?

MORGAN   Him? That's Leurins li Cavelaus—
  He can never get up at all.

ARSILE   Oh yes he can! He comes 'up'
  At the sight of any pretty piece!

CROKESOS   Madam, my duty summons me
  To return to my lord immdiately.

MORGAN   Then tell him that he should rejoice
  And be happy and joyful for evermore
  Because I shall be his loving mistress   830
  From henceforth all the days of my life.

CROKESOS   Madam, with those words, I'm gone.

MORGAN   I mean it; boldly repeat my words
  And take this present to him from me.
  But wait. A drink before you go?

CROKESOS   (*going*, *sings*)
  'How does my fancy head-dress fit?'

MORGAN   If it please you, gentle ladies,
  It seems to me it must be time
  To go away, before dawn breaks.   840
  We shouldn't stay any longer here
  Because we must not walk by day
  On ground where men pass to and fro.
  Let's go at once back to the Meadow—
  I know they're waiting for us there.

MAGLORE   Let us go there quickly then;
  The ancient women of the town
  Expect us there.

(*Dame Douce appears, still searching for the fairies.*)

MORGAN   Is this a trick?

MAGLORE   Look! Dame Douce has come for us.

DAME DOUCE   What's the matter with you ladies?
  It's a nuisance and a great disgrace   850
  That you have hung about so long.
  I have to be look-out tonight,
  And my daughter's waited up for you
  All evening by the Meadow Cross.
  That's where we expected you
  And kept a watch down all the streets.
  You've kept us waiting far too long.

MORGAN   Why's that, Dame Douce?

DAME DOUCE   They've been spreading
    Dirt about me in front of the crowd—
    Just let me get my hands on that man!   860
    He'll soon be buried if I do,
    Or turned inside out and backside up
    With his fingers where his feet should be!
    I'll soon have him where I want him—
    Stretched on his bed—just like I did
    Last year with Jakemon Pilepois
    And with Gillon Lavier the other night.

MAGLORE   Right! We shall come and help you out.
    Bring your daughter Agnes too,
    And the other one who lives in the City—   870
    She won't show him any mercy!

MORGAN   Walter Mulet's wife?

DAME DOUCE   That's her.
    Now lead the way and I will follow.

THE FAIRIES *sing*
    'This way go all dainty creatures,
        The way that I go.'

(*At this invitation, the women in the company follow the
fairies out of the 'place' into the streets, singing as they go
Most of the men follow, but Rikiers goes to sit at a table by
the tavern door, leaving Hane and the sleeping Monk sitting
in their 'audience' seats. The Monk wakes up.*)

MONK   Goodness me—how long I've dozed.

HANE   Holy Mary! I watched all the time.
    You'd best be on your way at once.

MONK   Brother, first we ought to eat—
    By my duty to Saint Acaire. (*He picks up his relics.*) 880

HANE   Monk, you know what's a good idea?
  Let's go to Raoul the Watchman's place—
  He has left-overs from yesterday
  And maybe he will give us some.

MONK   Splendid! Who will take me there?

HANE   No one can guide you better than me.
  I'm sure that we shall find a crowd
  Of regulars who gather there,
  All pleasant folk and no one brawling:
  Adam, Master Henri's son,   890
  Velet, and Rikier Auri,
  And Little Gillos, I expect.

MONK   By Jesus, I'll agree to that!
  My business here was a success.
  Look—here's a little pancake
  That some poor devil 'offered' me.
  I won't charge it to your account!
  That's a beginning anyway.

HANE   Let's get along before the crowd   900
  Get there and fill the tavern up.

(*They walk across the 'place' towards the door of the tavern.*)

  Look, the table's ready laid,
  And Rikier's sitting on one side.
  Have you seen the landlord, Richy?

RIKIER   He's there, inside. Raoulet!

(*The Taverner appears at the threshold.*)

TAVERNER   Here I am.

HANE   Whose job is it
  To draw the wine? Has it all gone?

TAVERNER   (*to the Monk*)
You're welcome, sir. By Saint Giles,
I want you to have a really good time.
See the stuff we sell in town—
Taste this. I sell it by special licence.   910

(*He pours wine.*)

MONK   Thank you. Here then!

TAVERNER   Isn't that good wine?
They don't drink that in monasteries!
I give you my solemn word on oath—
Not *this* year's vintage of Auxerre.

RIKIER   You'd better give me a glass of it then,
For old time's sake. Let's sit down here.
There's a handy window sill
That we can put the jug down on.

(*Gillos joins them, unnoticed.*)

GILLOS   That's true.

RIKIER   Who asked you, Gillos?
That's an end to our peace and quiet.   920

GILLOS   It certainly wasn't you, Rikier,
I've never been a friend of yours.
What's this? (*to the Monk*) Has my lord of Saint Acaire
Performed his miracles in here?

TAVERNER   Gillos, are you out of your mind?
Shut up. You're not welcome here at all.

GILLOS   Oh! Kind sir, I won't say a word.

(*Aside to Hane*)

> Hane, will you ask Raoulet
> If he has any scraps left over,
> Put in the pantry from last night?   930

TAVERNER   Yes indeed—one Yarmouth herring.
That's all, Gillos. I hear you all right.

(*He produces the fish.*)

GILLOS   I know what belongs to me—(*he snatches the
herring*)
Hane, why don't you ask for yours?

TAVERNER   I tell you, take your paws away!
It has to do for everyone.
It isn't fair one greedy guts
Should hog the food.

GILLOS   Pah! It's fair enough.

TAVERNER   Put that herring right back here.

GILLOS   There—I shan't even taste the thing.   940
But I *will* try a little drop of wine
Before you've drunk it to the dregs. (*He helps himself.*)
This keg was scalded out with water—
It tastes a bit like washing up.

TAVERNER   Don't go libelling the wine,
Gillos. Just you behave yourself.
The people here are all good friends
So don't go finding fault.

GILLOS   I'm not.

(*Adam and Henri walk by the tavern.*)

HANE   I see that Adam's being virtuous,
Because he's going to be a scholar.   950

I've seen the time that he has been
Glad to join us for his breakfast.

(*Henri attempts to steer Adam towards the tavern group.
Adam pulls away.*)

ADAM   No, sir. It's time that I grew up.
By God, I won't for anything!

HENRI   For Christ's sake, go in. You're all right—
You often go in when I'm not here.

ADAM   Well, I insist I shan't today,
Unless you come inside with me.

HENRI   Go on, I'm coming. After you. (*They enter the
tavern.*)

HANE   Well, for Christ's sake! Look at our scholar!   960
That's a fine way to spend your money!
Is that what the others do in Paris?

RIKIER   Hey, look! The monk has fallen asleep.

TAVERNER   Listen, everyone, I have an idea.
Let's fix it so that he pays the bill.
Say Hane gambled and threw for *him*.

MONK (*waking*)   Oh, ah! Good Lord, I've stayed too long.
Landlord, what's the reckoning?

TAVERNER   *You* don't owe anything, dear sir;
But you shall pay up all the same.   970
Now don't get angry—let me think:
You owe me twelve shillings in all.
You've got your friends to thank for that—
They gambled on your behalf and lost.

MONK   For me?

TAVERNER   That's right.

MONK   I owe for them all?

TAVERNER   That's right.

MONK   Have I been snoring then?
I'd have got as good a bargain
Shopping in Pickpocket Square.
I don't believe they ever diced
For me, nor at my request.   980

TAVERNER   Look for yourself. Each of them swears
That he was throwing the dice for you.

MONK   Oh, Lord! The man that trusted you
Would be well and truly tricked.
It's wicked to come here to drink
When folk get swindled just like that.

TAVERNER   Pay up, Monk. Come on—the cash
That you owe me. Are you quibbling?

MONK   If I pay you, may I become
As mad as that Idiot tonight!   990

TAVERNER   You may fret and get annoyed,
But you'll stay here until the cock crows
Or else you'll leave your cowl behind.

(*He starts to strip off the Monk's cowl.*)

You take the nut—I'll have the shell.

MONK   Are you threatening me with force?

TAVERNER   Certainly, if you don't pay.

MONK   I see that I've been properly tricked,
   But this is the last time it will happen.
   But meanwhile I'd better leave
   Before another bill turns up.   1000

(*The Doctor enters.*)

DOCTOR   Brother monk, if you've got sense,
   You'll clear off now, I'm warning you.
   Gentlemen, you're poisoning yourselves,
   You'll all turn into paralytics,
   If my prognosis isn't false—
   Still here drinking at this hour!

GILLOS   Doctor, you've taken leave of your wits;
   I don't give a fig for your prognosis.
   Sit down with us.

DOCTOR   Well, just this once.
   Please may I have something to drink?   1010

GILLOS   Here, take this—and eat this pear.

MONK   Landlord, listen to me a minute:
   You've made a profit out of me.
   Keep my relics here in pawn,
   Since I've not much money on me now,
   And I'll come back to redeem them tomorrow.

TAVERNER   Off you go! They're in safe hands.

(*Exit the Monk, leaving his chest of relics with the Taverner.*)

GILLOS   How true, O Lord!

TAVERNER   Now I'll preach to you.
   By the bones of Saint Acaire,
   I charge you, Master Adam and Hane,   1020

And each one here to mumble and moan
And make a solemn celebration
For the saint whose thirst has been assuaged
By such a curious circumstance.

(*He places the relics in a prominent position and leads the
company in parodic worship of the saint.*)

THE COMPANY sings:
   'Once she sat in a lofty tower.'
   Good old landlord, was that well sung?

TAVERNER   You are to be congratulated—
   It was never sung so well before.

(*The Idiot, his Father, and the Monk enter the 'place' below the
tavern terrace.*)

IDIOT   Look out! A fire, a fire, a fire!
   I can sing as well as them.   1030

MONK   You're carried away by a hundred fiends!
   You do nothing but cause me harm.
   Your father wasn't very clever
   When he brought you back again.

IDIOT'S FATHER   Oh, sir, it's very worrying—
   But all the same, what can I do?
   Unless he comes to Saint Acaire
   Where will he go for his sanity?
   Really, he's by now cost so much
   That I have to beg for my own bread.   1040

IDIOT   Jesus Christ, I'm starving to death.

IDIOT'S FATHER   Take a bite of this apple here.

IDIOT   You're a liar! It's only a feather.
   Go, go, go! (*He throws the apple.*) It's gone to Paris.

IDIOT'S FATHER   Dear Lord God, how ashamed I am,
   How wretchedly unfortunate!

MONK   The devil keeps him well employed—
   Why do you bring him back to me?

IDIOT'S FATHER   Oh, sir, it's terrible. All he does
   At home is violence and filth.   1050
   Yesterday I found him covered in feathers,
   Hiding himself inside his mattress.

(*Meanwhile, the Idiot enters the tavern porch and leans across
the table to grab the wine jug, upsetting glasses and causing
pandemonium.*)

HENRI   Good God! Who's that leaning over?

(*The Idiot drinks.*)

   Cheers! You glutton, glutton, glutton!

GILLOS   For God's sake, let's clear everything.
   The idiot's attacking us.
   Grab the cloth! You take the jug!

RIKIER   For heaven's sake, take them quick,
   Before he damages any more.   1060
   Everyone take his own belongings.
   We've all stayed up far too long.

(*The Monk enters the tavern porch.*)

MONK   Landlord, you have swindled me—
   And most of the others here are richer.
   But let that be; where are my relics?
   There's twelve shillings that I owe.
   Damn you and your blasted tavern!
   The devil take me if I ever come back.

TAVERNER   I shan't force you to come again.
Take your relics. .

MONK   Give them here.   1070
(*to Hane*) God blast you for bringing me here!
I never heard of such a thing.

(*He leaves the tavern, taking his relics, and rejoins the Idiot
and his Father in the 'place'.*)

GILLOS   Say, Hane, anything more to do?
Have we forgotten anything?

HANE   Nothing at all. I've cleared the stuff.
Let's wish the landlord all the best.

GILLOS   No. While I think of it, let's go instead
To kiss the statue of Notre Dame
And offer this candle to light her shrine.
It will bring us all good luck.   1080

(*The whole company leave the tavern, taking their own
tankards, napkins, etc. with them. They walk through the
'place' and go off. The Idiot, his Father and the Monk
remain in the 'place'.*)

IDIOT'S FATHER   Up on your feet, my lovely lad!
I still must go and sell my wheat.

IDIOT   What's that? Do you want to take me to hang,
You son of a bitch, convicted thief?

IDIOT'S FATHER   Shut up! I wish you were dead and buried,
You stinking fool! May God damn you!

(*Water is poured down from above.*)

S

IDIOT   By Christ, someone is pissing down
  On me from up above, I think.
  For two pins I would strangle you.

(*The Idiot attacks his Father, who beats him with his stick.*)

IDIOT'S FATHER   Ow, ow! Get a feel of this peastick!   1090

IDIOT   Didn't I make a noisy fart?

IDIOT'S FATHER   That's no use, you'll have to come.

IDIOT   Let's go. Look, I am your wife.

(*As the Idiot gesticulates obscenely, his Father leads him out of the 'place', leaving the Monk alone.*)

MONK   I'm not doing myself much good
  By staying, since everyone has gone.
  There's no one left except young girls,
  Little children and gangs of boys.
(*Addressing his relics*) Ah well, let's go. Saint Nicholas's
  Morning bells begin to chime.

(*Exit*)

Texts

Adam le Bossu, *Le Jeu de la Feuillée*, éd. Ernest Langlois, Classiques Français du Moyen Age, Paris, 2e éd., 1951.

Le Jeu de la Feuillée & Le Jeu de Robin et Marion, adaptés par Ernest Langlois, Editions Boccard, Paris, 1964.

Oeuvres complètes du trouvère Adam de la Halle, éd. E. de Coussemaker, Paris, 1872.

Staging and interpretation

Alfred Adler, *Sens et composition du 'Jeu de la Feuillée'*, Ann Arbor, 1956.

Gilbert Mayer, *Lexique des oeuvres d'Adam de la Halle*, Paris, 1940.

Marie Ungureaunu, *La bourgeoisie naissante*, pp. 69ff., 181ff.

Thomas Walton, 'Staging *Le Jeu de la Feuillée*', *Modern Language Review*, XXXVI (1941), pp. 344-50.

LE JEU DE ROBIN
ET DE MARION

by Adam de la Halle

PERSONS OF THE PLAY

MARION, also called Marot etc., shepherdess, Robin's sweetheart
THE KNIGHT, Sir Aubert
ROBIN, also called Robert etc., Marion's lover
GAUTIER THE HOTHEAD } Robin's cousins
BAUDON
PERONNELLE, also called Perrette, Marion's friend
HUART, Robin's friend
Two Musicians

LE JEU DE ROBIN ET DE MARION

Text

It is thought that Adam de la Halle composed *Robin et Marion* in about 1283, when he was in service as musician and poet to Robert II, Count of Artois, during the Count's stay in Southern Italy. The play—it verges towards musical comedy—is written largely in octosyllabic couplets and is in Adam's native Arras dialect. Three medieval manuscripts of it survive, one of them (*c.* 1300) containing all Adam's known works. This one manuscript contains an expanded version of the play, which was apparently revised for an Arras performance shortly after Adam's death in Sicily (*c.* 1287). Since these revisions (consisting of the *Jeu de Pèlerin* prologue and two interpolations in the play itself) are not the author's, we have followed Kenneth Varty's 1960 edition and omitted them from our translation. We have followed the line-numbering of Varty's edition and we have also gratefully adapted some of the stage-directions he provides, when they were appropriate to our purpose.

The music which occupies a substantial part of the play consists of songs and dance-songs. Although Adam de la Halle was a distinguished composer in his own right, the music he has incorporated here is of a popular traditional kind. Jacques Chailley has shown the dependence of these lively and attractive tunes on the *pastourelle* and *bergerie*. It is a normal characteristic of these little epigrams-in-song, as it were, to be in a different metre from the dialogue which surrounds them. In translating them we have attempted strict syllabic equivalence; the verses only make rhythmic sense with their music. The songs have been newly transcribed from the all-inclusive manuscript already mentioned

(Paris, B.N. fr.25.566). Unlike Adam's chansons in the same manuscript, the songs of *Robin and Marion* are written in unequivocally mensural note-values. This means that we can be certain of the rhythms to an extent to which we cannot be certain when dealing with most earlier songs for single voice. We can also be certain, from their context in the play, that they were sung unaccompanied, unless instruments are specifically mentioned in the action. As this is not an edition for scholars, no detailed commentary on the musical text is called for. A few observations may, however, be of interest to musicians: (i) the slurred or grouped notes are usually indicated in the manuscript by ligatures (two or more notes joined together); (ii) the line-endings in the transcription have been standardized (the scribe has not given his rests or phrase-marks a clear mensural meaning); (iii) the manuscript makes no distinction in pitch between male and female roles, but this is no sure indication by any means that men played all the parts; (iv) three songs (95, 97, 729) often interpreted in 6/4 or 6/8 metre (the dactylic mode) are here transcribed in duple time; the first part of the last song seems to call for this also.

Staging

Although the three manuscripts of the play have no stage-directions as such, the entrances and exits of the characters can be readily deduced from the dialogue; so too can most of the stage business. The dialogue gives little hint, however, of the means by which the pleasant pastoral 'place' of the action was suggested to the original audience. Obviously the play is well suited to outdoor performance—especially in the latitude of Naples.

The main action of the play takes place in a meadow by a wood, perhaps the traditional *bois d'amour* of thirteenth-century pastourelle dancing songs.[1] A grassy area with a central clump of bushes would provide all the main plot

[1] A fifteenth-century French tournament used a *pastourelle* centre-piece very similar to that needed for the play. At the *Pas d'armes de la*

requirements. When the play is acted indoors, an emblematic bush can be used on a conventional stage. When characters go 'off', they merely retire behind the bush. Robin and his cowardly friends hide 'behind the bushes' to spy on the Knight's advances to Marion (356), and at the end of the play the whole company leaves 'by the path beside the wood'. A small hummock is needed for the enthronement of the 'King' of the quizzing game (497). At the edge of the acting 'place' there could be a timber structure representing the house of Robin's cousins.

The dialogue makes explicit most of the properties and costumes needed. The Knight requires hunting clothes (a cloak, breeches, hat) and a falconer's heavy leather gauntlet. Robin wears leggings which he says are torn (213) and boots; he also says he has changed his rustic smock for a heavy long coat because of the cold (112) and when he runs he has to tuck this up into his belt (228). He has a purse and brooch (177). The other men are similarly dressed: they carry satchels containing food for the picnic. Gautier has a heavy stick and a pitchfork, Baudon a thorn club (258–9).

Marion should wear at least some of the clothes she sings about in her opening song: Robin has given her a fancy short coat made of 'scarlet', a long, square-necked dress or bodice, petticoat and ornamental belt. She and Peronnelle also have jackets or cloaks of some sort, because Marion claims that her own is dirty, thus tricking Peronnelle into using hers for the picnic cloth (682). The girls' bodices

bergère at Tarascon in 1449, King René d'Anjou defended his queen, who was dressed as a shepherdess, against challenges from 'shepherd knights'. The shepherd queen sat at the foot of a tree in a place at the end of the lists, 'as delightful as man knew how to devise, exquisitely adorned with trees and flowers and smooth turf, as was fitting . . . Her crook was about two yards long and wrought in fine silver. She had also a little silver barrel by her side from which to refresh her little mouth; and as well as these she carried a little food basket which was very dainty.'
(See Glynne Wickham, *Early English Stages, 1300–1660*, vol, I. p. 22.)

must be loose-fronted or else have deep pockets; this is where Marion carries bread and cheese (142) and Peronnelle's 'bumps' (bread and salt and water-cress) are the cause of Huart's joke (640). Marion has a basket and water jar and probably also a crook. Peronnelle has a straw hat which she presents for the play-king's crown (500). Marion should have nothing on her head except her *chapelet de fleurs*, the traditional garland of the shepherd queen.

Two musicians play *cornetts*, which are curved, wooden instruments making a pure sound; they were often used to double the boy-trebles in choir. Recorders would do as substitutes. Robin brings from the village at least one set of bagpipes for accompanying the dancing and says (216) that he will fetch a drum. If bagpipes are not available, a concertina, piano-accordion, or even mouth-organ would do.

The animals (the Knight's horse, his falcon, Marion's ewe) may have been real, for real animals were certainly used in medieval plays. But Marion's realistic comment, asking the Knight to back his horse a little (73) does not necessarily prove the use of a live animal. In Ben Jonson's *Masque of Owles*, presented at Kenilworth in 1624, the Ghost of Captain Cox begins the entertainment with,

> Roome, roome, for my horse will wince,
> If he come within so many yards of a Prince.

Captain Cox's Ghost was riding a hobby-horse. This was regarded in Shakespeare's and Jonson's time as a quaint and obsolete convention of folk drama and rustic pageantry. It was a much more sumptuous creature than its modern equivalent, and it would suit the purposes of *Robin et Marion* admirably. The Knight 'wears' his hobby-horse, caparisoned to the ground, like a skirt on a frame from which the horse's neck and head project. He requires only a pair of leggings hanging from the 'saddle' to complete the ensemble. There is no need for the Knight to dismount, but if he needs to do so, he can discard his horse behind the 'bush'. When he abducts Marion he can simply pick her up in his arms and trot out of the 'place.'

LE JEU DE ROBIN ET DE MARION

(*Marion is alone in the 'place' with her sheep. She weaves a garland of flowers for her head as she sings.*)

MARION (*sings*)

Robin loves me, Robin does; Robin asks, Can he have me? Yes, he can! He bought me a little jacket made of scarlet fine and fancy, petticoat and little girdle: Hey trolly lo! Robin loves me, Robin does; Robin asks, Can he have me? Yes, he can!

(*The Knight enters on horseback. He wears a thick leather gauntlet on which sits a hunting falcon with a leather hood over its head and a bell on its leg.*)

KNIGHT (*sings*)

I was com-ing homewards from the tour-na-ment, When I found this pret-ty Ma-r

të a-lone

MARION (*sings*)

Hey, Ro-bin, if you love me, please come and fetch me now

KNIGHT   Shepherdess, good day to you!

MARION   God bless and keep you, sir!

KNIGHT   Dear girl,
    Tell me now in the name of love,
    Why do you sing this melody
    So often, and so happily?

(*sings*)

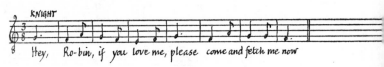

Hey, Ro-bin, if you love me, please come and fetch me now

MARION   Good sir, the reason's obvious—   20
    I love Robin, and he loves me.
    He's shown quite well that he holds me dear—
    This little basket he's given me,
    And my sheephook, and my knife.

KNIGHT   Tell me, have you seen a bird
   Flying over the meadow-land.

MARION   I've seen more birds than I can count,
   And in the bushes, here, there are
   Goldfinches and chaffinches,
   Singing away so prettily!   30

KNIGHT   Heaven help me, you beautiful girl—
   That wasn't what I asked at all!
   I asked if you had seen a duck
   Passing this way down the brae.

MARION   A dunck-ie? Are those the beasts that bray?
   Only yesterday I saw three,
   Going loaded to the mill.
   Is that what you had in mind?

KNIGHT   Look, what a helpful answer I get!
   Tell me, did you see a heron?   40

MARION   A herring? No, of course not, silly.
   I haven't seen one of them since Lent;
   We had them for dinner at Dame Em's,
   My grandmamma's—these are her sheep.

KNIGHT   Heavens alive! She strikes me dumb—
   Never been made such a fool of before.

MARION   On your honour as a gentleman,
   What is that animal on your fist?

KNIGHT   Why, it's a falcon!

MARION   Does it eat bread?

KNIGHT   No, no—good meat.

MARION   A beast like that!   50
   Look! It's head is made of leather!—
   Where are you going?

KNIGHT   Along the bank.

MARION   Robin doesn't behave like that.
   Robin is much more full of fun;
   He raises a din all over town,
   When he plays upon his pipes.

KNIGHT   Tell me, pretty shepherdess,
   Could you love a gentleman?

MARION   Please draw back a little, sir!
   I really don't know what 'gentlemen' are.   60
   More than all the men in the world
   I love Robin—and no one else.
   Every morning and every evening
   He comes to see me—it's his way.
   He brings me a portion of his cheese—
   I have a piece, here in my pocket,
   As well as a good thick slice of bread
   Which he brought me for my dinner.

KNIGHT   Tell me, pretty shepherdess,
   Wouldn't you like to come with me,   70
   And have a game on this nice horse
   By the side of the copse in the valley there?

MARION   Please, please! Back your horse a little!
   He almost did me an injury.
   Robin's never kicks out at all,
   When I walk behind the plough.

KNIGHT   Shepherdess, become my love,
   And, graciously, grant my request.

MARION   Now, sir, keep your distance, please!
        You've no business to stay here;   80
        Your horse will do me damage soon.—
        But tell me, please, what is your name?

KNIGHT   Aubert.

MARION (*sings*)

You will lose your la- bour, Sir Au- bert.

Ro- bin is   my   on- ly   on- ly   love

KNIGHT   Won't you?

MARION   No, upon my word!

KNIGHT   Do you want to put me in my place
        By such a forcible rebuff?
        You're a shepherdess, I'm a knight!

MARION   That won't make me love you more.

(*sings*)   90

I am a shep-her- dess, but may   have a lo- ver, spruce and gay.

KNIGHT   Sweetheart, may God give you joy!
If that's the case, I'll take my way,
And never speak to you again.

(*He begins to ride away.*)

MARION (*sings*)

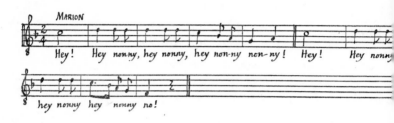

KNIGHT (*sings as he goes*)   97

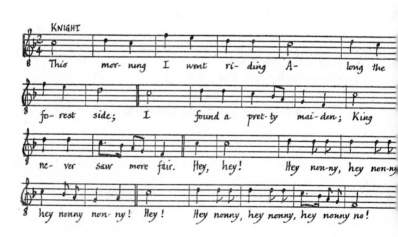

(Left alone, Marion sings; Robin (off) sings in answer as he approaches the 'place'.)

MARION & ROBIN

M: Hey, Ro- bi- kin! Trol- ly lol- ly lo, Do come to
R: Hey, Ma- ri- on! Trol- ly lol- ly lo, I come to

me,   Trol- ly lol- ly lo, And we will play of
you,   Trol- ly lol- ly lo, And we will play of

trol- ly lol- ly lo, of trol- ly lol- ly lo!
trol- ly lol- ly lo, of trol- ly lol- ly lo!

(Enter Robin.)

MARION   Robin.

ROBIN   Marion.

MARION   Where have you been?

ROBIN   Heavens above, I've taken off   112
   My cape (because it's got so cold);
   Put on, instead, my heavy coat
   And brought along some apples. Here!

MARION   Robin, I recognized your voice
   Singing, as you came along.
   Didn't you recognize me too?

ROBIN   Of course—your singing and your sheep!

   T

MARION   Robin, dearest, you'll never guess   120
   (But, please, don't go and take this wrong!)
   A man on a horse came down this way—
   He was wearing a great thick glove
   And carrying a sort of kite
   On his hand; and he kept on asking
   If I would love him! *He* got *no*where!
   Because I'd never do you wrong.

ROBIN   You would have killed me, Marion—
   But if I'd come along just then,
   And Gautier the Hothead with me,   130
   And Baudon, too,—you know, my cousin—
   The very devils would have joined us;
   He wouldn't have left without a fight!

MARION   Dearest Robin, don't get upset—
   Let's enjoy ourselves together!

ROBIN   Am I to stand? Or kneel down here?

MARION   Come along, sit down next to me;
   We'll have some food.

ROBIN   A good idea.
   I'll settle here, right by your side—
   Oh, but I've brought you nothing with me!   140
   I'm sorry that I've been so rude.

MARION   Don't worry, Robin! I still have
   Some cheese—here, in the front of my dress,
   And a big thick slice of bread
   As well as the apples that you brought.

ROBIN   Heavens! This cheese is really rich.
   Come, darling, eat!

MARION   You eat, as well.
   And when you want a drink, just say!
   I've got some water in a jar.

ROBIN   If only we had a bit of bacon   150
   Your Granny's—it would be just the thing!

MARION   Robin, we can't have any of that—
   It's hanging up on the beams for curing.
   Let us make do with what we have.
   It will see us through the morning.

ROBIN   Heavens! How my stomach aches
   From playing ball the other day!

MARION   Tell me, Robin—on your honour,
   Did you play? Bless you for that!   160

ROBIN (*sings*)

You will hear it tru-ly spo-ken; dar-ling, you will hear it.

MARION   Robin, anything more to eat?

ROBIN   No, really.

MARION   I'll put away the bread,
   And the cheese, then, in my bodice,
   Until we get an appetite.

ROBIN   No, put it in your basket, dear.

MARION   There it is! Now, what's to do?
   Yours to command—whatever you like!

ROBIN   Marion, I'm going to test   170
       Whether you are my sweetheart true,
       For I've been proved your own true love.

(Robin and Marion sing in alternation, while Marion takes the garland from her head and offers it to Robin. In return he takes off his belt, purse, and brooch, and offers them to her. Finally Marion places the garland on his head.)

MARION   Robin, let's have a little fling!   183

ROBIN   Shall I 'twist' or shall I shake'?
         I tell you, I can do the lot.
         Don't you know my reputation?

(*They sing in alternation. In answer to each of Marion's
demands Robin demonstrates the appropriate dance steps.*)

MARION

Ro-bin, by your father's soul, do you know how to dance the foot.

ROBIN

Ma-rote, by my mother's soul, yes, you will see it suits me well. Dancing forwards,

dancing backwards, dancing back & for-wards.   193

MARION

Ro-bin, by your father's spi-rit, will you do the Tour de Chief?

ROBIN

Ma-rote, by my mo-ther's spi-rit, I will bring it to a head! Is this how one

does it, dar-ling? Is this how one does it?

MARION

Ro-bin, by your fa-ther's spi-rit, will you do the Tour des Bras

ROBIN

Ma-rote, by my mother's spi-rit, I'll do just as you may wish. Is this how one

does it, darling? Is this how one does it?

205

MARION

Ro-bin, by your fa-ther's spi-rit, can you dance an Evening dance?

ROBIN

Yes, dear, by my mother's spi-rit, But my hair is much too short. Short in front, but long be-hind me; short, but long be-hind me.

MARION   Can you do the farandole?   **211**

ROBIN   Yes, but the pace is far too quick,
And my leggings are all torn.

MARION   We are very suitably dressed.
Don't mind that! Do it, please, for me!

ROBIN   Wait, I'll go and get the drum
And the bagpipe with the drone.
And I'll bring Baudon here with me,
If I can find him, and Gautier;
For they'll be of great use to me,   **220**
If your gentleman should return.

MARION   Robin, come back as soon as you can—
And if you happen on my friend
Peronnelle, invite her too.
It will be nice to have her with us.
You'll find her just behind the gardens
As you go to Roger's mill.
Now, be quick!

ROBIN   Let me tuck up my coat.
I'll run all the way.

MARION   Go on, then, go!

(*Robin runs across the 'place' and stops in front of his cousins' 'house'.*)

ROBIN   Gautier! Baudon! Are you there?   230
  Quickly! Open the door for me.

(*Gautier and Baudon appear.*)

GAUTIER   Hallo! It's good to see you, Robin!
  What's up to make you so out of breath?

ROBIN   What's up? Whew! I'm ready to drop—
  I'm so out of breath I can hardly speak.

BAUDON   Has some one hit you?

ROBIN   No, no one.

GAUTIER   Has someone done you an injury, then?

ROBIN   Listen a moment, friends, I'll tell you.
  I've come along to get you two,
  Because some wretched, dirty minstrel   240
  Came on horseback and made approaches
  To Marion; and I'm still afraid,
  He may be coming back this way.

GAUTIER   If he comes back, he'll get it hot!

BAUDON   He certainly will—I'll take a bet!

ROBIN   You're sure to have a splendid time!
  My friends, if you come back with me.
  As well as you, Huart will be there
  And Peronnelle—it's quite a party!
  You'll have the best bread from the baker's,   250
  Excellent cheese and cool clear water.

BAUDON   Come on, cousin! Lead the way!

ROBIN   No! you two get along the road,
And I'll be off to fetch Huart
And Peronnelle.

BAUDON   Then off you go!

GAUTIER   And we'll be off the other way
Along the road towards Le Pierre.
I'll bring my iron fork back with me.

BAUDON   And I will bring my heavy thorn-club.
It's at Bourguet's—she's my cousin.   260

(*Gautier and Baudon go through the 'place' looking for Marion. Robin continues round the 'place' to find Peronnelle.*)

ROBIN   Hey! Peronnelle! Peronnelle!

PERONNELLE   Is that you, Robin? What's the news?

ROBIN   Don't you know? Marion wants you.
We're going to have a splendid party.

PERONNELLE   Who will be there?

ROBIN   You, and me,
And Gautier the Hothead, too,
Baudon, Huart, and Marion.

PERONNELLE   Should I put on my party dress?

ROBIN   No, no, no—you're not to bother.
That outfit suits you very well.   270
But hurry up—I'll go ahead.

PERONNELLE   Go on, I'll follow straightaway,
As soon as I've rounded up my sheep.

(*Robin and Peronnelle go behind the wood. The Knight
returns to the 'place'. He no longer has the falcon, but carries
a game bird. He approaches Marion.*)

KNIGHT   Hallo, my dear, aren't you the girl,
   The one I saw this very morning?

MARION   For heaven's sake, sir, get along!
   I'll take it as a courtesy.

KNIGHT   Easy, now, my dearest one;
   I don't intend you any harm.
   I've come downstream to look around   280
   For a bird with a bell on its leg.

MARION   Go along this little hedge—
   I think that you will find it there.
   It's only this moment flown that way.

KNIGHT   On your honour?

MARION   Yes, absolutely.

KNIGHT   I wouldn't care for the bird, you know
   If I had a lovely girl like you.

MARION   For heaven's sake, sir, go away,
   I'm quite terrified, can't you see?

KNIGHT   Who're you afraid of?   290

MARION   Robin, of course.

KNIGHT   What, *him*!

MARION   Yes, indeed, for if he knew,
   He wouldn't love me any longer;
   And I love him more than all the world.

KNIGHT   You needn't be afraid of anyone,
    If you're willing to listen to me.

MARION   If you go on, they'll catch us at it.
    Get away, do! Just let me alone
    I've nothing I want to say to you:
    Just leave me to mind my sheep in peace!

KNIGHT   Really, I have descended low—   300
    Bandying words with a girl like you.

MARION   It'll be best for you to go.
    Besides, I can hear people coming.

(*sings*)

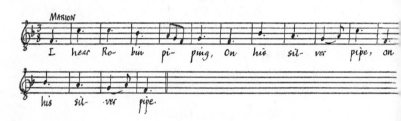

MARION

I hear Ro-bin pi-ping, On his sil-ver pipe, on his sil-ver pipe.

For heaven's sake get away from here!

KNIGHT   Shepherdess, goodbye! God bless you!
    I will not press you any more.

(*He retires and meets Robin, who clutches his falcon.*)

    You stupid lout! You've got it coming!
    Why are you massacring my falcon?
    If someone were to give you a beating
    It'd be the best thing he could do!   310

ROBIN   Easy, sir, you'd do me a wrong.
    I'm only afraid it might escape.

KNIGHT   Well, take this punch on the chin for hire
Since you're handling him so well!

(*The Knight beats Robin.*)

ROBIN   Help, help, for heaven's sake, help!

KNIGHT   What's that noise for? Take this too! (*boxes his ears.*)

MARION   Holy Mary! It's Robin's voice!
I think he must have been waylaid.
I'd rather lose my flock of sheep,   320
Than fail to help him in his trouble.
Oh Lord, I see the knight, I think;
He's beaten Robin on my account.

(*Marion runs to join them.*)

Robin, sweetheart, what are you doing?

ROBIN   Darling, he's killed me, he really has.

MARION   For God's sake, sir! It's a wicked thing
To have beaten the poor boy up like that.

KNIGHT   And how has he been treating my bird,
I ask you. Just look at it, my girl!

MARION   He doesn't know the right technique.   330
Please, sir, please! Don't treat him harshly!

KNIGHT   I won't then—*if* you'll come with me.

MARION   That I won't!

KNIGHT   I think you will.
I don't want any other girl,
And this is the horse to carry you off.

(*The Knight carries off Marion as she protests.*)

MARION   Then you'll do me a violence!
    Robin, why don't you rescue me?

ROBIN (*alone*)   O God, help me! Now everything's lost!
    My friends will be along too late.
    I've lost Marion—got a clout on the ear,   340
    And torn my jacket, and my coat.

(*Gautier approaches the 'place', singing, together with Baudon.*)

GAUTIER (*sings*)

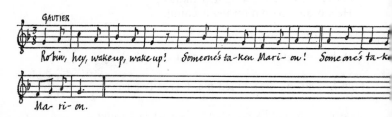

(*They enter*)

ROBIN   Oh dear, oh dear, is that you Gautier?
    Everything's lost! Marion's gone.

GAUTIER   Well, why don't you go and get her back?

ROBIN   Keep quiet! He would rush on us,
    Even if we were four *hundred* strong!
    It's a knight—right out of his mind—
    He carries a colossal sword.   350
    He gave me such a blow just now—
    I shan't forget it for a while!

BAUDON   If I had come along in time,
　He would have got himself a fight.

ROBIN   Now, let us see what becomes of them.
　I've got it! We must hide ourselves,
　All three of us, behind the bushes
　(For I *do* want to rescue Marion,
　Provided you two will stand by me.)
　I feel my courage coming back.   360

(*They all hide behind the wood and watch. The Knight brings
Marion back to the 'place' and tries to make love to her.*)

MARION   I must ask you—please get away
　From me! And do the proper thing.

KNIGHT   That I will not, my dear, for sure.
　Rather, I'll carry you off with me,
　And you shall have a—you know what.
　Don't you be so high and mighty!
　Look, take this bird, which I have caught
　Down by the river; it's yours to eat.

MARION   I far prefer my own fat cheese,
　And my bread, and my juicy apples—   370
　Not your bird for all its feathers.
　You can't get round me with anything.

KNIGHT   Is that so? Is there really nothing
　That I can do to give you pleasure?

MARION   You can be absolutely certain,
　There's nothing. Your case is hopeless—quite.

KNIGHT   Well, my dear, I'll say 'God bless you'.
　Really, I'm making an ass of myself,
　By coming down to an ass's level.
　Farewell, shepherdess!   380

(*He leaves the 'place'.*)

MARION (*alone*)   Good bye!
   Oh dear, now Robin's sure to be cross.
   He's bound to think he's lost me.

ROBIN (*from behind the wood*)   Hoo-ooh!

MARION   Heavens! That must be Robin calling.
   Robin, my darling, are you all right?

(*Robin, Gautier and Baudon emerge from behind the wood.*)

ROBIN   Marion, I'm happy as I can be
   And quite recovered, now I see you.

MARION   Come along here and give me a hug.

ROBIN   I will, darling, if that's what you want.

MARION   Now just look at this madman here—
   Kissing me right in front of them all!   390

BAUDON   Marion, you know, we're his relations;
   You need not be afraid of us!

MARION   It isn't you I'm worried about.
   But he's really such a lunatic,
   That he'd do it in front of all the folk
   In the village, just as he did here.

ROBIN   And who could resist it?

MARION   Not again!
   You see how impudent he is?

ROBIN   I reckon I'd be pretty tough,
   If that gentleman returned.   400

MARION   Really, dear? And to what end?
You don't even know what trick I used
To get away.

ROBIN   Oh, yes I do.
We watched everything that you did—
You ask Baudon here, my cousin,
And Gautier, when I saw you go,
What trouble they had to hold me back!
Three times I got away from 'em both!

GAUTIER   Robin, you are amazingly brave;
But now the affair is happily over,   410
It's better forgotten altogether.
Let's not go through it all again.

BAUDON   Now we'll wait for Huart to come,
And Peronnelle; they're on their way.
Look, here they come!

(*Enter Peronnelle and Huart.*)

GAUTIER   It's them all right.
Huart! Your bagpipes, did you bring them?

HUART   Yes I did.

MARION   Hallo, Perrette.

PERONNELLE   Hallo, Marion, it's good to see you!

MARION   We've been longing to have you with us;
Now it's time the singing began.   420

THE COMPANY (*sings*)

In this compa- ny so   merry, We shall, we shall happy be.

BAUDON   Have we all arrived, at last?

HUART   Yes.

MARION   Now let us choose a game.

HUART   Shall we play at 'Kings and Queens'?

MARION   Or, perhaps, some present-giving game—
The kind we play round Christmas Eve?

HUART   Saint Coisne, then?

BAUDON   That's a good idea.

MARION   It's a nasty game—a silly farce!

HUART   Mind you keep your face straight, then!   430

MARION   Well, who will tell us how to play?

HUART   I will, surely. Whoever laughs,
When he 'offers' before the saint,
Has to sit in Saint Coisne's place;
The one who gets away has won.

GAUTIER   Who shall it be?

ROBIN   Me.

BAUDON   All right, then.
    Gautier, you 'offer' first!

(Robin sits on the hillock as 'Saint Coisne'. Gautier kneels before him in solemn pretence of making a religious offering. The rest try to provoke him to laugh.)

GAUTIER   Receive, Saint Coisne, this offering!
    E'en if but little you may profit,
    Receive!

ROBIN   Ah! He's lost. He's laughing.   440

GAUTIER   All right, I was.

HUART   Marion, your turn !

MARION   Who's sainted now?

HUART   It's Gautier.

(Gautier takes Robin's place. Marion and the rest 'offer' in turn.)

MARION   Receive, Saint Coisne, reverend Sire.

HUART   Heavens! She's managed not to laugh!
    Who's next? Come on, Peronnelle.

PERONNELLE   Saint Coisne, reverend Sire, receive.
    I bring this offering here to thee.

ROBIN   You're doing very well indeed.
    Now you, Huart! And you, Baudon!

BAUDON   Receive, Saint Coisne, this fine gift!   450

GAUTIER   You're laughing, idiot! Now you're 'out'.
    U

BAUDON   I'm not!

GAUTIER   Huart, your turn.

HUART   Coming.
  Here are two shillings.

GAUTIER   That's no good.

HUART   Now, quiet, you! Stay where you are!
  I haven't even *begun* to laugh.

GAUTIER   What's that, Huart? Do you want a quarrel?
  You're always asking for a beating.
  You'll be sorry you ever came!
  Now pay up quick, and don't be awkward.

HUART   All right, I don't mind, I'll pay.   460

(*Huart takes Gautier's place and Robin 'offers'.*)

ROBIN   Receive, Saint Coisne! (Is it settled?)

MARION   Ho! You lot! This game's a bore.
  What do *you* think, Peronnelle?

PERONNELLE   I agree.
  Surely, it would be very much nicer
  To play some other little game—
  Here we are: two of us girls,
  And, between you, four men, too.

GAUTIER   Why don't we fart to amuse ourselves?
  I can't think of anything better.

ROBIN   Gautier!
  A fine idea of fun you have—   470
  In front of Marion my sweetheart,
  To mention such a filthy thing.
  You must have a dirty nose,
  If you really think that's funny.
  Don't you let it occur again!

GAUTIER   All right, forget it! Let's not quarrel.

BAUDON   And now, a game.

HUART   What's your idea?

BAUDON   If Gautier will help, I want
  To play the game of 'Kings and Queens'.
  I shall ask some splendid questions   480
  If you're willing to make me King.

HUART   Certainly not, by all that's holy,
  We'll count out to decide the thing.

GAUTIER   All right, have it your own way!
  The person who gets the 'ten' is King.

HUART   I think we're generally agreed?
  Well then! Let's put our hands in a ring.

(*They stand in a circle and each puts out an arm towards the
centre. As they number off they raise their arms in the air
and drop them again in turn.*)

BAUDON   Is that all right? Are we all ready?
  Who shall begin?

HUART   Gautier.

GAUTIER   I am perfectly happy to start: 490
    Number one.

HUART   And two.

ROBIN   And three.

BAUDON   And four.

HUART   You next, Marion! Don't waste time talking.

MARION   All right—sorry!—And five.

PERONNELLE   And six.

GAUTIER   And seven.

HUART   And eight.

ROBIN   And nine.

BAUDON   And ten.
    There we are! Gentlemen, I'm King.

GAUTIER   Holy Mother, how appropriate!
    I think we all accept the fact.

ROBIN   Up with him! He must be crowned.

(*Robin, Gautier and Huart ceremoniously lift Baudon on to the
hillock for the 'coronation'.*)

    That's good!

HUART   Peronnelle, be a darling!
    Since he hasn't got a crown,
    Present the King with your straw hat.   500

PERONNELLE   Take it, Your Highness.

(*King Baudon is crowned with Peronnelle's hat. He summons each of them in turn before him.*)

KING BAUDON   Gautier,
   Come to court! Quickly, come!

GAUTIER   With pleasure, sir: yours to command!
   Anything that I can do, sir,
   Be it not against my will,
   I will expedite for you.

KING BAUDON   Tell me—were you ever jealous?
   (Robin's the next one I shall summon).

GAUTIER   Yes, sir, I was—of a certain cur,   510
   That I heard knocking on one occasion
   At the door of my sweetheart's room—
   I had my suspicions it was—a man!

KING BAUDON   Come on, Robin.

ROBIN   King, welcome!
   Put to me any question you like.

KING BAUDON   Robin, when an animal's born
   How do you tell that it's a female?

ROBIN   Well, that's a fine question to ask!

KING BAUDON   Come on, answer!

ROBIN   I certainly won't.
   But if you really want to know,   520
   Your Majesty, look at the tail.
   You'll get no details out of me;
   Are you trying to make me blush?

MARION   Robin's quite right.

KING BAUDON   Who asked you to speak?

MARION   All right, but it's a dirty question.

KING BAUDON   Marion, I wish him to fulfil
  His deep desire.

ROBIN   I dare not.

KING BAUDON   No?
  Go on, give Marion a kiss,
  As tender as she likes it to be!

MARION   Look at the fool! He's kissing me!   530

ROBIN   I'm not really.

MARION   You are a fibber!
  The mark's still there—just have a look!
  I think he's bitten me in the face.

ROBIN   I thought I had my teeth in a cheese,
  When I felt you soft and tender!
  Come here, sweetheart, and give me a hug
  And make it up.

MARION   You silly devil,
  You've no more sense than a lump of wood.

ROBIN   Now, for Christ's sake!

MARION   *You*'re angry, are you?   540
  Come over here, and calm yourself down.
  I won't say another word about it.
  Don't be so abashed and sheepish!

KING BAUDON   Come to court, Huart! Come!

HUART   I'm coming, since your Highness wishes.

KING BAUDON   Now say, Huart, as God is your judge,
   What kind of food do you like the most?
   I shall know if you're telling me the truth.

HUART   Good rump of pork, heavy in fat,
   With a strong nut-and-garlic sauce.
   I ate so much the other day   550
   It turned my bowels upside-down.

KING BAUDON   Ooh! But gorgeous venison!
   Just like Huart to talk like that.

HUART   Peronnelle, come to court!

PERONNELLE   I daren't.

KING BAUDON   Yes, you must, Peronnelle! Now tell me
   By the allegiance you owe to me,
   The greatest joy you ever had
   In love, wherever it may have been.
   Speak now, speak! I shall you hear.

PERONNELLE   Your Majesty, why, willingly.   560
   I swear it is when my dear love
   Who's given me his heart and hand,
   Keeps honest company, a-field
   With me, amongst my flock of sheep;
   Not once, but many, many times.

KING BAUDON   That's *all*?

PERONNELLE   It is, it is.

HUART   The liar!

KING BAUDON   By God, I really do believe you!
Marion, your turn! Come to court!

MARION   Make sure you ask me something nice!

KING BAUDON   Of course, I will. Now, Marionette,   570
Tell me how much you love young Robin,
My cousin here, this splendid fellow.
(Evil to those who tell a lie!)

MARION   I promise you I'll tell the truth:
I love him, Sir, with a love so deep,
I love him more than I love my sheep—
Even this one, with the little lamb.

KING BAUDON   I must admit he's loved a lot;
I'd like it to be widely known.

GAUTIER   Marion, something awful's happening—   580
The wolf is stealing one of your sheep.

MARION   Robin, quickly, run, my dear,
Before the wolf has gobbled her up.

ROBIN   Gautier, lend me your heavy stick—
You'll see what a gallant squire is like!

(*Robin runs out of the 'place'.*)

Ho, there! Ho, there! Wolf, wolf, wolf!

(*Robin returns to the 'place' with a sheep in his arms.*)

Well then, who said I was a coward?
Here you are, Marion.

MARION   The poor, poor thing!
She's come back looking very poorly.   590

ROBIN   Just look at her, how dirty she is!

MARION   How *are* you holding the animal?
Her bottom's right up by her head.

ROBIN   What does it matter? There wasn't much time
When I picked her up, Now, Marion, feel
Where the wolf got hold of her.

GAUTIER   You'd better look where she's been pricked!

MARION   Gautier, you're a dirty lout.

ROBIN   Marion, hold her in your hands:
Be careful that she doesn't bite!

MARION   No, no, I won't! She's far too dirty;   600
Just let her wander back to the field.

BAUDON   Do you know, Robin, what I would say?
If you really love your Marionette
As much as it appears you do,
Then candidly I would advise
That you should take her, if Gautier's willing.

GAUTIER   I'm quite willing.

ROBIN   That's what I want.

BAUDON   Take her, then!

ROBIN   Is it up to me?

BAUDON   Yes, no one's going to interfere.

MARION   Hey, Robin! You're squeezing me to death.   610
Can't you learn to behave yourself?

BAUDON   It really rather surprises me
That Perrette isn't jealous of them.

PERONNELLE   Who? Me? No man I know
Ever concerned himself with me.

BAUDON   There *could* be one. Yes, there's a chance,
If you were willing to try it out.

PERONNELLE   Nonsense! Who?

BAUDON   Why me, or Gautier.

HUART   No, I'm your man, Perrette, my dear.

GAUTIER   It's true, I must admit, at *piping*   620
No-one on earth can rival you.
But I'm the owner of a cart-horse
Good harness, harrow, and a plough;
And I'm the big man in our street.
I've top-coat and overcoat, all to match,
And Mother owns a drinking-cup
Which'll come to me, when she is dead;
And a steady income which she's paid,
In grain, for the letting of a windmill;
And a cow which gives us every day   630
All the milk and cheese we need.
Don't you think I'm eligible?
What do you say, Perrette?

PERONNELLE   Why, yes
But I wouldn't dare to 'go with' anyone.
It's because of my brother Guiot;
You and he are a pair of madmen—
We'd very soon have a fight on our hands.

GAUTIER   If you don't want me, I don't care.
Let's attend to this other wedding.

HUART   Peronnelle, what've you got in these 'bumps'? 640

PERONNELL   Bread, and salt, and water-cress.

(*Peronnelle produces her items for the picinic from her dress.
The others bring out food from satchels and pockets.*)

   Have you got anything, Marion?

MARION   Nothing, honestly,—you ask Robin—
   Except a bit of this morning's cheese,
   And some bread which got left over,
   And some apples which Robin brought:
   Here you are, look—if they're any use.

GAUTIER   Who'd like a pair of salty hams?

HUART   Hams? Where?

GAUTIER   Here, I've got them by me.

PERONNELLE   And I've a couple of cheeses—fresh
    ones.   650

HUART   Tell us what kind they are!

PERONNELLE   They're sheep's.

ROBIN   Friends, I have some roasted peas.

HUART   Do you think you'll get away with that?

ROBIN   Oh no, I've got baked apples, too;
   Marion, would you like to have some?

MARION   Is that *all*?

ROBIN   No.

MARION   Tell me, be honest,
What is it you've been hiding from me?

ROBIN (*sings*)   658

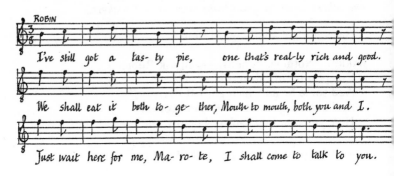

Marion, do you want more from me?

MARION   Yes, please go on!

ROBIN   I'll say this then:

(*sings*)

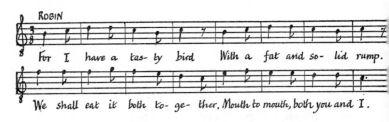

MARION   Robin, come back as quick as you can.   672

ROBIN   Dearest one, I will, I will.
And in the meantime help yourselves
Till I come back—that's the thing!

MARION   No Robin, it wouldn't be polite;
 To be sure, I'd rather wait for you.

ROBIN   Oh, don't do that! But spread your coat
 On the ground for a table-cloth,
 And then put all your food out on it.   680
 I shall be back here in a flash.

(*Robin runs out of the 'place'.*)

MARION   Spread out *your* coat, *dear* Peronnelle!
 It looks much cleaner than my own.

PERONNELLE   All right, Marion. I'm quite willing,
 If you really want me to.
 Take hold your end! It's ready, look!
 Spread it out wherever you like.

HUART   Now! Good people, kindly bring
 Your contributions over here!

PERONNELLE   Look, Marion! Look, over there! 690
 If I'm not wrong, I see Robin coming.

MARION   You're right. He's dancing his way along.
 Don't you think he's a lovely fellow?

PERONNELLE   Honestly, Marion, he's awfully nice,
 And puts himself out to make you happy.

MARION   He's bringing the men who play the horn.
 Look!

HUART   Where are they?

GAUTIER   Don't you see them
 Holding their two instruments there?

HUART   By all that's holy, I certainly do.

(*Robin re-enters the 'place', carrying bagpipes and bringing two musicians.*)

ROBIN   Here I am, Marion, Now, look   700
   Tell me!—Do you really love me?

MARION   I do, really.

ROBIN   Thank you, darling
   Thank you for saying it so frankly.

MARION   Hey! What are those there?

ROBIN   They're bagpipes.
   I got them in the village. Hold it,
   Now, isn't it a pretty thing?

MARION   Robin, please love, sit down here!
   And your companions over there.

ROBIN   Sweetheart, with the greatest pleasure.

MARION   Now let us really enjoy ourselves.   710
   Take a bite, my dearest one!
   Hey! Gautier! What are you thinking?

GAUTIER   Honestly, I was thinking of Robin.
   For if we two had not been cousins,
   I would have loved you, truly I would.
   You have the daintiest little figure—
   Baudon, just look what a body she has!

ROBIN   Gautier, kindly remove your hand!
   Marion does not belong to you.

GAUTIER   Are you jealous already, Robin?   720

ROBIN   Yes, I am.

MARION   Don't worry, Robin.

ROBIN   I can still see him fondling you.

MARION   Gautier, please behave yourself!
    I don't care for your playing about.
    Now, give your attention to the party.

GAUTIER   I'm very good at singing ballads.
    Would you like to hear me sing?

BAUDON   Yes.

GAUTIER   Well then, listen to me.

(*sings*)

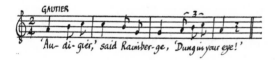

'Au-di-gier,' said Raimber-ge, 'Dung in your eye!'

ROBIN   Now Gautier! That's enough of that!   730
    Ugh, tell me, won't you ever grow up?
    You're singing like some filthy minstrel.

GAUTIER   I pity the fool who makes a joke
    At the expense of my fine phrases!
    Didn't you think my song was good?

ROBIN   Certainly not!

PERONNELLE   Come on, let's dance,
    The farandole! Robin shall lead,
    If he doesn't mind, and Huart will pipe;
    The other two will play their horns.

MARION   Quickly, let's pick up all these things.   740
    And now, please Robin, lead us off.

ROBIN   Good Lord! You do impose on me!

MARION   Go on! There's a hug for you!

ROBIN   You'll see me a master of my trade
    As a result of your kissing me!
    But first we ought to dance together,
    The two of us—we dance very well.

MARION   Very well, since you desire it.
    Come on! Keep your hand to your side.

(*The musicians play. Robin leads the company in a dance.*)

    Splendid! Robin, that *was* well danced!   750

ROBIN   Was that a good dance, Marion?

MARION   It *was*! My heart goes hippety hop
    When I see you dancing so beautifully.

ROBIN   Now I'm ready to lead the farandole.

MARION   You're ready indeed, my dearest one.

ROBIN   Now all you gentlemen, stand by!
    Just wait a bit! I'll go in front.
    Marion, lend me your glove.
    I'll dance all the better for it.

PERONNELLE   My word, it's going marvellously: 760
    You should be lauded to the skies!

(*Robin leads them in a chain dance around the 'place',
behind the wood and off.*)

ROBIN (*sings*)

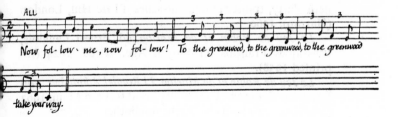

Now fol-low me, now fol-low! To the greenwood, to the greenwood, to the greenwood take your way.

X

Texts

Adam de la Halle, *Le Jeu de Robin et de Marion,* ed. Kenneth Varty, transcriptions musicales d'Eric Hill, London (Harrap), 1960.

— *Le Jeu de Robin et de Marion,* éd. Ernest Langlois, Classiques Français du Moyen Age, 2e éd. 1924 (reprinted 1958).

— *Le Jeu de Robin et de Marion. Li Rondel Adam,* her. von Friedrich Gennrich, Langen bei Frankfurt am Main, 1962 (Musikwissenschaftliche Studienbibliothek, Hft. 20).

— *Le Jeu de la Feuillée & Le Jeu de Robin et Marion,* adaptés par Ernest Langlois, Editions Boccard, Paris, 1964.

— *Oeuvres complètes du trouvère Adam de la Halle,* éd. E. de Coussemaker, Paris, 1872.

Staging and interpretation

Jacques Chailley, 'La nature musicale du *Jeu de Robin et Marion', Mélanges d'histoire du théâtre du Moyen-Age et de la Renaissance offerts à G. Cohen,* Paris, 1950, pp. 111–17.

Ernest Langlois, 'Le jeu du Roi qui ne ment et le jeu du Roi et de la Reine', *Mélanges Chabaneau (Romanische Forschungen,* XXIII), Erlangen, 1907.

Gilbert Mayer, *Lexique des oeuvres d'Adam de la Halle,* Paris, 1940.

Record

The songs of *Le Jeu de Robin et Marion* are recorded by the Pro Musica Antiqua of Brussels on Archive (History of Music Division of the Deutsche Grammophon Gesellschaft) ARC 3002.

THE NOTES TO THE PLAYS

LE JEU D'ADAM

In the Introductory stage-directions God is referred to as *Salvator*, thereafter as *Figura*. This could mean, as Auerbach has suggested (*Mimesis*, ch. 7) that God is seen as a prefiguration of his own son, *Figura Salvatoris*. It is more likely a way of avoiding blasphemy: the actor is only the shadow or 'figure' of God.

In principio: this lesson for Matins of Sexagesima would have been Genesis I, 1-27, and would have been intoned. It may be sung, or said, in Latin or English.

280-6. The division of the dialogue between Adam and Eve is clearly faulty in the MS. at this point. We have followed Aebischer.

290. Adam refers of course to the fall of angels.

382. With this poignant anachronism the poet makes Adam the first of the prophets of Christ.

400. Half a line is missing in the MS. We have translated Studer's conjecture.

489. Root: i.e. the stem of Jesse, the lineage of Christ, visualized later in the Prophet play.

546. Line supplied from an emendation adopted in Studer's edition.

LA SEINTE RESURECCION

13. The Guards do not belong at the Tomb until they are sent there (391). Their 'place' is obviously with Pilate's 'chivalry'. The Expositor mentions the Guard by association perhaps.

22. The Tower of David is not mentioned in the Paris prologue. In 1185, the Patriarch of Jerusalem urged Henry II of England to lead a force against the Mohammedan warrior Saladin, offering him in return the keys of the Holy Sepulchre and of the Tower of David. Thus the inclusion of this Tower may be of topical English interest as well as being an attempt at local colour. Bartholomew is probably included as being a saint specially revered at Canterbury.

43. Hercules: (from *P*; the *C* scribe wrote *Herodes*). This probably refers to the second and tenth labours.

203-4. The Anglo-Norman Text Society editors note that these lines on the Immaculate Conception are probably a late addition to the original text and closely follow a well-known Latin formula, attributed to St. Bernard, for the paradox.

325–6. The Easter Sepulchres of English churches were often hung with crimson palls whose inner white lining, revealed on Easter Day, symbolized the miracle of the Resurrection after the blood of the Passion. The liturgical symbolism of colour is still in use today.

428. The *P* fragment ends here.

443–8. These two feats were considered by the medieval Church as prefigurations of Christ's Easter triumph over death.

LE JEU DE SAINT NICOLAS

(W indicates F. J. Warnes's edition, H, Albert Henry's).

5. the Confessor: i.e. who professed the faith. According to tradition St. Nicholas was Bishop of Myra in Asia Minor around 325 A.D.

8. Life: Wace's *Vie de Saint Nicolas* (Anglo-Norman, c. 1150), which has many features in common with the play, is the likeliest of several.

12ff. This account does not quite tally with what happens in the play. This is one of the reasons Henry gives for doubting the authenticity of the Prologue.

105. i.e. Dec. 5.

126. A strikingly, but characteristically, anomalous reference.

167. This is line 170 in W. T.B.W. Reid has shown that the line was misplaced by the scribe of the MS.

200. This odd form of binding oath is attributed to Saracens in other medieval texts.

231. Prester John: (Presbyter John) an Eastern king, a Christian of fabulous wealth and power.

254. Arras taverns used a barrel hoop as their emblem. Presumably Benedictine monks were notorious drinkers.

258. The price of wine was strictly controlled by local magistrates.

274ff. Though for small quantities wine prices could be reckoned in (the equivalent of) farthings, there was no coinage smaller than a halfpenny.

300. 'Highest Points': Fr. *as plus poins*. The highest throw (here, Auberon's) wins.

316. Coine: the ancient Iconium in Phrygia, now Konieh.

322. Orkenie: Hyrcania(?) in ancient Persia.

328. Oliferne: Aleppo, where Holofernes had his head cut off by Judith while he slept.

333. Withered Tree: Fr. *Arbre sec*, a tree near Hebron, said to have been blighted at the moment of Christ's death.

349. Mahound: Mahomet.

355. Fields of Nero: *Prata Neronis* (now the Vatican Field around St. Peter's), the site of Nero's circus and scene of a great massacre of

Christians. At about the time of the play, Pope Innocent III had the Vatican rebuilt and its famous gardens were surrounded with a great wall.

447. Berengiers: proverbial figure of fabulous strength, reaper or blacksmith.

454 s.d. The unbracketed direction is the only one in the original MS.

458. The first of a number of derisive references to the 'horns' of the mitre on St. Nicholas' image. A miniature in the MS. of the play shows the Saint wearing such a cloven mitre.

604, 609. The City was the quarter around the Cathedral; the Town a separate area around the Abbey of St. Vaast. Clashes of jurisdiction were apparently of frequent occurrence.

704-9. This exchange is notoriously obscure because of the use of slang words and multiple puns. Our version owes most to Henry's comments.

748. CAIGNET (H) MS. and W give to Rasoir.

764. RASOIR (H) MS. and W give to Pincedé.

813. See above, 281.

815. Cf. 679-80, where Cliquet accepted the Taverner's 'rounded-off' reckoning of fivepence.

817. For elevenpence borrowed Cliquet must pay back twelve. See below, 1329.

831. RASOIR (H) MS. gives to Cliquet (obviously wrong) and W to Pincedé.

852. PINCEDÉ (H) MS. and W give to Rasoir.

884. PINCEDÉ (H) MS. and W give to Cliquet.

944. Cf. 693.

1016. H corrects W's *Preu* to *Pren*.

1060. Rasoir means, of course, that they should begin to use the treasure, which they have stolen at the risk of being hanged. But to touch a hangman's rope was a superstitious practice ensuring luck at gambling.

1062. Hazard is explained below, 1111.

1074-93. The first game is merely to decide who has the first turn at Hazard. Pincedé wins the dice with 17.

1111ff. *Hazard.* The numbers from 3 to 7 and from 14 to 18 are Hazard numbers. The thrower wins outright if his first three dice give him a total within the Hazard numbers. If, however, on his second throw he gets a Hazard number, he loses. If, as is more likely, he gets Hazard with neither, then his first total becomes his opponents' 'chance' and the second his own 'chance'. He continues to throw until he repeats one of these two numbers; if it is the first, he loses, if it is the second, he wins.

Cliquet hopes (1112) that Pincedé will get 7 with the first two dice because the third dice would be bound to bring him a total between

8 and 13. Pincedé calls for Hazard—or a 16 (an upper Hazard) will do as well! His first 13 is claimed by Rasoir as his and Cliquet's 'chance' (1114); they would now like Pincedé to get Hazard. On his second throw Pincedé calls out to claim the fallen dice (1117) because he sees that with a 3 for the first his chances of getting between 8 and 13 for the total are better than if he risked a rethrow. He gets 8 safely and this becomes his 'chance'.

Pincedé then throws several more times (the number and the totals inferred from the players' comments are uncertain) until he finally repeats his 8 (1139) and wins.

1142. Cf. 796.

1151–2. We have followed H's interpretation of these lines.

1269–70. These lines have the character of a 'refrain' and may have been intended to be sung; some editors believe them to be an interpolation.

1305. A common man's garbling of the Latin formula.

1329. See note above, 817.

1370. Fresnes-les-Montauban, 8 miles N.East of Arras.

1371. Gavrelle, 6 miles N.East of Arras.

1404. Herakles: probably Heraclius, Byzantine Emperor of the seventh century.

1429–30. These further miracles of St. Nicholas are related in contemporary Latin plays (*Tres Filiae, Tres Clerici*).

1460. We have adopted Reid's emendation *tant t'ai respité*.

1476–7. MS., H and W give to King. Reid suggests this is a mistake.

1478, 1482. EMIR OF ORKENIE (MS. and H). W gives to Withered Tree.

1498, 1500, 1505, 1506, 1512. The speakers follow H's emendation. W follows the rubricator of the MS., who probably inverted the names of the two Emirs. It is the outlandish giant who gives so much trouble.

1517–20. The nonsense language Tervagan speaks is similar to that used by Salatin to conjure up the Devil (*Théophile*, 160–8).

COURTOIS D'ARRAS

26. The game mentioned here (*tremeriel*) is something like backgammon, involving both draughts and dice.

75. *Hazard:* the dice game played by the thieves in *Saint Nicolas* (see note to line 1111).

81. Lenoir died in 1228, possible *terminus ad quem* for the play's composition. His wealth was apparently 'tied' by some legal restriction.

90. In one MS. there follows here a scene of 36 lines in which Courtois' sister pleads with his father in vain not to turn the boy out of doors.

103. Soissons wine is praised in the thirteenth-century *La disputoison du vin et de l'iaue* (Debate between wine and water).

147 s.d. These three lines belong to the 'A' text but were excluded from Faral's edition on the grounds that they do not occur in any of the other three MSS.

179–80. The inversion of these lines is authenticated in two of the MSS.

195. Lit. 'it's not made of lime or aspen'. These were apparently held to be unlucky (or perhaps poisonous?) woods to drink from. According to tradition, Judas hanged himself on an aspen or elder.

207. Cf. *Saint Nicolas*, 253, *Feuillée*, 914.

213. The wine of Rochelle is condemned in the *Debate between wine and water* as being sweet and weak.

220–5. There is some obscurity in the original here, owing to the *double entendre*. Mancevaire's feigned (or real) shock proves that the obscenity is intended.

247. Sir Gawain: the knight of Arthurian romance, renowned as *le Chevalier aux demoiselles*.

290. Malta is cited as a land of wealth and luxurious delights.

358–9. Renard the fox was the hero and Isengrin the wolf his traditional enemy in the twelfth-century beast-epic, *Roman de Renart*.

360–1. Possibly allusions to historical persons.

394. Béthune: a village some twenty miles from Arras.

471. Saint Rémi: 1st October.

664. *Te Deum:* Liturgical church plays were most often played at the end of Matins, immediately before the *Te Deum*. The practice of ending with the *Te Deum* was borrowed by the popular vernacular drama.

LE MIRACLE DE THÉOPHILE

16off. A magical formula, apparently meaningless as a whole, but containing some words resembling Hebrew and Arabic. Cf. *Saint Nicolas*, 1517.

390. Lit. 'I am caught upon the elder'. According to one tradition Judas hanged himself on an elder. The contrast in Théophile's mind is also between the sweet 'balm' of Christian life and the sourness of elderberries, symbolic of betrayal and despair.

566. Lit. 'With Cahu' (a Saracen god mentioned in the *chansons de geste*).

585 s.d. This action is depicted in the sculpture of the miracle above the north porch of Notre-Dame in Paris.

663. *Te Deum*. Cf. *Courtois*, 664.

LE GARÇON ET L'AVEUGLE

33. St. Gilain: Ghislain, also known as Gislenus, Flemish hermit and martyr of the seventh century.

63–4. This may just mean 'the true soldiers of Christ', but it is more likely to refer to those serving in Sicily (83). The 'king's own son' may be Charles I of Anjou (the *roy de sesile*), brother of Louis IX. His royal parentage is specifically mentioned by Adam de la Halle in his epic *Du roi de Sezile* and by Rutebeuf in his *Diz*. Charles called up troops in 1265–6 to enforce his claim in Sicily. Alternatively, the reference may be to Charles' son, the Prince of Salerne, who commanded troops in the invasion of Sicily after the Vespers Massacre in 1282.

83. See note above.

129. We have assumed that the obscure original reference to one *Gillot* is to a local dandy.

175–6; 183–4. The lines are obscure; no satisfactory interpretation has yet been proposed.

191. Ramegnies, Village N. of Tournai.

LE JEU DE LA FEUILLÉE

General Note
Most, probably all, of the people referred to in the dialogue of the play are historical persons who actually lived in Arras. Many of them have been identified as members of the *Carité des Ardents* (a fascinating study of the Arras background to the *Feuilleé* has been made by Marie Ungureaunu, in *La bourgeoisie naissante*). However, proper names referred to in the dialogue will not be commented upon unless the meaning of a passage is in question.

11. Adam's proverb is deliberately mystifying. The broken pot is an image for his own life and for his wife, whose lovely former shape and beauty he pays tribute to behind the grotesque catalogue of features he describes, 86ff.

52. The French has a conventional phrase used by master architects.

170. Adam puns on *Vaucheles* (Little Valleys), the name of a village near Arras and also of the Cistercian abbey in the diocese of Cambrai. Is this an obscure reference to Adam's own schooling? Or did Adam's wife come from the local Vauchelles-les-Authie? This reading would underline the double meaning intended in *le grant saveur de Vaucheles*.

194. The French *K'i a*? has the same obscene double meaning when spoken quickly.

213ff. Most of the names mentioned here with hatred are of influential *bourgeois* and patrician families.

234. Saint Leonard's disease: presumably obesity, but St. Leonard also freed debtors from chains. Henri may need his help.

271. Rainelet is redheaded and so, like Judas, quarrelsome and traitorous.

404–5. The *Puy* was the exclusive literary society of Arras. Its members were mostly patrician families and the wealthier *bourgeois*.

Robert Sommeillons was a rich burgher and probably a successful rival of Adam's in song competitions.

414. The instrument referred to here in the original text is the *cornett*. See *Robin et Marion*, 698, and the Introduction to that play, p. 262.

425. The Idiot's Father apparently refers to the ladies in the audience rather than to the (not very imminent) arrival of the Fairies.

426ff. The bigamists: this refers to tonsured *clercs* (those who had received the tonsure as a sign of their clerical education, but who were not in orders) who had married more than once, or had married widows or prostitutes. In 1274, at the Pope's instigation, 'bigamous' *clercs* were stripped of all ecclesiastical privileges, including exemptions (448) from secular justice and from civil taxes. It seems that for the purposes of Arras taxation married *clercs* who pursued certain commercial activities were considered in the same category as *bigames*. In all events, the honesty of one's wife was the crucial factor.

434. Almost certainly Pope Gregory X (*d.* 1276).

468–9. The precise meaning of the obscenity is obscure. Married clerks were said to have left the 'flower' to feed on dung, like the *escarbot* (dung beetle).

502. Marie le Jaie: Marie or Marion 'Magpie', possibly Henri's daughter-in-law, Adam's wife.

536. Hesselin: an Arras *jongleur*, singer of *chansons de geste.* Anseïs: King of France in Bodel's *Chanson des Saxons*. Marsile: Saracen King of Spain (*Chanson de Roland* etc.).

561. Cf. Chaucer's *Wife of Bath's Tale*, 8ff.

578. Hellekin's people: in folk-lore mischievous and murderous night-riding spirits with diabolical associations, specially active at midsummer.

589. Rainelet's exit is confirmed by the fact that he has no more lines to speak. He is terrified of the Fairies because it is they who will eventually promise to help Dame Douce to beat him up for his part in revealing her scandal (858ff.).

590. Crokesos's opening line, *Me siet il bien li hurepiaus?* is apparently intended to be sung, though there is no musical notation in the MS. *Hurepiaus* (the word is not found elsewhere) may be some kind of head-dress or possibly a cape. The words may be an echo of the magical formula *Sedet michi bene capuchinum?*

602 s.d. Dame Douce must leave at this point, since she reappears, out of breath and angry at the Fairies' delay, after the feast (848) which she clearly has not witnessed.

723. Round tables: social gatherings of knights for courtly games, including jousting, in imitation of the practices described in contemporary Arthurian romances.

770. Adam follows conventional mythology in identifying the three sisters as the *weirds* or *parcae* who control Fortune.

(802). There is apparently a line missing in the MS.

822. Leurins li Cavalaus: the Hairy One.

844. Meadow: a quarter of Arras to the North.

860. The man is Rainelet. See note (589) above.

1025. No music is recorded for this, which seems to be the first line of a lost *chanson de toile*, a short dramatic song with refrain, telling of love from a woman's point of view.

(1057). There is apparently a line missing in the MS.

1061. It was customary in thirteenth-century Arras for patrons of a tavern to provide their own crockery, napkins, etc., as well as to pay for the candles used. See s.d. after 1080.

LE JEU DE ROBIN ET DE MARION

6. Hey trolly lo: *A leur i va*! traditional nonsense refrain.

9–10. This snatch of song occurs in several *pastourelles* earlier than the play.

158. The game Robin refers to (the Picard *choule*) is something like croquet. Cf. *Feuillée*, 541.

186. Not much is known about the movements of the dances mentioned here. Many kinds of popular and courtly dance required a leader whose movements were followed or complemented by the rest of the dancers. The formula of invitation and reply 'by my father's soul' etc. is traditional.

206. Evening dance: the French *au seriaus* (Varty's emendation of MS. *seraiu*) seems to refer to an *evening* dance.

208. For this dance Robin has to move his head so that his hair swirls about. A thirteenth-century pastourelle song tells how 'Perrins became very agitated in his new jacket of baize . . . played upon the bagpipes and danced, swirling his hair about.' To be really successful Robin would have to have his hair cropped short at the forehead and grown to his shoulders at the back, in the manner represented in thirteenth-century miniatures.

212. The line, *Oil, mais li voie est trop freske*, is obscure. Robin may simply mean that the path is too fresh or dewy, but a metaphorical meaning seems to make better sense: the dance is too lively and Robin's reference to his torn breeches in the next line explains his hesitation.

240. The French word *menestreus* often has a derogatory sense, suggesting that minstrels were vagabonds. Cf. 732.

425. (Cf. 479) The game of 'Kings and Queens' is played later (501ff.). It consists of the election and crowning of a 'king' who summons his subjects to court and asks them provoking questions about love as a means of getting them to declare their affections. The subjects then have a chance to question the King, who must not lie. In the play the episode of the wolf cuts the game short.

The questions were probably often indelicate. The Statutes of the Synod of Worcester (1240) ordered clergy not to tolerate *ludi de Rege et Regina*.

428. Saint Coisne (Cosmo?) is among the games mentioned by Rabelais as diversions for the young Gargantua. In the *Feuillée*, devout offerings to the patron saint of lunatics, Saint Acaire, are the object of amusement to the more sophisticated characters in the play.

461. 'Is it settled?'. We have followed the MS. reading *pais* rather than Varty's emendation *plais* (which gives the sense, 'Are you quarrelling?') because Huart has agreed to give in already.

681. In one MS. there is an interpolation here of 70 lines. It involves Robin and three new characters, Warniers, Rogaus, and Guios. The latter is referred to at line 635 of our text as Peronnelle's obstreperous brother.

706. A second interpolation of 28 lines follows here.

729. This is thought to parody a *chanson de geste* telling of the popular hero Audigier. The music of the fragment gives some idea of the way in which the Old French epics were sung.

Adam de la Halle's own *chansons* receive the same foul-mouthed treatment from Rogiaus and Warniers in the *Pèlerin* prologue.